Praise for
Dude Making a Differen...

Part Henry David Thoreau and part Robinson Crusoe, Rob
Greenfield — a former marketing man who suffered his own
Don Draper moment a few years ago and chucked it all for an
eco-mindful lifestyle — is truly a dude making a difference.
His journey across America is by turns hilarious, gripping, and
eye-opening. A must read for anyone interested in living an environmentally conscientious life.

—Mike Sager, writer at large, *Esquire.*

I love many things about *Dude Making a Difference*, but what I
love most of all is that it's not about a guy gifted with super-hu-
man strength, sublime skill or mind-blowing intellect; instead,
it's about an ordinary guy doing extraordinary things. Greenfield
is a man with a huge heart, incredible integrity and an infectious
spirit for adventure — things we've all got the potential for. The
fact he writes about his story so beautifully makes it very easy for
the rest of us to be inspired by it.

—Mark Boyle, author, *Drinking Molotov Cocktails with
Gandhi* and *The Moneyless Man*

Rob Greenfield is my cousin. Well, not really, but that's just a
technicality. When it comes to humanistic values and commitment to making the world better for all of us, Rob is definitely
family. Cousin Rob not only has an incredible imagination but
also the joy, energy and generous spirit to turn that imagination into magical experiences of environmental sustainability.
It makes one proud to be a Greenfield. Cousin Rob, you rock!

—Jerry Greenfield, co-founder, Ben & Jerry's

Rob Greenfield reminds us that humanity's urgent need to live more in harmony with nature shouldn't be about doom and gloom: he shows us it's about living a rich, rewarding and ultimately more beautiful existence — without creating garbage, pollution, or consumer demands that cannot be satisfied. Rob glows with the simplicity and sincerity of his message and has inspired so many to take small steps to a more sustainable lifestyle.

—Tristram Stuart, author, *Waste: Uncovering Global Food Scandal*, and founder, Feedback

Dude Making a Difference is a thought-provoking meditation on what it means to be both part of and apart from our natural world. Rob's writing strikingly captures a snapshot of America today – a moment in time where our country tiptoes on the precipice of great environmental deterioration. Through this story Rob offers a humble example of the divine art of living simply to impact echoing positive change on our planet.

—Marion Haberman, Development Producer, Discovery Networks International

Rob is an amazing guy. This is his story of how to live a life based on your principles — and have fun in the process. If you don't have an opportunity to meet Rob in person, this book is the next best thing.

—Ben Cohen, co-founder, Ben & Jerry's

The stories in *Dude Making a Difference* are an inspiration to anyone who aspires to create positive impact in the world — even if that means breaking convention. It's a refreshing, eye-opening reminder that life is about more than things and paychecks; that we can, in fact, use less while accomplishing more; and that all it takes to make a difference is to have a little motivation and a lot of gumption. This is truly a worth-while read.

—Liz Core, writer, Grist.org

Rob Greenfield told me during an interview one time, "I don't think it's really possible to do something that's going to make serious change in the world without a fair number of people thinking that you're insane." Rob is the best kind of insane, and he is one of the most amazing characters I've ever met. I rarely get the pleasure of interviewing someone who is real, sincere, and absolutely out of his mind at the same time. More importantly, Rob has also been one of the few people to actually teach me something about... how badly we are screwing up the planet. I wish I had the discipline and the positive attitude he has towards everything. *Dude Making a Difference* is a testament to the insanity that all of us should follow. It's a great story, from the Earth's best friend.

—Joe Little, reporter, KGTV 10News, San Diego

When Rob set out on this ride destined for 1% for the Planet headquarters, we had no idea how epic and examined a trip it was. Through his trash talk, resourcefulness, stick-to-it-iveness and hopeful romanticism, he is inspired in every sense of the word. The world is a better place because of Rob.

—Barbara Friedsam, Director of Brand and Marketing,
1% for the Planet

With intelligence, humor, and heart, Rob Greenfield takes readers on a journey across America that redefines what it means to be self-sufficient. By uncovering a valuable food resource in what most Americans throw away, he exposes our misconceptions about poverty and hunger being irreversible social problems. His determination to show Americans how little one needs to be healthy and happy fuels his journey, and will delight and inspire even the most skeptical reader. Greenfield is more than just a "Dude Making a Difference" — he's an energetic and caring steward of the earth.

—Barrington Irving, National Geographic Emerging Explorer,
and founder, Experience Aviation, Inc. and The Flying Classroom

Rob's book is one part cycling travelogue, one part exploration of the greener (and not so green) side of America, and one part educational experience about how to lessen your environmental impact, one small step at a time. His story is also a great window into what can happen when we make a commitment to make conscious and low-impact choices about how and where we get our food, water, and energy, and it has the potential to inspire positive changes, both large and small, in the lives of many.

—Derek Markham, environment and sustainability writer

We can all learn from Rob's low-impact lifestyle and be inspired that, even while traveling across America by bike, he was able to stay true to his values. Rob is making the world a better place and empowering others to do the same. He shows that leading a more sustainable existence is not only doable, but incredibly rewarding.

—Claire Cummings, waste specialist,
Bon Appétit Management Company

DUDE
MAKING A
DIFFERENCE

Bamboo Bikes, Dumpster Dives AND Other
Extreme Adventures Across America

Rob Greenfield

new society
PUBLISHERS

Cover design by Diane McIntosh.

Cover Images: Map background: © iStock: ixer; Cover and interior images courtesy of ©Brent Martin.

Printed in Canada. First printing January 2016.

New Society Publishers acknowledges the financial support of the Government of Canada through the Canada Book Fund (CBF) for our publishing activities.

This book is intended to be educational and informative. It is not intended to serve as a guide. The author and publisher disclaim all responsibility for any liability, loss or risk that may be associated with the application of any of the contents of this book.

Paperback ISBN: 978-0-86571-807-4   eISBN: 978-1-55092-600-2

Inquiries regarding requests to reprint all or part of *Dude Making a Difference* should be addressed to New Society Publishers at the address below.
To order directly from the publishers, please call toll-free (North America) 1-800-567-6772, or order online at www.newsociety.com

Any other inquiries can be directed by mail to:
New Society Publishers
P.O. Box 189, Gabriola Island, BC V0R 1X0, Canada
(250) 247-9737

New Society Publishers' mission is to publish books that contribute in fundamental ways to building an ecologically sustainable and just society, and to do so with the least possible impact on the environment, in a manner that models this vision. We are committed to doing this not just through education, but through action. The interior pages of our bound books are printed on Forest Stewardship Council®-registered acid-free paper that is **100% post-consumer recycled** (100% old growth forest-free), processed chlorine-free, and printed with vegetable-based, low-VOC inks, with covers produced using FSC®-registered stock. New Society also works to reduce its carbon footprint, and purchases carbon offsets based on an annual audit to ensure a carbon neutral footprint. For further information, or to browse our full list of books and purchase securely, visit our website at: **www.newsociety.com**

LIBRARY AND ARCHIVES CANADA CATALOGUING IN PUBLICATION

Greenfield, Rob, 1986-, author

Dude making a difference : bamboo bikes, dumpster dives and other extreme adventures across America / Rob Greenfield.

Includes index.
Issued in print and electronic formats.
ISBN 978-0-86571-807-4 (paperback).—ISBN 978-1-55092-600-2 (ebook

1. Greenfield, Rob, 1986—Travel. 2. Sustainable living--United States. 3. Environmentalists—Travel—United States. 4. Cycling-—United States. 5. United States—Description and travel. I. Title.

GE197.G74 2015   333.720973   C2015-905416-8
                                                     C2015-905417-6

This book is dedicated to every person who is leading the way into a happier, healthier existence for all beings and creatures on Earth. I hope that includes you. If it doesn't, I hope you'll choose to include yourself after reading this book.

CONTENTS

ACKNOWLEDGMENTS

Thank you Brent Martin for helping me to tell my story through your incredible photography. These photos have served as such an important tool in my ability to spread health and happiness and thus help the earth. Many inspired people, including me, have you to thank for your dedication and skills both as a photographer and a friend.

THANK YOU Sean Aranda for being the man behind the scenes of almost everything that I do. Without you I don't know if any of this would have happened. Thank you for sticking with me for so long, trusting in my words, and being one incredibly loyal dude.

Cheryl Davies, your love and friendship has guided me into this happy healthy way of living. I've become a better man in your arms and by your side. You've been here for every step of the transformation. You were in my mind for nearly every moment of this story even when it doesn't show in the writing.

THANK YOU to my family at One Percent for the Planet, for inspiring me to use business for good and to be a good person: Barbara Friedsam Egan, John Egan, Kerry Blanchard Newton, Brodie O'Brien, Melody Badgett, Leah Cameron, Pauline Stevens, Jon Cocina, and Brittany Nunnink.

THANK YOU New Society Publishers for stumbling upon me online and inviting me into your family. You've brought this book to life. Thank you for all the tools you have created for a world of change and for leading by example in the publishing industry.

THANK YOU to all of my family. Thank you to my mom and dad for making me, raising me and teaching me to care about and protect the earth and all the creatures on it. Thank you Louise Greenfield for helping me on the road and always. You've kept me company from afar so often. I think you are the reason I started to explore, with your stories from abroad. Thank you Myrna Greenfield for thinking this idea was nuts but hearing me out, helping me to make my mission clear, and then being a part of the journey. Thank you for all that you are doing for the local food movement with your life and Good Egg Marketing. Thank you Arthur Greenfield for taking me on some of my first adventures abroad and instilling in me a desire to travel. Thank you to my brothers Joe and Levi, my sister Rebecca, and to Michelle, Hazel, Laurence and my late grandpa Harold for being supportive of everything I do and for being kindhearted people.

THANK YOU Jessica Baron for your support and your never-ending contributions to my cause. You were there every step of the way, practically pedaling across America with me.

THANK YOU Jared Robinson Criscuolo for helping me plan, connecting me with key people and encouraging me all along the way.

THANK YOU Rebekah Uccellini for being a steward of the earth and facilitating all of the seed planting on this journey. You've inspired me more than you'll ever know, and I admire you greatly.

THANK YOU Dane Gottschall, Wes Zolecki, Mitch Hunter, Marc Teichmann and Heidi Wanta Cabout for your contribution to the journey, for your support and for your friendship.

THANK YOU Jenna Leilani Tallman and to your father for brainstorming this crazy idea up with me and helping me figure out all the guidelines to stay off the grid on this journey.

THANK YOU to my sponsors for trusting me to represent your organization and for supplying me with gear to spread the message of sustainability: Prana, Dr. Bronners, James Atkin of Goal Zero, Craig Calfee of Bamboosero, Mary Turk of Drips Water, Riley Swenson, David Toledo, Matt Ford, and Kenyon Ellis of PowerPot, Rachel Ostroy of neat-os, Kala Brand Music, and Andi Lucas of Dinkum System.

THANK YOU to all of the nonprofits that supported me and for all the work you are doing to make the earth a happier, healthier place. Thank you as well for the knowledge of sustainability you have imparted upon me: Rich Points and Wanda Pelegrina Caldas of Community Cycles, MaryEllen Etienne of Reuse Alliance, Erin Barnes of Ioby, Eva Radke of Film Biz Recycling, Harriet Taub and Rachael Kuo of Materials for the Arts, Growing Power, Surfrider Foundation San Diego, Solar Sister, and Jonathan Zaidman of The 1 to 1 Movement.

ACKNOWLEDGMENTS

THANK YOU to my Warm Showers hosts for taking me into your home and being stewards to the cycling community.

THANK YOU Tina Davies for being such an amazing supporter of my adventures. You welcomed me to Northport like it was my own hometown, and I'm so appreciative of all the help you have given me.

THANK YOU Gavin Glatting for helping me create the videos that bring my ideas to light. To think it all started with a CFL bulb.

THANK YOU Brian Blum for being my partner in sustainable endeavors long before I embarked on this journey. You've taught me so much.

THANK YOU to all of my friends that supported me, hosted me and kept me company along the journey: Greg Radicone, Yael Sverdlik, Giulia Stasi, Maggie Scrantom, Katie Scrantom, Holly Hatcher, Dan Dougherty, Craig and Sherry Czarnecki, Lars Fiorio, Grant and Vanessa Reynolds, Miranda Willer, Kyle Bredeson, Claire Mullarney, Casey Hubner, Darryl Kotyk at Loving the Bike, Adam Houzner, Megan Dunovan, The Jenkins (Kestrel, Forest, Linda and Jim), Abby, Tom, Patti, Mike and Allison Carroll, Loren Groeschl, Aaron Hussman, John Miller, Basilio Ceravolo, Maria Breshkova, Talia Ceravolo, Bryan May, Dave Mullen, Joey Perez, Kevin Davies, Greg and Melissa Davies, Kenny Craft, Andrea Gordon, Didi Emmons, Patagonia Boston, David Elkin-Ginetti and his mom Debbie, Matt Lane, Kyle Pfister, Jamie Serenstara, Patty Bertram, Ari Joshua Hoffman, Meghan Lipsett, Nathan Woody, Marsha and Brad Eastep, Kris Moody, Chrisane Jarosz, Kristin and Keith Hogheem, Rob Williams, Laura Ehret, Wreford Stewart, Sarah Alderman, David Dougherty, Sheila Powers, Jo Hagney, Mary and Morgan Vittengl, Cheri Cordova Baca and Elicia Amber Baca, Jim Brown of Sac Bike, Rachel Marcotte, Mark Kennedy at Saturday Cycles, Audrey Huffman and Candice White of Sugarbush Resort, Bruno Bustos and James Bachez.

THANK YOU to Organic Valley and all of the farmers that invited me to their farms the Stollers in Ohio, the Beidlers in Vermont,

The Wilsons and the Ihms in Wisconsin, and Michelle Pedretti and Jonathan Reinbold.

THANK YOU to Nicole Ravlin, Michelle Searer and Alicia DeMartini of People Making Good PR for helping get the word out.

THANK YOU to everyone who has supported my adventures, who has helped me along the way, and who has doubted me.

I know you won't be reading this, Earth, but **THANK YOU** for the life you have given to me, to everyone I love and to anything and everything that has ever lived. Thanks for being.

INTRODUCTION

Cycling 4,700 miles across the USA, that's the easy part. So what's the hard part? How about doing it off the grid?

That means:

Traveling via my own human power, without the assistance of fossil fuels

Eating locally produced, organic and unpackaged foods, and forgoing long-distance-shipped, conventional, packaged food unless it is being wasted

Using water from natural sources and forgoing water from municipal systems unless it is being wasted

Using electricity generated by portable alternative-energy devices and forgoing electricity generated by fossil fuels

Creating near-zero trash or recycling and composting all of my food waste.

That is exactly what I'll be doing. The adventure is called "Off the Grid Across America," but it would better be called "Low-Impact Living Across America." Off the grid typically means not connected to public utilities such as electricity and water, but it is a very subjective term with different definitions depending on who you talk to. It almost always includes living in a self-sufficient manner.

In this adventure I'll mostly be off the grid, but more precisely I'll be living an extremely low-impact lifestyle and living in a manner that causes minimal harm to the planet and all the people, creatures and plants that call it home.

To live in this manner and stick to my guidelines I will:

- Use resources as they are naturally provided by the earth
- Get these resources from the source, or as close to it as possible
- Use only as much of the resource as I absolutely need
- Be resourceful and find ways to meet my needs while causing no unnecessary harm.

This will mean giving up many of the convenient ways I am accustomed to using resources. Take water as an example. The water we get when we turn on our faucets is of course from nature. However it has been treated with chemicals, electricity was used to extract it and deliver it to the faucet, and it may have traveled a long distance from the source. On the other hand water in a river or lake has not been treated with chemicals (at least not intentionally), uses the earth's natural life cycles to move and is at the source. This water takes no human input or added resources and causes no harm in its creation or existence, whereas water from the tap often does. So on this adventure I will get my water from natural sources rather than taps.

Water is just one of the five key aspects of sustainability that I will be paying attention to. The others are transportation, food, energy and waste. I'll dive into those more in a minute but first, you're probably wondering, Why I am doing this. Why take on all of these strict rules and shoulder such a burden? I am doing this to inspire Americans to live more sustainably. I think the best way to effect positive change is to lead by example, so that is what I'll be doing. I've learned a lot about sustainability over the last few years but there is so much left to learn, and in turn to teach. What better way to do this than to thrust myself into an adventure that explores every nook and cranny of personal sustainability? What better way to inspire sustainability than to be extremely inspired about it myself? And of course it has to be enjoyable and entertaining, too or most people just won't be interested, hence the adventure being a little extreme. At times I will be doing things in an extreme way to draw attention to a core issue. Don't worry — there will always be simple, take-home lessons from the extreme actions, so you won't have to take on something so extreme. For example I'll be cycling across America, which you of course don't have to do — but you could cycle to work or school instead of drive.

I also have a strong desire to live a more earth-friendly lifestyle, and this adventure is going to help me do just that. I want to live in a manner that is beneficial to the earth, my community and myself, and I don't want to cause harm anymore to anyone or anything. The problem is that we have lost touch with our resources. We have outsourced everything, and we don't realize how our actions affect the earth and everything on it. Our simple daily actions revolving around food, water, energy, waste and transportation are causing all sorts of destruction to the planet and many of the people and creatures on it. We just aren't taught this at school or by the government, or (in most cases) by our parents.

I want to start with the basics and analyze all the details of how my simple daily actions affect my world, both near and far. By creating the guidelines for this adventure I will be forcing myself to pay attention to my surroundings, where the resources I use come from and how they get to me. At the same time I will learn more about how my actions affect the earth, both negatively and positively. And that's what this book is here to share with you.

So here are all of the guidelines that I set for myself before departing on the adventure, in more detail.

TRANSPORTATION

I commit to crossing the country on my bicycle using human power only, without the use of fossil fuels. I will not take a ride in a car for any reason, including a broken-down bike, unless my life is seriously threatened. I will not take public transportation and will not even get in an electric vehicle. On my off days I will still not use a vehicle to move my body, not even an escalator, elevator, or moving walkway. Simply put, no fossil fuels will be burned in my transportation.

FOOD

I will eat locally produced, organic and unpackaged foods and forgo food that has been shipped long distances, was conventionally grown, or is packaged. The food must be local AND organic AND unpackaged, not just one or the other.

MAKING A DIFFERENCE

LOCAL For the purpose of this adventure, locally produced means that the food was grown in the state I am in or within 250 miles of where I purchase it. I will be getting local food directly from farms, gardens, farmers' markets and environmentally conscious grocery stores such as co-ops, and to a lesser extent through hunting, fishing and foraging. (Foraging may sound like a fancy word but if you've ever eaten a wild berry off a bush, you've foraged.) If I buy a food item with multiple ingredients, all of the ingredients have to be local, even the salt.

ORGANIC This means that the food was grown naturally without using any chemicals on the plant or in the soil. I do not care about certifications and will simply be taking the word of the grower.

UNPACKAGED This means there is no packaging on the food, even if it is recyclable: no paper, no plastic, no cardboard, no tinfoil. I will even avoid fruit stickers. The purpose of this guideline is to not create waste. I can, however, buy food in a reusable package, such as milk in a returnable bottle or eggs in a carton from a farmer. I will also make an exception for some jarred items when I can give the jar to someone who will get good use out of it or give it back to the distributor to be reused.

WASTED FOOD The exception to all of these guidelines is food that is going to waste, which I can eat. This primarily means eating food that I find in grocery store dumpsters or trash cans. Other sources of wasted food include table diving (food left on people's plates at restaurants) or food going bad in my host's fridge. I will be very strict in only eating food that was already thrown away or most definitely will be thrown away; if I have any inkling that the food is not in fact going to waste, then I will not eat it. In this way no "helpful" friend can pretend to be not finishing his sandwich and trick me into eating it.

WATER

I will use water from natural sources and forgo water from municipal systems unless it was being wasted.

Natural sources of water include rivers lakes, rain, and groundwater. Means of accessing ground water include wind-powered pumps and artesian wells. When needed I will purify the water I harvest using a Katadyn Pocket filter. I will not use water that has been transported from the source with the use of any resources, such as electricity. This means I will not turn on a faucet, use a shower, use a flush toilet, or wash clothes in a washing machine. Despite these challenges I intend to remain clean, presentable and pleasant-smelling.

Again, the exception to these guidelines is water that is going to waste, which I can use. This waste could come from leaky faucets, water bottles found on the roadside, or broken sprinklers. I will also be bathing and washing my clothes using natural sources of water. For the purpose of keeping track of statistics I will only include water that I actually consume or take away. So for example if I swim in a lake I won't count that as water used.

ENERGY

I will use electricity generated by portable alternative energy devices and forgo electricity generated by fossil fuels or that has been put into the grid.

I am equipped with Goal Zero solar panels and a PowerPot to generate electricity to charge my laptop, cell phone, bike lights and headlamp. I will not turn on a light switch, plug into an outlet, turn on anything in a house, take a hot shower, use a stove, eat at a restaurant that uses electricity, or use any electronic device powered by electricity, unless it was powered by my alternative energy.

Electricity is so engrained in my daily life that I will really only understand the challenges of this part of the requirement once I have begun the journey. I will likely use some electricity indirectly by walking through automatic doors, accidentally triggering automatic lights, buying food with cash registers or getting money at the bank, but I will avoid all these actions wherever possible. I will make an exception with wireless Internet, so that I can connect to social media, contact the media, communicate, etc.; but again, my laptop will be solar-powered.

I will only cook using fires made with wood that I harvest myself.

WASTE

My aim is to create near-zero waste on this adventure. I will do this by following the 3 Rs — reduce, reuse and recycle — in that order. First I will reduce my consumption and needs, then I will reuse what I can, and only after failing to reduce or reuse will I then recycle. What can't be recycled will be considered trash, but both recyclables and trash will be considered waste.

Many of these terms are subjective so I'd like to define them for this adventure.

Waste is both trash and recycling. Any item that needs to be sent to the landfill or a recycling facility is waste. Trash is any item that needs to be sent to the landfill, or ends up becoming litter. Recycling is any item that needs to be sent to a recycling facility (and is actually accepted there; otherwise it's just trash).

You may be surprised that I am including recycling as waste because you've likely been taught that recycling is the green thing to do. But recycling is actually a highly energy- and resource-intensive process, and though it is far superior to sending waste to the landfill, it still has a far greater impact on the environment than not having that item to recycle in the first place. I will be weighing and logging both forms of waste. I will not be throwing away any of the trash I create this summer, but will carry it all the way across the country. So if I purchase something wrapped in non-recyclable plastic, it will be traveling all the way to Vermont with me. In this manner I'll deal with my own burden, which should keep me from creating much trash. I will put recyclable materials into a recycling bin after I've logged their weight.

I am not including food scraps in my waste. I will either bury these in the dirt, throw them under a plant, or put them in a compost pile. In this way the nutrients will be recycled into the earth without using any added resources or energy. I will also be using bokashi to help break down food scraps so they can be absorbed into the earth. Of course I will make sure I don't throw any food scraps in places where the earth can't put them to good use, such as sidewalks, because that would be littering.

What about human waste — you know, poop and pee? I will not waste it, as it is a valuable resource for the natural world. I will not be using a toilet so you may be dying to ask, "Where will this guy be pooping and peeing?" When I am cycling through nature, which will be often, I will go in the woods or the desert so that the nutrients can be recycled naturally back into the earth. While in cities I will have to be a little more creative; I will be carrying a small portable toilet. I'll use this when needed and bury the waste when I get back into nature.

I would recommend trying nearly everything else discussed in this introduction EXCEPT THIS, unless you have a very sanitary and responsible way of dealing with your waste. At home you can easily set up a composting toilet, but as a traveler this is going to be the most burdensome aspect of creating zero waste.

CONSUMPTION

I spent many hours preparing for this trip, making sure I will have everything I need for the next three and a half months. So I should not need to buy much besides food. More importantly, though, I intend to reduce my needs greatly to reduce my consumption. When I do need to make purchases I will follow these guidelines to reduce their impact:

- Rather than purchase something I will try to go without it or find a way to repurpose other items, such as finding things in the trash.
- I will purchase used products over new products when possible.

- I will purchase sustainably made products.
- I will buy locally made products from small businesses.
- I will support businesses that are putting serious effort into minimizing their negative impact on the earth, like those that practice corporate social responsibility and the triple bottom line. These businesses are not operating solely for profit but are also trying to minimize their negative impact on people and the planet in their business operations.
- I will support businesses that are doing their part to make the earth a better place. Many of the businesses I support will be members of One Percent for the Planet, a growing global movement of over 1,000 companies that donate 1one percent of their sales to environmental organizations worldwide.
- I will keep the money in the hands of the small businesses by paying with cash. I will not be carrying a credit or debit card so that the bank doesn't get a cut of the transaction. Plus not having a card will reduce my consumption by limiting the funds available to me and keeping the transactions more noticeable, as it's all too easy to swipe a card without visually seeing the money leave my hands.

The previous guidelines were all designed to decrease my negative impact on the earth and to lead by example in living a more earth-friendly lifestyle. But I realize one of the best ways to have a happy, healthy earth is to have a happy, healthy me. So I've also created some guidelines to make myself a better person and lead by example in that area, too. Many of these also decrease my environmental impact, as everything on this earth is connected whether we realize it or not. And I do not want to focus solely on reducing my impact but also want to increase my positive impact.

I intend to leave each place a little better than I found it and to have a positive impact on the earth. I will do this by:

- Inspiring and teaching people how to live in harmony

with the earth, their communities, and themselves. This will be done simply by leading by example.

- Planting seed bombs full of native wildflowers all along my path. These flowers will help the endangered bee populations and beautify the earth. A seed bomb is a little ball of clay, soil and seeds that you can toss anywhere you want. The seeds are protected within the clay while they wait patiently for the rain (or a sprinkler) to soak them so they can grow into food or flowers.

- Having a positive mindset. Although my actions will speak much louder than my words I strongly believe that my thoughts and my words shape my actions. Because of this I aim to think and speak positively in order to act positively. One way that I will control and monitor my mindset is by giving up swearing and keeping track of how many times I break this rule. Every time I swear I will do ten push-ups and donate $10 to Below the Surface, a nonprofit that protects America's water supply.

- Living 100-percent alcohol-and drug-free for the entire summer. Although I typically enjoy beer or wine in moderation and occasionally smoke marijuana, I realize that my mind and body perform on a higher level when I am alcohol-and drug-free, so I will not drink or smoke for the entire summer.

- Raising money for One Percent for the Planet non-profits. I've set a goal of raising $10,000 for Guitars in the Classroom, Below the Surface, Worldbike, Ioby, Surfrider Foundation San Diego Chapter, Reuse Alliance, Growing Power, Solar Sister, and Community Cycles, so they can carry out their missions of creating a more sustainable planet.

- Practicing natural personal hygiene. You've heard the saying "one earth" and it's true — this is the only one we've got. Well, what we do to our bodies we are doing to the earth. To treat my body (and the earth) with respect I will only put natural things on it and will forgo all chemically derived products. I will only use Dr. Bronner's organic biodegradable soap to wash my body and hands; organic coconut oil to moisturize; and natural toothpaste and essential oils for cleaning as well as scent. I will not use any body-care products that contain synthetic chemicals or petroleum-based ingredients.

All of these guidelines are self-created and self-imposed: I conjured them up, and only I can hold myself to them. You will see that I really took on some extreme challenges. You may also see that at times I overlooked certain aspects of the guidelines and did not always succeed in following them. I was, however, transparent with my successes and failures throughout the journey. I recorded every instance when I broke or bent one of the guidelines and kept statistics wherever they could be kept.

The journey was set to start in San Francisco, California on April 20, 2013 and end at the One Percent for the Planet headquarters in Waitsfield, Vermont on August 1, 2013, after 104 days of riding. So that I could plan events and media, I had a pretty

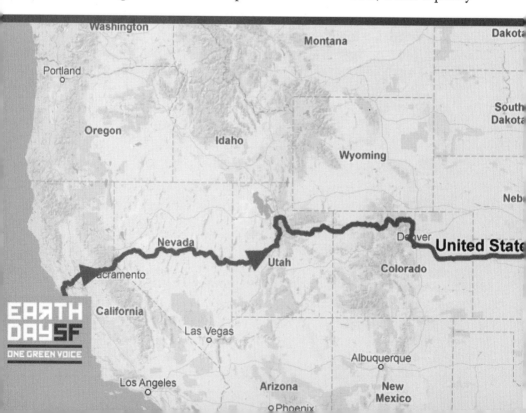

solid route and schedule, but had left some flexibility across the great expanses of land. I planned to travel mostly via local highways and roads, avoiding the interstates whenever possible. I wasn't alone — my friend Brent, whose two favorite things in life are cycling and photography, was tagging along, videoing the whole adventure. We were planning to create a documentary out of the journey.

This book is a journal of my adventure. I wrote about my experiences most nights — in my tent, on a picnic table, or from the couch or bed I was sleeping in — and posted each day's story straight onto my blog and Facebook page. What follows is an edited version of that blog. By "edited," I mean that I have had a chance to correct my grammar, cut repetition and add factual information. But for the most part I have not altered the feelings I expressed on my journey or changed my thoughts to reflect new perspectives I may have developed in the two years since. This is the 104-day journey as I experienced it: the highs and lows, the successes and failures and, always, the truth.

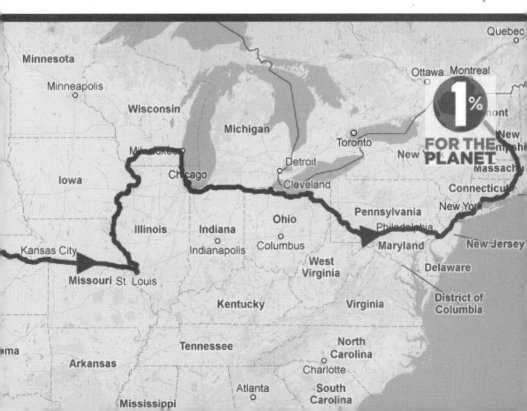

PART 1
THE WEST

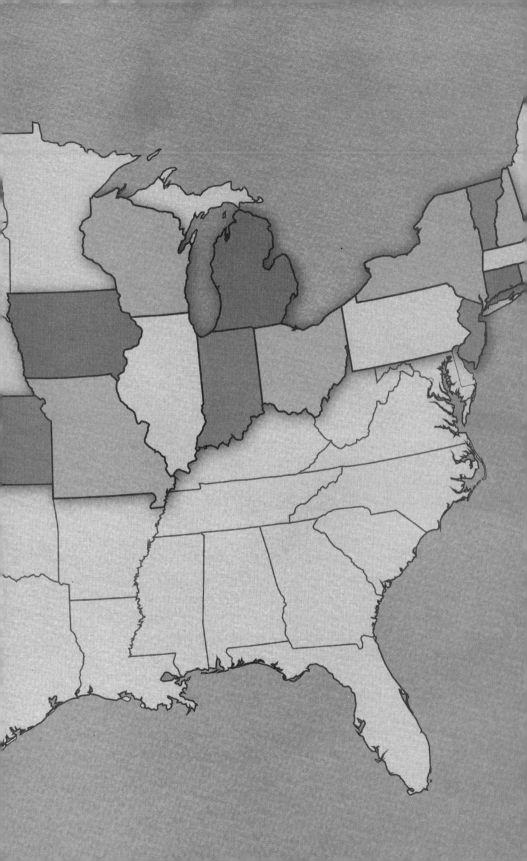

DAY 1: TRAPPED IN SAN FRANCISCO

Today was the day. The months of brainstorming and countless hours of planning were at an end, and it was time to finally put it all into action.

Upon awakening I took a shower, the last I'd be taking until I reached Vermont in 104 days. Then I made plans to stock up on food and water. My host, Meghan Lipsett, was a huge help here. She directed me to a nearby farmers' market that is well known for its bounty of local, organic food as well as Lake Temescal, a small lake 2.5 miles east in Oakland. This would also provide me an opportunity to test out the trailer on the bike.

So Brent and I headed to the lake with high hopes. But just a mile from the house the trailer started rubbing really hard on the frame. I adjusted the set-up and was able to make it to the lake and fill up my three-gallon jug with water, but the little five-mile roundtrip adventure took two and a half hours.

Back at the house I knew I had to drop some weight to make this manageable so I spent a good amount of time going through my gear getting rid of things I did not need. I took out about ten pounds of gear including the blender and fishing pole. Meghan kindly stocked me up with locally produced olive oil, honey, rice, beans and produce from the Berkeley market.

By 4 p.m., way behind schedule, I finally headed into San Francisco to the official launch point, the Earth Day festival in Civic Center Park. I got onto the BART knowing this would be the last time I stepped foot in a fossil fuel-powered vehicle for 4,700 miles. At the festival I was invited onto the stage to speak for a minute. I spent the next few hours talking to many of the good people out celebrating Earth Day and was now even further behind schedule.

At 6 p.m. I began the journey. But as I pedaled up the ridiculously steep hills of San Francisco it fully sank in that this trailer would not do the job; it was way too heavy and was throwing the tire off kilter, making it rub on the frame. We spent about two hours biking up and down the steep hills of San Francisco and only made it about four miles. Much of the two hours was spent pushing the bike up hills too steep to ride and trying to put the rear wheel back on after it had been pulled off by the weight of the trailer.

Pushing the bicycle up the steep hills of San Francisco. Notice the rear wheel is not even touching the ground.

It was obvious we weren't making it out of the city that night so Brent got ahold of a buddy from a past bike ride, and we crashed at his house. I had my solar light set up as I lay in bed charging my laptop with energy stored from the day's sun, so I was successful at remaining off the grid. A few hours earlier, around 9 p.m., I had a huge pit in my stomach and was questioning how I was going to make this happen. We came up with some solutions, and it looks like we will spend tomorrow in the city setting up a new rig.

It's not a question of if I will make this work, only a matter of how. I've had some moments of doubt and some moments of worry but right now I feel joyful and confident.

DAY 2: A NEW TRAILER

Upon awaking I got online and found a better bike trailer on Craigslist for $160 just three miles away. This was exactly what I needed, for the right price, just down the street! I called the number from the ad and he got back to me right away saying the trailer is still available. Score!

So I rode over there and picked up the trailer. It fit on my bike perfectly, and I was on my way home trailing it behind me in no time. I had a lot of work to do though so we decided to not rush things too much and leave tomorrow morning after a full day of reconfiguring everything. I had to figure out how to mount the solar panel, which I accomplished fairly easily. The harder part was dropping more weight, and a serious amount of it, if I wanted to bike out of San Francisco, let alone over the mountains, which were just a few days ahead.

I laid out everything on our host's garage floor and chose what I didn't need. The biggest thing I ditched was the 28-pound battery. I'll have to get a smaller battery to charge my laptop, but for now I'll still have the small kit to charge my cell phone. I also ditched my three-gallon jug, deciding to carry no more than one and a half gallons at a time. Those two changes alone add up to 40 pounds.

Sorting through my gear in search of stuff to send home to lose weight in the trailer.

I remembered two things today that let a load of stress off my back. First, I am allowed to eat from the garbage, so if I can't find local organic unpackaged foods I have that to fall back on. Second, I can find water bottles in garbage cans, in the gutter, etc. and purify it. So if there isn't a natural body of water nearby I can scour for water in that way.

I'm definitely behind schedule, but with this lighter load we will jam over to Tahoe.

DAY 3: THE ADVENTURE BEGINS (AGAIN)

We took off from San Francisco around 9 a.m. and headed north to the Golden Gate Bridge. The new trailer pulled along nicely, and I could tell this new setup would be manageable.

North of the bridge navigation was pretty tough and we spent a good portion of the afternoon making wrong turns. Food consisted of drinking honey straight from the jar and fruits and veggies I still had left from the Berkeley farmers' market.

After a couple of hours we started to make good time. When we hit Highway 37 we had a fun half hour dodging thousands of honeybees in wine country. Towards evening I saw a sign for fresh eggs and stopped in at a farm. Fresh eggs indeed. I cracked them right open into my mouth for some good protein.

Now for those of you who just cringed at the idea of eating raw eggs, let me explain. The odds of being exposed to salmonella from raw eggs are extremely low. How low? About one in 20,000. So if I ate a raw egg every single day of my life it would take 20,000 days — nearly 55 years — for me to begin defying the odds. Then you have to take into account that I've got a healthy immune system and salmonella doesn't fair too well in healthy individuals, so even if I do ingest the bacterium, the odds are I'll fight it off. Here's where it gets even better though. The one, in, 20,000 statistic is for eggs produced by the industrial farming system, which come from hens that live their entire lives in tiny cages. These are the eggs you'll find on your average grocery store shelf. Studies have shown that *all* of the egg recalls for salmonella come from factory farming, not fresh, cage-free, organic eggs like I ate raw today. There is much reason to believe that the salmonella problem is primarily fueled by the money-driven practices of large-scale industrial farming. I live with less fear than many because I aim to think rationally, and by living naturally I've found there is less to fear.

I spent the evening with Matt, the working owner of the farm, and he showed me this wonderful place of his. I ate kale, chard and bunching onions straight out of his garden. We hung out with him for a while and ended up setting up a tent right on the farm for the night. I couldn't have asked for a better situation.

DAY 4: GRUELING

We woke up early and I grazed from the garden and had another four raw eggs before hitting the road. We've made it 15 miles from the farm and are in downtown Napa. I made a stop at a local organic market and found some California-grown organic avocados and kiwis that I mowed down. It's about 50 miles to Sacramento from here, and I would love to make it there tonight.

After leaving Napa we climbed an unexpected mini, mountain for hours. Every time we went downhill for three or four miles we were met with a more-than-hour-long climb shortly after. We didn't see that coming at all. Food consisted of more honey, greens at the farm, California avocados and kiwis, a score from a farm stand with locally grown oranges and grapefruits, a caterpillar, and, of course, more raw eggs straight from the chicken. I harvested and purified water from a beautiful stream.

Swimming in cold streams today was not only refreshing for the body but also for the mind. The hot day cooled down and we hit flat ground, allowing us to jam out about 30 miles, finishing the day at about 50 miles. I was exhausted but feeling energized after eating leftovers off a plate in a food court. I've been able to get ample food that is local, organic and unpackaged, but the only thing I've been lacking is carbohydrates since I haven't taken the time to make a fire and cook grains and haven't found dumpster carbs.

DAY 5: GOING IN CIRCLES

I woke up just after sunrise and planted a few seed bombs full of native California flowers and chowed down about a half dozen oranges from a tree nearby. It was a hot morning riding over to Sacramento from Davis and I was feeling a bit sluggish. The capital city was gorgeous, and it was refreshing to pull into town where bikers were happily pedaling along in every direction.

To solve some issues I was having with the bike, I found the Sacramento Bike Advocacy office figuring that they could direct us to a good place for used bike parts that would not be in packaging. Jim directed us to his friend Mark over at Edible Pedal. We ended up spending four hours in the shop and the parking lot. By far the coolest bike shop I've ever been to and the people were just awesome.

A friend from Facebook came down and delivered me a bunch of seed bombs as well as local produce and well water. I was in need of food so it was a true blessing and he was a cool dude. Drained of energy after shattering my full jar of olive oil in the parking lot, I was rejuvenated by finding a full bag of fresh bread in the dumpster. CARBOHYDRATES. Just what I needed.

Next stop: the bank, to pull out $1,000, with the intention of not going back for a month. Except I ended up spending $450 on new bike gears, a backpacking woodstove so I can finally cook grains to get more carbohydrates, straps to properly attach the solar panel and gear to the trailer, a tent for Brent so we don't have to sleep together, a connection piece for the solar panel and a few other things. The problem is that it created some waste. Luckily much of it was minimally packaged and mostly in cardboard rather than plastic.

The rig was looking good and everything was tight, which was exciting. But it was now 10 at night and quite cold. So what to do? We decided to bike and were soon flying along the moon-lit bike path. My bike was riding smoother than ever and every pedal felt like a hot knife through butter. My energy was at its peak. The path wound along the river, and we even had an owl fly along with us for a while. Life was good and we were cruising.

We stopped a few times and looked at the GPS on the phone, but the blue dot was just not showing us where we were. I couldn't figure it out. An hour of night flying and we probably made close to ten miles. Again we looked at the GPS and thought it was just not working. That's when we realized we had gone in a big loop, passed where we started and were now farther from Vermont than when we left. Wham. A hit to the stomach. So we pedaled backwards, and I felt horrible.

We found a spot just a mile or so later and camped just off the bike path. I felt more comfortable than ever on the bike and began to think things would go smoothly tomorrow. We have the Sierra Nevadas to start climbing, which will be one of the more physically challenging things I've done in quite some time, maybe ever.

There was a lot of talk of One Percent for the Planet today with everyone in town and Sacbike is going to become a recipient, Edible Pedal a member, and Jim is going to talk to a bunch of businesses in the area about becoming members. I'm pretty certain it was a big day on the One Percent for the Planet front. I'm also certain Sacramento was left a slightly better place by our visit. I threw a lot of the seed bombs along the bike trails and hoped they'd sprout into beautiful wildflowers for the bees.

DAY 7: DAYS BLURRING TOGETHER

The days have blurred together. My comfortable home in San Diego seems like another life. I can faintly imagine my brown couch in my living room and vaguely remember my life back home. I am fully immersed in this adventure and everything else has ceased to exist. I'm sure home still exists, but I can't fathom myself residing there or even conjure up an image of what my roommates might be doing.

Today... Words that come to mind are *progress* and *success*. Here's the play-by-play. I woke up behind a church in Jackson, California, and the hot sun was beating down upon me. It was late, past 8:30 a.m., and it was good to sleep in but I felt as groggy as a troll waking up from a three-week nap under a bridge. Shaky body, puffy eyes and a rear end ready to explode. The morning was very slow, and after planting some native wildflower seeds around the area I got out around 10 a.m. We were on the road with a lot of elevation to gain.

But first I found a grocery store and decided to see what was in the dumpster. JACKPOT. The treasure chest held so much food I could afford to be picky: a bag of oranges with only one bad orange, a bag of perfectly good potatoes, zucchini, melons, soy yogurt and, best of all, a still-frozen half gallon of chocolate chip vanilla ice cream. It wasn't even past the sell-by date, just a small hole in the cap, and I happily ate half of the box.

From there I got a flat tire — the first of the trip — and fixed it in a little under a half hour. Okay, now maybe I'll make some distance, I thought. One mile later I found a bike shop and stopped in to get some spare 16-inch tubes for the bike trailer. Lucky me, they had used ones so I didn't have to create any waste. He even gave them to me for free. Of course I hung out and chatted about One Percent for the Planet, cycling and the environment for about 30 minutes.

I stopped at a roadside creek to pay some much-needed attention to my body. I bathed in the cold creek and washed off with my Dr. Bronner's soap. I washed my clothes, cleaned and emptied my compost container, and purified 1.5 gallons of water for the day. I then brushed my teeth, stretched and rubbed my whole body down with Dr. Bronner's coconut oil. I felt like a new man, and for the first time on the trip, my body felt really good.

An hour later, climbing, climbing, climbing and I was amazed how easy it was. Now that I'm accustomed to the trailer and I'm balanced, I can stand up while I climb, which is my preferred way of pedaling.

The mountain air is keeping my spirits high and the creek water is keeping me hydrated. Best of all, the bamboo bike is running perfectly and the trailer is pulling along well. My last blog post was powered by the sun. Thanks to the earth for being magnificent!

Wow. At the very moment that I put the exclamation point after "magnificent" my trailer got run over by an SUV. Amazingly, it appears to be fine.

Back on the road at 4 p.m. and the climbing really began. I was very excited at how well it was going. We continued gaining elevation, from 1,500 to 2,500 to 4,000 to over 5,500 feet at the end of the day. To all those who think you can't, YOU CAN.

I knew I was going to make it when I started to take notes with pen and paper while ascending the Sierra Nevadas.

I was amazed and excited at the relative ease of the ascent — which is not to say that it wasn't challenging. The evening was beautiful: crisp mountain air, pine trees all around and a smooth road to climb. My energy level was high and I was well nourished and hydrated all day. This whole trip got off to a very rocky start, but today was the turning point. It's only going to get better from here. I have managed to not plug into a single outlet, turn on a light switch, use a drop of water from the grid, or buy any food that is not locally grown, organic and unpackaged, and have only sworn one time. I've planted seeds every day, inspired many people, taught dozens of people different ways to better the planet, talked about One Percent for the Planet and supported good businesses. I haven't taken a shower or used a toilet (and am very clean and smell good) and have created almost no garbage. All of this in the first week. I feel very proud of it all and look forward to what's to come.

DAY 8: OUT OF THE SIERRA NEVADAS

I made it out of the Sierra Nevadas after an amazing day yesterday. More than 6,000 feet of total climbing through jaw-droppingly gorgeous mountains. I took a two-and-a-half-hour break by crystal-clear Silver Lake to make my first hot meal in seven days.

Harvesting the energy of the sun for my cell phone and bike lights.

Arrived at the 8,500-foot peak in late evening and then did 30 miles of downhill, dropping a mile in elevation in one and a half hours through bitter cold fresh air. Pitched tent outside a government building last night in Minden, Nevada. I'm happy, healthy, hydrated and well nourished. Coming up is a week of cycling through the Nevada desert along Highway 50.

DAY 9: MORNING VISITORS

Imagine spying a tent tucked away in the shrubbery of your town's courthouse — that's what the Minden police came across this morning. Given that we were sleeping at a government office I knew we'd have to get on the road early, but my actions failed to meet my knowledge. I woke to the police snooping around my tent, but they quite enjoyed my story and were happy to continue conversing with me after running my license and coming up with a clean record.

I passed the morning catching up online until close to 11 a.m. From there it was 14 miles to Carson City, Nevada. I found a little organic store where I stocked up on locally grown apples, grapefruit, carrots, broccoli and a few other foods, most importantly, honey. I live off of that stuff. It has 17 grams of carbohydrates per

tablespoon, and it revs me up every time I take a gulp from the jar. I also stopped at a little farm lake and filtered my gallon of water to last me the day.

After 20 miles or so of pedaling we wound up in Dayton, where gold was first discovered in the state of Nevada. I struck gold here too: I mined a dumpster with four bags of perfectly good bread and three bottles of water. This will serve as my reserve food and water as I cross the desert. I have so much rice and potatoes that I don't need the bread, but for quick carbs it will serve its purpose.

The night was surprisingly warm and with the fire was downright hot. I cooked up a trout I was given in the Sierras along with golden beets, sweet potato, yam, garlic and rosemary,

and man, was it good. Even with the slow start we cranked out 55 miles today, which makes me realize what can be done with a full day of biking. We decided tomorrow we would shoot for 100, a first for me.

DAY 10: THE LONELIEST ROAD IN AMERICA

When I woke up at 7:30 the sun was already shining bright and it was warm enough to comfortably get out of bed. The lake was awaiting, but first I cooked up today's energy: a pot of wild rice, potatoes, onion, garlic and kale. Then I bathed and swam in the 60-degree water, washed my clothes and purified my water for the day. What a beautiful morning to spend on this lake surrounded by desert. By 10 a.m. we hit the road, which for the first mile was the sandy gravel road to the lake. It was tough pushing but easier than I was expecting. Then on a downhill I picked up too much speed and fishtailed out of control. The bike and trailer crashed into the road, and I skidded across the rocks on hands and feet for five feet. My gloves kept my hands unscathed, and the trailer was undamaged minus a bit of a tear in the waterproof bag. The tires were spinning, but the bike was fine. This bamboo bike is one tough ride.

Onto the main road and I jammed like I never have before. I'm powered by the heat of the sun, fresh cold water, natural whole food, clean desert air, ample sleep and honey. My spirits are high and my body is running like a finely tuned machine. I knocked out 25 miles in 1.5 hours, averaging 16 mph. The late start might not make it possible to hit 100 miles today but 75 plus without a doubt.

What's that you say, Highway 50? Slow down, you want to spend more time with me? NO WAY. I'm going to roll through you like there's no tomorrow, and I'm going to let you keep the title of "The Loneliest Road in America." I've got my short shorts on, and you'll have to flatten my tires and blast me with 30-mile-per-hour winds to slow me down.

More pedaling on "The Loneliest Road in America" and the

41

Camping out under the expansive Nevada sky.

road was starting to become true to its name. Big vasts of brush land surrounded by mountains on every side. The road was smooth, wind was minimal, and there was a bit of cloud coverage keeping me cool. All those ingredients made for a good day of cranking out the miles. A few trucks flew by in the opposite direction and blasted their horn at me while flipping me the bird. I don't understand why some drivers hate people on bikes so much. I can only conclude that it is ignorance. To judge someone based on the type of vehicle they are riding just makes no sense to me. Sadly this has been a daily occurrence and the honking definitely gets to me. Sometimes it's friendly and other times it nearly scares me right off the road. But the road was beautiful and it was nice to be out there.

For miles and miles people had written their names and love messages and the like in stones right along the highway. It was a very interesting sight. We also saw a sign to an earthquake fault that was six miles off the road. I can only imagine what that fault would have looked like. Earlier in the day we saw some giant white sand dunes to the north that looked like a scene from Aladdin. It would have been fun to visit both of those spots, but I have other lands on my mind. You might think that riding through the Nevada desert would be boring, but it is all but that. You just never know what you are going to see and today was a unique day in my life.

Purifying water from a well of sorts.

Around 7 p.m. I still had the energy to bike for a few more hours and had every intention of doing just that. Then I saw a concrete structure on the side of the road that looked like a well. Sure enough it was. And it was powered by a windmill that appeared to pump water into it when it was spinning. I was a bit dehydrated and had been rationing my water so it was a very exciting find. I guzzled the rest of my water down and filled up my bottles. As I was in the well I decided it would make the most sense to stay in the area for the night. That way I'd have unlimited water all night and in the morning and start out with a full load of water. So we set up camp while it was still light out and were in bed by 9:30 p.m. It ended up being a 71-mile day, and I was satisfied with that. Maybe tomorrow will be a 100-mile day.

DAY 11: NEVADA ANSWERS MY CALL

I had a good morning start. Woke up at 6:30 and cooked myself up a huge pot of beans and rice, took down camp, and

Taking down my tent while cooking breakfast and lunch.

purified water for the day. A fair amount of work just to eat, drink water and sleep but that's the way it is on the road when you're cooking your own meals, drinking from natural sources and pitching a tent.

By nine I was on the bike and had a slight tail wind. Things were looking good and I had that 100 mile day in mind.

Then Nevada said "no," over and over again. She blew cold wind straight at me all morning long. I was still managing ten mph but it was hard-fought and draining. On top of that she put hills in front of me for miles and miles. She wasn't going to take it easy on me, it was obvious. We hovered at around 5,000 feet of elevation for most of the morning, and the wind was chilly enough to keep me fully clothed.

From there Nevada gave me a six- or seven-mile climb up to Austin, a small town of about 150 people at 7,500 feet above sea level. I had no idea Nevada had peaks this high or that I would be climbing them. In my hectic preparation for the trip I had done only the research I absolutely needed, and the geography of Nevada was not included. I assumed it would be low-elevation desert, but it actually has the fifth-highest average elevation of all the states in the country.

The gas station in town provided me with warmth for a short time, and although there was nothing there I could eat, the owner went back to his house and got me a pound of venison from a deer he had killed that year. It was frozen so I'd have to wait a day for it to thaw out. It was getting colder outside by the minute, and I contemplated getting a hotel in town but stuck to my mission and decided to climb on to the campground that Champy, the gas station owner, said was eight miles east of town.

As the light faded behind the snowcapped mountains I saw a shiny jet on the horizon beaming through the sky. Tears nearly fell to my cheeks as I imagined all the comfortable people inside peeking out their windows at the earth below or napping away on their way to their comfortable homes or hotel rooms. I imagined warm dinners with friends and family around an oak dining

44

table. Laughter, hugs, love and friendship in the air. A table full of delicious things like mashed potatoes, warm bread, steamed vegetables and glasses of red wine. And here I was on this freezing cold, snowcapped mountain all by myself.

I climbed another 1000 feet in elevation from Austin, and when I reached the campsite after dark it was below 40 degrees already at 8,000-plus feet above sea level. I made a fire and sat there for a while listening to the coyotes that had made a kill not too far away. It was forecasted to get down to 26 degrees tonight, and I was sure I'd make it through the night, but it could be a miserable one. My sleeping bag is only rated for 40 degrees, but I have warm clothes on and wrapped a blanket around my feet and legs. Plus I filled a pan full of hot coals and brought it in the tent with me, which warmed the air and my hands as I typed.

DAY 12: TOO COLD FOR COMFORT

I've underestimated Nevada. It is way colder, way more mountainous, and way windier than I was hoping. It got down into the mid-20s last night and didn't warm up for me for almost the entire day. I woke up a dozen times during the night in my sleeping bag with the little kid's blanket I had wrapped around my feet. A few times I wanted to call out to Brent but was scared I wouldn't hear back so I didn't. I actually thought the Florida boy might be dead. Around 9:30 a.m., when I finally was ready to get out of bed, I called his name half expecting not to hear back from him, but he responded with a muffled "Yeah." A big relief for me. Our morning conversation revolved around figuring out how to not have another night like this.

The riding started with six to eight miles of fast, freezing, downhill cycling. The next three hours were agony. The goal was to get to Eureka, 63 miles east. A cold wind was blowing straight into my face and I just kept pumping my legs but much of the time I was only going 6 mph. I was downright miserable from the wind, not to mention a lot of climbing. We were

Bundled up to stay warm in the cold Nevada desert.

between 6,500 and 7,500 feet all day. I thought Nevada was low desert, not over a mile high. Without the freezing wind it would have been quite nice out. The only way out of this torturous place is by pedaling.

The afternoon did get easier. The wind died a bit and we hit a fair amount of downhill. In 63 miles we did not sight a single service station, but there were plenty of dust tornadoes, snowy mountains and wide-open expanses full of shrubs. We arrived in Eureka, a town of 1,500 people, at around 7 p.m., a solid hour before dark. First stop was Rainee's grocery store, and the only local food they had was eggs. I stocked up on two dozen. Even those were in a package though.

It's amazing how little local food most small markets carry. Most of our food comes from thousands of miles away. The most common statistic is that the average meal in America travels 1,500 miles from farm to fork. And I've seen firsthand that much of our fruits, vegetables, cheese and other food items travel 3,000 to 7,000 miles from places like Chile, Spain and New Zealand. Check the label next time you are buying something and you'll see for yourself. I have no interest in purchasing food from the other side of the country or the world. On this trip my food on average has traveled less than 250 miles to reach my stomach with a majority of it coming from within an hour's drive. In the near future, I hope we will get back to communities that create their own food. It's looking promising, and it does seem to be coming back, but we've got a long way to go.

Just behind the market there's a little park where I set up camp. There's a grill that made it much easier to cook my food. I ate four eggs and boiled up another dozen. I also cooked up about a quarter pound of the venison. I was completely out of water and very thirsty, but there's a spring behind the police station a few blocks away and I planned on filling up in the morning. It was way too cold to walk over there tonight.

DAY 13: YEARNING FOR CIVILIZATION

The only way to the promised land, which at this point is any state besides Nevada, is to keep on pedaling. So of course that's what I did today. I yearn for civilization so bad.

The day started with a long but easy climb which took a solid hour, and from there it was almost ten miles of downhill. That was followed by a long valley with some short uphills and a lot of wind blasting me in the face.

A second summit, at 7,500 feet, was just a bit taller than the last and was followed by another long downhill where I was able to tack on the miles. I hit another long valley and then had a third climb through a beautiful pass followed by a looooong downhill through beautiful terrain. I thought, "This is Nevada?" Every day the terrain is changing and some days it changes a fair amount.

The day was coming to an end and there was one more nine-mile climb in between me and my goal of 63 miles and I knew I just wouldn't be able to do it. Plus it would have been colder up there. So we scoured the roadsides as the sun set and ended up setting up camp in what appeared to be a quarry/mining site. We were a good one hundred feet off the road and completely hidden from everyone. It was flat and open and I was very happy to have found this spot. I built a fire, cooked some rice with zucchini, artichoke, tomato and garlic and ate a few more of the eggs I had bought yesterday.

DAY 14: WARMTH

The sun is shining, the wind is at my back, and I'm free of burdensome clothing. But that doesn't mean I'm sticking around Nevada.

There was about six miles of climbing and twice I stopped to shed clothes, leaving me in just my underwear. I'm free. I perform so much better in minimal clothes. They tend to slow me down physically and mentally. Things sure are looking up. The sun is shining bright, I'm getting a tan, the wind is at my back and there was about 15 miles of downhill into Ely. In celebration of all this

I pedaled seven miles naked. Only 30 or so trucks and cars passed me, and I don't think most of them even noticed. I was just happy not to see a police car — it remains a mystery what their reaction to a nude biker would have been.

Compared to yesterday when I didn't even get on the road until noon, I had pedaled 23 miles by noon. Then I spent a few hours in the small town of Ely catching up on the computer.

I stopped at a beautiful creek to collect water and cleanse my body. It had been a few days without washing, and I came out of the creek feeling like a new man. The earth gave me more fortunate wind along with warmth from the sun, which allowed me to push on for a total of 64 miles. I spent the night on BLM (Bureau of Land Management) land, which is public land free for anyone to enjoy and camp in. BLM land spreads far and wide across the western half of the United States, totaling 250 million acres, over twice the size of California (the third-largest state in the country). For anyone traveling by road it's excellent to know you can pull off and set up camp anywhere on this land.

DAY 15: GOODBYE NEVADA, HELLO UTAH

I made it out of Nevada. And I'm proud of my stats:
- Six days, seven nights
- 400 miles, seven or so passes at around 7,500 feet
- Zero light switches turned on
- Not a drop of water from a faucet
- One outlet plug to charge my computer for 1.5 hours
- All food purchased was locally grown and organic and only two packaged items, which were eggs in cardboard cartons from a local farm
- Seven naked miles biked
- Swore only one time
- Planted wildflowers every day.

On to Utah. Life elevated. Excited to visit Goal Zero and the PowerPot in Salt Lake City this week and learn more about their sustainable products.

You know that good kind of exhausted where you are excited to get in bed and when you do you can hardly keep your eyes open to read a page of a book or watch an episode on TV? That kind of exhausted when you know it was a good day and you accomplished a lot? That's the exhausted I felt tonight. There were some tough days back in Nevada, and lying there with only one sleeping bag on and my hands out in the open it was hard to fathom that just four nights ago I thought Brent might have died in the night of hypothermia.

It's not like I haven't been out in the elements. I grew up camping every month for many years in Boy Scouts and fondly remember building igloos and sleeping snugly on sub-zero nights. I've trekked solo into the jungles of Borneo and spent multiple, consecutive lonely nights in remote jungles searching for wildlife, eating bugs and chopping down banana trees to get at the goods. I just wasn't prepared for or expecting what Nevada had in store for me. When it comes to survival situations, preparation makes all the difference and can make a torturous scenario quite enjoyable. My last few years in sunny San Diego may have weakened me a bit, too.

But here I am now in Utah and it was an exquisite day. The first hour and a half was all climbing, but it was smooth and enjoyable. A small creek provided me with water for the rest of the day. Once I reached the Sacramento pass at 7,154 feet it was downhill for ten-plus miles. That took me into the Great Basin, a valley 30 to 40 miles wide.

Then came the "Welcome to Utah" sign, which brought me great joy. The instant difference in terrain when I enter a new state gives me great pleasure. The land was drier, the mountains were sculpted differently, the air felt different, and the environment was more alive. I've learned to become very thankful for biting insects because they are a sign of warmth. When the temperature drops below a certain threshold most insects die off. With warm weather comes biting insects. That is a tradeoff I am completely willing to take because it's better than biting cold. When I called it a night I had hit my goal of 80 miles for the day, my longest day yet. That's why I had that good kind of exhausted.

Tonight I gave thanks. To the earth, just for being. To my parents, for putting me on earth and leading me in the direction of a sustainable life. To my Aunt Louise, for always being a vital part of my life. To my Boy Scout leaders Mike Hines, Ron Cline, and Owen Gorman, for preparing me for life and making these tasks I am dealing with easier today. To my fellow Eagle Scouts Paul Hines, Kyle Schulz, Dan Hudak, Neil Belsky and Pat Cline for challenging me, motivating me and keeping me in Scouts long enough to attain the rank of Eagle Scout. To John and Sheila Schulz and Mike and Dawn Hines, for helping to sculpt me during my adolescence into the man I am today. I love you all, thanks for being such an influential part of my life.

DAY 16: A LITTLE BIT OF LUCK

Today I was feeling as grateful as ever. Tears of thankfulness and appreciation streamed down my cheeks this afternoon as I pedaled across the western Utah desert thinking of the people that shaped my adolescent self into the man I am today. Particularly the tears came when I thought of my mom back in my hometown of Ashland, Wisconsin. Every one of the approximately 842 million seconds I have lived on this planet has led to me being exactly where I am today, and every one of the hundreds of thousands of human interactions has made me who I am.

Looking back on the people that came in and out of my life and the experiences they've created for me brings deep feelings of appreciation to what I call my heart. I am who I am today because of each of the people that have entered my life, whether it was for a day, a semester, my entire childhood, or decades.

I've learned that good creates good. So my advice to anyone who wants to make the world a better place is to start with yourself. Be a good person, live a healthy lifestyle, go out of your way to help others, share your knowledge, your possessions and your life. By being a good person you will inspire others to be good and that is the ripple effect that can change the world. By starting with yourself and eating healthily, exercising, drinking plenty of water, and getting fresh air and ample sleep you will find you are living a planet-friendly lifestyle and that will make you feel even better. A happy you is the best thing you can do.

It was quite the morning and by noon I had ridden about 30 miles. I found a tree full of shoes that I climbed and played on for a half hour or so and towards the end a branch broke, crashing to the ground five or ten feet below, with me underneath. I was fine but when I looked around I realized barbed wire lay just inches from my behind and a broken bottle just inches from my right leg. A dear friend, Cheryl, recently wrote to me, "I always admire your secret power of being lucky." I thought of her in this instance as I sat on the desert floor and felt very lucky. Much of what people consider luck is hard work and dedication that they don't see, but this was an instance of pure luck. Back on the bike with just a few scratches, another hour of pedaling led me into Hinckley and then Delta.

I expected to knock the miles out in less than two hours but the evening had other plans for me. Rain was visible from all four directions, but for some reason none was coming down on me. Big winds pushed me up the hill and rain came from behind. I cranked the pedals as hard as I could, thinking if I could make it over the hill, maybe the winds would push me away from the rain. Well the rain indeed never caught up except for a couple dozen drops, but the sudden exertion stirred up pain in my already sore knees.

Still 15 miles from the camping area, the next hour or two was a hard fought battle, but I just couldn't make it. A half hour after dark I finally settled just off the side of the road after completing a total of 75 miles, probably a few miles short of the campground. Instead I was on the roadside in a nice field. This works just fine, but there was no wood to build a fire, leaving me with a head of purple cabbage, tomatoes, salad and raw onion for dinner. I was craving a cooked meal with some serious carbs, but I was full and will make that happen in the morning.

DAY 17: PUSHING THROUGH THE RAIN

This morning I awoke in the field very exhausted after a night full of dreaming. My knees were still aching and I was quite lethargic, but I managed to pack up and hit the road a short 40 minutes after awakening.

I pedaled reluctantly up hills and made slow progress. On through the fields I pedaled, and the clouds continued to roll in as I gently climbed. Then steeper climbing led me to Eureka, Utah, one of the most rundown yet compelling cities in America. Most of the buildings on Main Street were half-standing and had so much character to them. The ones that were still together mostly had closed signs on their doors reading "Open Wed–Sun." It was Monday. I thought, am I in America?

A new challenge had arisen — rain. My time in the desert appeared to be over. I wasn't exactly ready for the rain, especially the

Eating my meal under a carport while waiting for the rain to pass.

cold rain, but while I waited for it to pass I cooked myself a badly needed meal of eggs, mushrooms, potatoes and onions. While eating, I also prepared a similar meal for later on, except I replaced the eggs with tofu and made a soup instead. Many of these ingredients I had gathered earlier from a grocery store that was tossing them out. I didn't even have to dig through the dumpster — an employee who had heard about the mission I was on had given me them, inviting me into the back to take whatever I desired from the boxes that were bound for the dumpster. I had very little cell phone service all day and the lack of sun meant my drained batteries wouldn't be getting recharged. Not much communication with the outside world today.

The rains let up and I continued on. I spent ten miles descending a steep mountain, and as I lost elevation the rains dissipated. Ten miles later the road started to wind along Utah Lake. With snowcapped mountains in the distance and rolling hills surrounding the blue lake, I saw beauty in every direction and around every corner. Twenty miles after the gloomy mountain town of Eureka I decided to reach out to my contacts in Salt Lake City. I now had only 27 more miles to go until Bluffdale, a southern suburb where Goal Zero is located.

At 9:30 p.m. I started looking for a spot to sleep. It took a little while but I ended up on Porter Rockwell Road on the edge of a rock quarry with my own panoramic view of the city. It was gorgeous up there and I felt good inside my tent. The rain was sprinkling down as it had been for much of the day and the wind was ruffling the rain fly. I was completely parched as I did not do a good job of harvesting water today, but I knew I would sleep well. Maybe I'd dream of waterfalls pouring into my mouth and drinking fresh cold milk straight from the cow. It was a long exhausting day, and I felt like I was just barely dragging myself into civilization. A spoke broke on my wheel today and it was wobbling like an egg down a hill. My gear needs attention, my body needs healing, and my mind needs rest. I still managed to pedal 65 miles

Sunrise in Utah with our tents in the foreground.

and I'm just five miles from Goal Zero, who I'll visit in the morning. If not waterfalls and fresh milk maybe my dreams will be of the flat Midwest states of America where food and water will be abundant.

DAY 18: SALT LAKE CITY

I woke up much earlier than usual, around 6:30 a.m., and was greeted by a gorgeous sunrise over the mountains to the east. I found a big rain puddle, used my microfiber towel and soap, and before I knew it was looking spiffy enough to go to a formal event. I threw on some clean clothes, moisturized with coconut oil, put some essential oils on, and I swear you would have thought I was a civilized man.

I went over to Goal Zero and spent three hours hanging out with them. They have about 100 employees and I probably met about 70 of them, from sales to social media to research and development to shipping. It was very cool to check out the many processes of their businesses and I learned a lot about solar power. Their staff is incredibly fun. What I like the most about Goal Zero is they are bringing the idea of solar power and alternative energy to the public. They are showing people that the sun can in fact produce electricity and that we can have energy that causes less harm to the environment and is much more sustainably produced. It's more about the grand idea than the energy that is created, although they are doing a serious amount of business and generating a pretty solid amount of solar energy. The tricky

thing is the amount of energy and resources that is being used to create these little solar panels and batteries. Most of the people who buy them will never use them enough to offset the impact of their creation. Hence the importance of nationwide alternative energy rather than each of us having to have our own gadgets to create it. Goal Zero is a big part of the awareness in this process because people have to actually see solar power to realize its reality.

Then I was off to REI to give some attention to my bike and pick up a few small items that would make my daily life on the road a little simpler. Again I was very impressed by their acts of sustainability, particularly with their lack of packaging on their line of gear. Most of it just has a simple tag. They fixed the spoke and got the bike working. By now it was already 5 p.m. and I still wasn't even in Salt Lake City. I had close to 20 miles to ride to get to Riley's house downtown, and rain stopped me from knocking that all out in one piece. Huge rain clouds came from the eastern mountains, and I had to duck inside a restaurant for an hour to let them pass over.

Next I went on a mission to find locally produced food, with minimal success. First I went to Whole Foods where I found cheese, mushrooms and honey. Then I stopped in at Sprouts and they didn't have a single local item. I spent an hour in the two stores learning about products and when and what local items they carry. In the summertime, during the growing season, Whole Foods gets some local produce, but overall a very tiny percentage of what they sell comes from the state of Utah. I've been in at least a dozen larger grocery stores so far on this trip and have found that many of them carry no food from within the state, and the ones that do have a mere handful of items. It's crazy. Food is one of the only things we need to survive, yet for the most part we don't create it in our communities or even nearby. Instead we have it grown thousands of miles away and shipped here. We have the ability to produce and eat local food; we've just decided we want tens of thousands of choices of food in packaging that seems to be showing off a prize rather than food. The average supermarket today has 47,000 products on its shelves. I was not discouraged and it was a great learning experience.

DAY 19: A DAY IN TOWN

It is Day 19 and I have not yet turned on a light switch or used a drop of water from the grid, and have plugged in to just one outlet. The areas I have used electricity are automatic doors, automatic lights, cash registers, Wi-Fi and getting cash at the bank. I avoid all of these when possible but have used all of them on a few occasions. If an automatic light turns on I usually go unscrew it.

I was off to Liberty Heights Fresh where I was told I would be able to find local food and wow, was it an amazing little market. They had dozens of local products even though it was not the growing season. Beef, lamb, pork, goat, milk, yogurt, eggs, honey, dozens of cheeses, jams and dried fruits, all from the state of Utah, mostly within 100 miles. No fruits and veggies shipped from the other side of the world here. It was great to see this. I purchased milk, two dozen eggs, goat yogurt and 32 ounces of honey, all in packaging, but the best part is all of it will be reused when I bring it back to them tomorrow: the milk jug is refillable and has a $2 deposit, the yogurt cup and the egg cartons will get used again at the market by the vendors, and I will give the honey jar to someone to store food in once I have emptied it. It's zero-waste shopping while still buying food in packaging, which is new to me. Janet the "fresh foods wrangler" showed me all around the store and it was such a great learning experience. In a few weeks they will start to have all sorts of local produce. Another great thing about Liberty Heights Fresh is they don't let anything go to waste. Food that will go bad is given to people for free, given to local farmers to feed animals, or composted.

It was great casually biking around town with a much lighter than usual trailer, and I cruised through some nice parks, though I was hoping to not get on the bike at all on my "rest day." I stopped at the bank and got cash for the next leg of the trip, made a quick stop at home to eat some of my fresh food and then headed to Saturday Cycles to get my bike tuned up. They were very busy with the spring season, but Mark Kennedy, the owner, managed to squeeze me in. It was such a wonderful experience spending time at his cool shop. Mark was a very nice guy, and he did everything for me for free to help with the cause. His kindness touched my heart. The most exciting part of my experience there is he is going to join One Percent for the Planet.

One Percent for the Planet is a very simple concept. It means your business gives one percent of its revenue to environmental non profits. There are over 3,000 approved organizations in the network that you can donate to, from bike advocacy and alternative energy to water conservation and music in the classroom. It's a simple, easy process to join, and besides the fact that you are giving to great organizations it is an excellent branding and marketing move for nearly any business. A few awesome members are Jack Johnson, Clif Bar and New Belgium Brewery, and the people at Patagonia who founded the organization.

I spent a few hours at the PowerPot in the afternoon, and it was an extremely educational experience. I learned how they use thermoelectric conductivity to charge USB-powered devices like cell phones, lights and steriPENS from fire and boiling water. They hand-make the pots right there in the shop and showed me the process from start to finish. The room was full of tech dudes who really knew what they were doing and had passion in their product.

It is an absolutely amazing concept. While I cook dinner I can plug my phone, or any USB-powered device, into the pot, and it will charge the battery by using thermoelectric technology to create electricity from excess heat. Thermoelectric generators produce electricity based on the difference in temperature between the liquid in the pot and the bottom of the

pot where the generator is. The technology takes energy that would not have been otherwise used and turns it into usable electricity. The beauty of the PowerPot is that you can turn any fuel source into power for your mobile devices. Wherever your adventures take you, all you need is fire and water to keep charging. Besides being an awesome product for camping and emergency preparedness, the people in developing countries who they donate to cherish it.

DAY 20: BACK INTO THE WILD!

It felt so good to be back on the road. My bike was running smooth thanks to Mark, and it was a picture-perfect night to be pedaling along Interstate 80 in Utah. This might be the only 20 miles of the 4,700 miles that I will ride on the interstate. There wasn't a direct way to get out to Park City off the interstate and this cut out some time. It was a solid three hours of climbing, but I was very happy with how easy it was. The ride started at around 4,200 feet and ended at 7,000 feet. Today was a short day of riding and I am staying with a friend of a friend tonight. I have one more night in the comforts of a home before a week or so of roughing it through the Rocky Mountains.

DAY 21: CHANGE YOUR PERSPECTIVE AND CHANGE YOUR LIFE

It felt real good to wake up inside a warm house. We all tend to take for granted the things we have. Every day I try to remember that many people are not fortunate to have simple things like food, clean drinking water and a warm bed. One thing I have learned on my adventures around the world and in the USA is that by putting myself in challenging situations and removing the luxuries of life I come to appreciate them so much more. Most people who know me realize I am an extremely cheerful and happy person. I'll let you in on a secret. I appreciate the simple things in life and try to be happy with whatever comes my way and that makes it very easy to feel content. Change your perspective and you'll change your life.

A relaxing cruise with multiple distractions through Park City led me to Highway 40, which I will be on for the next 450-plus miles. It was a beautiful day to be on the road, and I was able

One of the many summits I crossed during the journey.

to crank out 72 miles with a good deal of ascending but an even greater amount of descending. There were some seriously long downhill stretches. I love watching my trip odometer on the long downhill slopes. All day long beautiful creeks meandered along the roadside and that is where I got my drinking water.

Tonight I found a rest stop with a quaint tucked-away area to set up my tent. I'm hanging out inside the heated building very much appreciating the shelter and lights that are providing me a comfortable evening. I am amazed that I could bike over 70 miles today, communicate with my business back home, talk to friends on the phone, return e-mails, write and have a relaxing morning. So much can be done in a day.

DAY 22: MY MOBILE OFFICE

The fight for a healthier planet stepped up a notch today. I picked up a headset with a microphone in Salt Lake City and have turned my bamboo bike into a mobile office of doing good. I will strive to make it the most productive office on pedal-powered wheels in the USA from now until I reach the One Percent for the Planet headquarters in Vermont on August 1. I can now talk with sustainable nonprofits and business, brainstorm with peers, inspire friends and family, and make arrangements for gatherings along the route as I pedal. Also I've loaded up my phone with sustainability podcasts to increase my knowledge during my "down time." I will be sharing this knowledge

A typical highway that you could have found me pedaling on across America. Sometimes the shoulders were drastically narrower but this was typical.

with anyone wanting to learn how to live a more earth-friendly lifestyle.

The purpose of this crazy adventure is to inspire and teach others to live a happier, healthier life and in turn lead a life that is more earth-friendly; a life with less consumption, less waste and less usage of valuable resources. A life with more health, more happiness, more physical activity, more time in the outdoors and more nutritionally wholesome food. A life with more community, sharing, giving back, and love and friendship. A life that makes the planet smile as well as the people around you.

The 75 miles I pedaled through the eastern Utah high desert today flew by as I chatted away on the phone brainstorming ideas of how to help others live a more sustainable lifestyle. I talked to friends and family, and everyone is so excited about this adventure. People are inspired and I am excited about that. The sun beat down on me fiercely all day on Highway 40.

I arrived in Vernal, Utah with a solid hour of daylight left. I am staying with a host from WarmShowers, which is a community for touring cyclists and hosts. Sometimes the host has a room for you, sometimes a couch and sometimes just a yard to camp in. Patrick, my host for tonight, has a cozy little home, and it's splendid to sit in his living room in a comfortable chair as I write. Brent and him are in the kitchen sharing a spaghetti dinner telling stories of adventure. A perfect stranger is now a good friend who is sharing his life, his food and his home with us. We live in a wonderful country with so much to offer.

So are you inspired to live a more earth-friendly life? Here are a few ways you can get started that take minimal effort but will make a big difference:

- Conserve water and electricity
- Avoid single-use items
- Bike or walk instead of drive
- Shop local and buy unpackaged food

- Donate to sustainable causes
- Reduce–Reuse–Recycle
- Buy real whole foods that are not full of chemicals and dozens of ingredients
- Share with family and friends
- Be good to each other, yourself and your body, live a healthy life and be good to each other. In turn you will be good for the earth.

Just make an effort to be good and do good. Doing something good that makes you feel good will make you want to do more good so it becomes easier. It's a ripple effect that can change the world. Start small. Start simple. But just do something today.

DAY 23: DO GOOD

We've really got it made in America and I am so thankful for this. Patrick sent me off with a pound of meat from an elk he killed just five miles from his home. I'm not much of a meat eater, but if I'm going to eat meat I prefer it to be from a wild animal that lived freely and ate wild food from the land. Back home I stick to a vegetarian or vegan diet, but on this trip I am taking the opportunity to eat any local natural food I find.

I was off at noon and it was a scorcher. The sun beat down hard and the land was dry. After pedaling for about 16 miles I came across the Green River, where I spent an hour sitting under a shady bridge and purifying drinking water from the very muddy river. At 4 p.m. I hit the Colorado border and let out a yelp of joy. I've pedaled over the Sierra Nevada Mountains of California,

With Patrick, my Warm Showers host in Vernal, Utah.

Purifying drinking water from the Green River in Utah.

across the entire barren state of Nevada, through the elevated state of Utah, and now here I am in Colorado. Driving here in a car would have been a bit of a task in itself, and I've managed to bike here. What a cool thought that is.

The first town in Colorado was Dinosaur, a tiny town with next to nothing in it. Outside of Dinosaur the hills continued to rise above me, and as I neared the top of each hill I kept expecting a long downhill. Again and again I was met with just a small downhill and a long uphill afterwards. The day was coming to an end, and I was hoping to make it to a water source that Patrick had told me about at Elk Springs. I didn't arrive until after dark, but it was a great little spot to camp with well water, a picnic table and a streetlight. All these things made for some serious comfort. I cooked up an elk soup with ginger, garlic, potatoes and onions (all from a grocery store dumpster in Vernal) and enjoyed it as I sat at the picnic table.

Today was an inspiring day. I can feel big things coming in the future and it excites me. Without a doubt in my mind, this earth is going to be a happier, healthier place because of my efforts.

Do something good today!

DAY 24: OVERCOMING THE DARKNESS

So much inspiration churned inside my body today that shivers erupted from my skin and tears exploded from my eyes. The inspiration coursed through my veins from head to toe all through the day as I pedaled up and down the green Colorado hills. My elated spirits soared the highest as I flew downhill and jammed out on flat land, but all day they were present. Jack Johnson, Trevor Green and Xavier Rudd — along with some educational sustainability podcasts — inspired me to keep on pedaling through the intense heat and in turn to keep inspiring others to live a happier, healthier life.

The tears came as I thought of the amazing changes that are to come and the people out there doing good, bettering their lives and inspiring others to do the same. Not for the sake of religion, or government, or any organization, but solely for the sake of us as individuals, community and the planet we call home.

The morning continued to heat up as the sun moved overhead and the rolling hills continued on as far as the eye could see. By 2 p.m. I had pedaled 50 miles and was exhausted. I stopped in a cool building in the town of Craig as I could not bear the heat any longer. At 4 p.m. I moved on, still feeling lethargic from the heat. Out of water and quite thirsty I saw a grouping of about 30 bee boxes I couldn't resist investigating. I sat amongst the honeybees as thousands buzzed around me going about their business. Occasionally they flew into me or landed on me, but they had no qualms with me being in their presence. Many cleaned themselves as they rested on my arms and legs and seeing this made me realize they were quite comfortable. I've wanted to do this for many years and to finally spend time amongst masses of bees was a dream come true. As I child I very much feared bees and wasps but I've grown more comfortable with them over time. I learned recently that some beekeepers do their work without bee suits so I knew that with the proper mindset (be calm) and this knowledge, I too could spend time amongst the bees unprotected. Experience is always king though, so today was a landmark day for my development in being comfortable with these creatures.

Not to mention all the honey I sipped from my jar while they buzzed around me.

Sipping honey from my jar while the bees buzzed around me.
Bee boxes are in the foreground.

After an hour I pedaled on in search of a river to quench my thirst. I found one just five miles east and spent time sitting on the bank guzzling water as I purified it. I topped off my water bottle and was back on the bike. Conversations with friends helped the miles fly by. I had another 45 miles to make it to my friend John Miller's house in Steamboat Springs and wasn't sure if I'd be able to do it, but his home beckoned me to continue on.

As the sun set and the light faded in the sky I received a call from a friend that changed everything. I had 25 miles left to pedal and the conversation led me into darkness. Immersed in the conversation, it was becoming night as a change in topic launched a dagger into my heart. I was on the verge of a new type of tears, very different from the tears of inspiration earlier — tears of sorrow. This conversation marked the end of a deep love for me, she was moving on, and I felt left behind. Two years of emotions churned inside of me.

I pedaled on for miles through the darkness feeling great depths of sadness. It was pitch black now, and I texted John to let him know that I was still riding but would make it to his home that night. I needed the comforts of a home and a hug from a friend to help cure my sorrows and bring me comfort. As I texted I realized I was not on the road anymore but in the ditch on the opposite side of the road. Very confused but still on my bike I managed to stop safely before hitting anything; simultaneously, coyotes began to howl nearby. I pulled myself out of the ditch and continued on. I had no lights on as the batteries were dead and shortly later was blinded by the flashing red and blue lights of a police car. Wes, the officer, was very friendly and wanted to make sure I was safe, but in my sorrowful state the flashing lights added to my disorientation. I wrangled up some rechargeable batteries with a bit of energy left and was on my way.

The dagger still in my heart, I felt like I couldn't go on. Hopelessness overwhelmed me. I knew I must though and I knew a positive attitude and a smile would overcome s,orrow and despair. Looking at it from a different perspective I could see light beginning to shine upon me. Wait, is that a headlight? No. It is a light representing a new beginning. With every end there is a new beginning. I had shed an unneeded weight that was holding me down and now I was free.

The inspiration flowed back into my body and a smile grew on my face. Just five minutes prior I had felt like my world had ended. This is proof that life is a matter of perspective, and as I've said before, happiness is a choice.

Pedaling my bike enhanced my ability to move on. Every physical mile forward, every mile closer to Vermont, helped me to move on and move forward in my own emotional battle.

I continued on for ten more miles to Steamboat Springs through the darkness and the cold to the house of a fellow Wisconsinite, John Miller. He welcomed me into his warm home, and I sat down on his comfortable couch, where I ended the long day 97 miles down the road from where I had started.

DAY 25: DARE TO BE YOURSELF. LIVE FREE

The sadness left within me from yesterday provided great contrast to the high spirits and inspiration that overcame it when I gave them a chance. The contrast provided me with deep appreciation for happiness and reminded me that whenever things are bad they always get better with time. This contrast is what makes us feel alive. This is what life is. Life is ups and downs. The ups make the downs and the downs make the ups. Without one you don't have the other. You just have to push through the downs. The biking is not so much of an issue for me. That's the easy part. It's the mental part that causes the great struggles, the distractions of emotions. Biking is mostly mental, so as long as I can muster up the strength to get past that I know anything is possible.

It was a slow, but needed, start to the day. I was really feeling the 97 miles from yesterday in my legs, unlike any other day so far. I spent the morning on the computer (powered by my solar panel) in a beautiful home with a view of the valley of Steamboat Springs. I made a fire in the pit and cooked wild rice, butternut squash, potatoes, garlic and ginger. It was a pleasant morning, yet I was feeling like I should be on the road to Boulder. I left the house around 2 p.m. and stopped at Bamboo Market, where I was very pleased to find many locally grown organic foods. I picked up raw honey, rainbow chard and some potatoes, all from

Colorado. There was much more in the store, including mixed greens, arugula, meats and cheeses, but most was in packaging. I am still too early in the season for most fruits, but they will have a lot in the summer. It was a wonderful market that has been open for 22 years, and the owner, Anne, told me a lot about Colorado food production.

I took a break on my way out of town to eat some food I had stocked up on. I had grabbed most of it at a health food store dumpster: almond milk, hummus and pita, strawberries, peaches and pastries. It was 4 p.m. when I got back on the bike and rode up to the monstrous steep slope of a road that would lead me over the mountains.

This is the Rockies. A mountain range that many dream of but few conquer. The largest mountain range in the continental United States. The soundtrack of *180 Degrees South*, my favorite documentary, beckoned me up to the summit, the songs ranging from high to low in spirits. An inspirational documentary indeed that creates a stirring inside me every time I watch it. If you enjoy what I am doing take the time to watch this documentary. You will be inspired to achieve greater levels of elevation in your life.

I found myself mocking the mountains, "Come on Rockies! I'm trying to get into shape here. Could you at least put up a fight? You're supposed to be a mountain not a little speed bump!"

On the other side of the pass the world around me transformed. Snow five feet deep surrounded me when just yesterday I had been baking in the heat. This new world held white flat land surrounded by deep green coniferous trees all backdropped by a sunset with a hue of beautiful colors and a bit of blue sky. It stirred up a new emotion inside me. I continued until the only light left came from the glow of the snow surrounding me. This was an unknown world for me, 9,500 feet high with beautiful snow-melt rivers running through the white fields, veins of ice-cold water pouring out from the melting created during the heat of the day. It was magical and I could feel the magic inside me. Incredible creatures were surely hidden in the forests encircling me, yet they were nowhere to be seen. Moose, elk, wolves, bears; I can only guess at what might have been peeking at me from the tree line.

Hop on a bike and pedal somewhere. There are wonderful places waiting to be discovered right in your own backyard.

DAY 26: PEDALING THE ROCKY MOUNTAINS

It was a long night with an undesirably minimal amount of sleep. The night was cold and to conserve heat I had to fold myself up into a ball. This position did not give my weary legs a chance to recover and between the cold and my aching muscles I found myself awake for too much of the night. The morning did come but alas, it was a cloudy one and cold on top of that. When I awoke at 6 a.m., I thought about breaking down camp but instead spent a few hours in my tent on my computer. Even with the cold, it was an enjoyable morning in the snowy Rocky Mountains. I was on the road by 9:30 a.m. and was happy to leave the 9,400 feet of elevation and spend a good portion of the 40 morning miles descending. The winding road was likely the most enjoyable I've pedaled in the last four weeks; the sun even came out to greet me.

Throughout the day birds of prey accompanied me, soaring alongside me guiding me through the Rocky Mountain flats as they scanned the green pastures for prey. Midday I was fortunate to see a hawk succeed in its hunt and come up with a small rodent in its talons.

In the early afternoon rain decided to change my plans of pedaling 80 to 100 miles today. Instead I found myself ducked under an overhang of a local bar, where I spent an hour and a half waiting for the rain and hail to pass. That it did around 4:30. I continued onward, somewhat lethargically but feeling good that I had already done a fair distance of riding. Three individuals at the bar had told me the road would continue downhill to Granby but the next 16 miles were quite the opposite of downhill. In town I took a break and then continued on, intending to make it to Winter Park 20 miles away before nightfall. Just outside of

Granby the climbing resumed, past herds of beautiful cows in the pasture as more water fell from the sky. It was dark and gloomy but quite enjoyable. The sun just peeked out over the foothills behind me, creating a majestic sun shower, and in front of me a magnificent rainbow presented itself. I was astonished to see it growing across the sky and increasing in brightness with each second. It was a fabulous near-end to the night, but I was still 10 miles from the comforts of my tent and sleeping bag, where I hoped to make it an early night.

As the sun faded completely behind the foothills a new set of rain clouds opened up on me. It was downright miserable but at the same time downright awesome to be exposed to the harsh elements. Many of us forget we are a part of this earth, but the harsh elements make for a good reminder. I was happy to see a sign for a YMCA, where I pulled in to find they had rooms available. I thought about taking one but realized it would compromise my mission even if I did not use any electricity or water. They would clean the room and wash the sheets even if I did not use them, and this would use water from on the grid. Instead I stealthily explored the large complex and found a basement room with a back entrance where I hid away for the night. This simple accommodation kept me out of the rain and cold and gave me confidence that I would get a fair night's rest.

DAY 27: FLATLANDS AWAIT

Minutes after I hit the road, snow-covered mounds thousands of feet above me presented themselves in a daunting manner. Rather than feeling fear I saw them as a right of passage to my freedom. Simply by pedaling one pedal at a time I would find myself climbing the snow-covered mountains and reaching the summit, where my freedom would lie before me. From there I knew I'd see many miles of downhill, and the Great Plains of the Midwest would open up to me in the near future. My challenges of frigid cold, snow and mountain passes would be over in just a few more hours of hard pedaling. Freedom awaited.

I'd shed my long underwear, bulky sleeping bag and any other gear that would not serve a purpose on the populated eastern side of the country. Flat lands would yield easy pedaling and they were on my mind. Cities full of welcoming friends and family were in my imagination. The hardest work would be over. I felt nothing but excitement for what was to come and appreciation for the challenge that stood before me.

I casually climbed the mountain, switchback after switchback, taking in the natural beauty. The hardy green pine trees and the dazzling white snow provided a backdrop for astonishing views. 9,000, 10,000, 10,500, and then the elevation began to take its toll on me. Pedaling became forced, breathing became a challenge, and it was obvious I was over two miles above sea level.

And then before I knew it I had reached Berthoud Pass, 11,306 feet up, and the climbing was over. I was cold, short of breath and fatigued. Miles of downhill awaited me and with little hesitation I bombed down the mountainside, eager to lose a mile of elevation where I knew my body would be warmed by the heat of the sun. It became warmer by the minute, and in great admiration I whizzed past beautiful cliffs, roaring snowmelt rivers and a bountiful forest. The beauty was not quite enough to stop me from moving on, but I was certain there would be days in the flatlands of Kansas when I would yearn for the Colorado Rockies.

The warmth I was waiting for did indeed present itself, and I continued to descend for the entire afternoon. Fifteen miles on service roads weaving north and south of Interstate 70 eventually led me to Highway 6, which cut through to Golden, Colorado. It was 20 miles more downhill through Clear Creek Canyon. The shoulder was narrow, which made the beautiful road quite perilous and hard to fully take in. At one point a snowplow pulled me off of the road and told me that bikes are not allowed on this route. I felt I had no choice but to continue on since the only other option would have taken me hours out of the way so I kept pedaling after he drove off. I passed through tunnels carved into the mountains and continued along the riverside. Ten miles down the road another snowplow (or was it the same one?) gave me quite the shock. He hovered behind me as I traveled at 25 mph, either trying to run me off the road or protect me from the traffic behind him. I'll never be certain of his intentions but the rush of adrenaline kept me pedaling as fast as my legs could manage. Once at Golden I took a short break and then continued north along Highway 93 to Boulder, Colorado.

In Boulder I cleaned up in a river and was welcomed by Rich Points from Community Cycles, a bike advocacy nonprofit and One Percent for the Planet recipient. He took me to a party nearby and hosted me at his home. What a feeling it was not only to be back in civilization but to be in the world-renowned city of Boulder, where bikes are as welcome on the roads as cars, and there is a booming local food movement.

Each day on the road is unique and the scenery changes constantly. Each day you must adapt to new surroundings full of different challenges and stimulations. The challenges make the rewards even greater, and the lonely roads make the cities all the more welcoming.

DAY 28: BOULDER STEALS MY HEART

If I didn't have a country to cycle across I'd settle down right here in Boulder. This town has stolen my heart, and I am certain I will come back here to live a portion of my life. I'll start with a summer and see where it goes. What impresses me most is the number of entrepreneurs and change-makers it holds. The intentions of the people here seem to be in line with creating a healthy planet, and they actually get things done. I love a person whose actions speak louder than their words.

For lunch I met with Quayle Hodek and Tom Drzewiecki of Renewable Choice Energy to learn about their efforts. They provide sustainability consulting services to help their clients measure, understand and offset their environmental impact. A main priority of theirs is to get large corporations to use wind and solar energy rather than energy from fossil fuels. They help many companies, including Facebook, to build solar and wind farms as they expand. Sometimes they advise them to build these energy farms on site to use the electricity directly, and other times they build off-site farms to offset the energy they use. My time with these guys really opened my eyes to how electrified my life is.

So far on this trip I've made an honest effort to avoid using electricity in every way possible. I've avoided automatic doors and lights. I've taken the stairs instead of elevators even when it meant carrying my bike up with me. I haven't pushed buttons, such as the walk button for crossing the street. I've not used anyone else's phone or computer.

I have allowed myself to be around electricity that was already in use, such as sitting in a room full of people. However, I've made sure that my presence didn't affect the volume of electricity being used, e.g., by keeping people up later than usual. It has been a challenge to stay with hosts who've wanted to cook me dinner, turn on lights for me and wash my clothes. They often open their electric garage door for me to put my bike inside before I can tell them not to. I've been able to avoid electricity pretty easily on the streets, but once I've been with other people this has become much more difficult.

I've started to see how deeply electricity is interwoven into my day-to-day routine. I've been able to almost completely remove the use of fossil fuel-based electricity from my life. The major exception to this is signing onto wireless Internet; I'm not sure how much extra electricity a router uses for each computer that is added to it. However, I've had a lot of blogging and social media to do to spread inspiration, so I feel really comfortable with using this electricity.

But today I've realized how much electricity my cell phone is using. It's easy to overlook my dependence on electricity now that so much of life is wireless. Even though I'm powering my phone with solar it is consuming electricity from the grid by using cellular data at the server. On top of that, I have about 20 GB of data stored in the cloud, which is using electricity 24/7 where it is being hosted. Even my Facebook profile uses electricity!

I can take steps to greatly reduce my electricity usage while still using my phone and the Internet, but I can't control how the electricity to host my Facebook page is being created. I can, however, choose to offset the electricity I consume with green power in the form of renewable energy credits and carbon offsets. I'm hopeful that the United States will embrace alternative energy so that every single citizen doesn't have to pay such close attention to these details. And I'm more hopeful for the success of companies like Renewable Choice Energy. They are teaching and helping big energy users to use green power. If every company started to embrace wind and solar as clean forms of energy, I wouldn't have to worry nearly as much about my wireless consumption. I also wouldn't have to worry about where my electricity was coming from back home in San Diego.

DAY 29: FROM BOULDER TO DENVER

I woke up and got busy, preparing myself for a morning in Boulder and the ride to Denver. I weighed and assessed my trash and recycling created since Salt Lake City 11 days ago. I found that I had created 0.9 pounds of trash and recycling combined. That is less than 0.1 pound per day. The waste consisted of receipts, a box and a few pieces of food packaging; 95 percent of it was recyclable. At this point I have created 3.8 pounds of waste and have been able to recycle 95 percent of it. I have created 0.2 pound of trash and 3.6 pounds of recycling, leaving me with just a couple of ounces of actual trash to carry across the country so far.

Boulder is ranked a platinum-level bicycle-friendly community by the League of American Bicyclists (only three other cities have achieved that rank: Davis, CA, Fort Collins, CO, and Portland, OR). It truly is one of the best cities in the USA for cyclists. Then there's the Boulder Farmers' Market, the largest in Colorado. This was my first market since I left San Francisco, and I was able to eat local organic food to my heart's content. I picked up arugula, wheat berries, apple cider, granola, ice cream, peach jam, honey, and jarred fruits and veggies from last season but there was so much more on offer. The five pounds of wheat berries will be a lifesaver as I'll be able to sprout those over the next month for a high-energy food.

Purchasing some locally grown wheat and fruit jam at the farmers market.

Fixing a flat tire on the roadside.

From the market I was off to Denver. The 30-mile bike ride was quite miserable. The arugula I ate was so spicy it was causing my stomach to churn, and the roads had some unexpected hills to climb. The roads in the suburbs of Denver were in horrible shape with huge potholes and very narrow shoulders. On top of the exhaust from cars, over a half-dozen fire trucks and ambulances blared by, deafening my ears. Just 1.8 miles from my destination, Adam's house, I got a flat tire, which really added insult to injury. I wanted so badly to be on his couch relaxing but instead found myself on the side of a busy road failing at changing my tire. I got back on my bike eventually and made it to Adam's place before nightfall.

DAYS 30-32: FREESTYLE GARDENING WITH FRIENDS

Sunday was my first relaxing day since I left San Francisco. My friends Wes and Adam helped throw a get-together at Washington Park, and it was heartwarming to spend time with them. Some people I had met online made over 1,300 seed bombs for us to plant, and five of us rode our bikes around

A few of the thousands of seed bombs we planted across America.

Out on a bike ride with friends chucking seed bombs around Denver.

Denver Freestyle Gardening. We planted over 500 seed bombs full of daisy, poppy and cornflower seeds. It was really great to go on a casual bike ride on a beautiful bike path on a pleasant Sunday afternoon. Then we headed back to the park to meet up with a bunch of people and I made a lot of new friends. We laid blankets out and just relaxed in the park. It was one of the most enjoyable days yet this summer. We played guitar and Frisbee, told stories and chilled. It was so nice to just hang out and enjoy the company of good people.

Monday was a major social media and Internet day. I pretty much hung out at Adam's house the entire day sitting on the couch. It rained for a good portion of the day, which made it hard to get my battery charged enough on the computer. The humid air reminded me of Wisconsin and excited me for the Midwest. At night some friends came over. I hadn't taken much time to just hang out on this trip because I'd been so busy, so it was nice to socialize.

Tuesday the plan was to take off in the morning, but I ended up sticking around in Denver for one more day. I spent the morning on the computer and headed down to the river in the early afternoon to finally wash my clothes and cooking gear after nearly a month of not doing so. While there I went for a real nice swim and cleaned myself up. Cleaning up everything felt like a new start. It was a sunny day, and it was nice to be still chilling in Denver while being extremely productive. I was a little anxious about not being on the road, but it was important to get all of this stuff done.

I'm Barefootin' for Sustainability! Tomorrow when I walk out of the house I'll put my shoes into my bike trailer and leave them there until I reach Kansas City, 600 miles away. I'm pedaling barefoot to raise money for One Percent for the Planet nonprofits and asking people to pledge per barefoot mile that I ride. My goal is to ride every one of the 600 miles barefoot.

THE GREAT PLAINS

DAY 33: A DAY TO RANT

Inspired again to be on my bicycle, I was flooded with joy. I felt as if there was a party balloon full of happiness expanding inside me ready to burst as I pedaled along the open Colorado road barefoot and bare-chested. A bike is a magical thing, and I often find that I can cure boredom or sadness of any sort just by getting on a bike and going for a ride. It's fun, good for me and good for the planet. What a great combination.

I woke up at 6 a.m., at the crack of dawn, at Adam's house and was excited to get back on the road after nearly five days of hanging out in Boulder and Denver. A new world awaited me. A world of flat open spaces, vast fields of green and endless skies of blue, and roads that would be a breeze to pedal on compared to the mountains. The sun was hot and the wind was in my face, but for most of the day that didn't stop me from cruising at 15 to 20 miles per hour, excited to break my record of 97 miles in a day. By 2 p.m. I had already pedaled 60 barefoot miles. The possibilities were endless with my feet on the pedals, and I had my first 100-mile day in sight with a shot at even more.

I turned myself into a giant tumbleweed in the Great Plains.

I recorded the following rant on my phone later in the evening: "I'm so freaking mad right now...20+ mph winds are coming straight from the east blasting me in the face. Winds are generally supposed to go from west to east in this country, but for this entire trip it's been coming from the east and making everything so much harder. The wind this morning was subtle but as of a few hours ago I'm going just 3 to 4 mph per hour rather than the 15 to 20 mph I should be doing. It's not even a matter of gusts of wind. It's a consistent, non-stop 20-mph wind straight at me. Yeah right, downhill to Kansas City, it's been uphill most of the day. This is no easier by any means than crossing the Rocky Mountains and one million times more frustrating. I've been roaring in anger at the top of my lungs over and over and over. I'm so mad right now. This is just absolutely horrible. But I'm getting close to a 100-mile day. Imagine with the wind at my back this could have been a 100-mile day two or three hours ago. Instead it's eight at night and I'm pedaling at a quarter of the speed of what I could be doing. Ahhhhhh, I thought the hard part was over and instead I am the most frustrated and mad that I've been so far on the trip. And to make matters worse the forecast for tomorrow is for even stronger winds straight out of the east. STRAIGHT OUT OF THE EAST. If I had this wind at my back I could be breezing through this dang stretch of the highway. And what is with all of these hills? Every time I go over a hill there is another one straight ahead of me with the wind blasting me backwards. I'm going to make it. I am going to make it. I just wish the wind was going in my direction but I'm going to make it. And on the bright side I just found a half a bag of Chex Mix on the side of the road. Yeah, baby."

Eventually I made it to Anton and ended the day after pedaling 102 miles: my first 100-mile day, and it was barefoot. Two pretty big achievements but man, did it destroy me. Anton had nothing but a few horses and a gas station and before pitching my tent behind some old buildings I walked over to the horses to say hello. I didn't know if it was possible after the frustrating evening but they brought happiness back into my body. I fed them grass and pet them and their presence rejuvenated me. Pledges for "Barefootin' for Sustainability" were up to 72 cents per mile so I raised about $75s today. Now that is something I could be proud of.

DAY 34: NO MERCY FROM THE WIND

What a completely miserable night. I stayed up until almost 12:30 in my tent writing and catching up on e-mails, and when I finally went to bed I was awoken just three hours later by the wind blowing my tent around like a rag doll.

The tent walls were blowing in from every direction, and I felt like my tent was punching me repeatedly. It was so noisy I couldn't sleep at all. I was wide awake and filled with anger and frustration. I lay there for a good half hour or more not knowing what to do and eventually dragged my tent and everything inside into an old, dusty, abandoned

building. In there I could hear the wind howling like a banshee through the trees but I was mostly protected. The wind must have been blowing at close to 30 mph.

When I woke up I was amazed to find that it was 9:30 already. I felt horrible. My throat was hoarse, my pee was bright yellow, it was cold out, and the skies were dreary and gray in every direction. It was looking like a horrible day ahead. The forecast called for wind all day long, picking up every hour and reaching 20 to 30 mph.

My goal as of last night was to leave early this morning before the winds picked up too much, but the cold, mist, clouds and horrible night destroyed any chances of that happening. Besides all that horrible news there is no local food out here, and the signs inside the tiny market advise against drinking the water due to high levels of nitrates. So I'm expecting today to be a battle and on top of that I'm going shoeless. My legs are also the most sore they have been yet on the trip from battling the wind all evening yesterday when I was expecting a breeze.

It was noon by the time I got on the road, and the dreary skies appeared as if they would accompany me all day, along with the daunting winds. I set my goal at 50 miles for the day but hoped to somehow manage 75. The winds whipped across the open land all day long, rarely letting up for a second. I fought hard for every foot, every yard and every mile. I wanted to give up all day and just 25 miles in I even laid down on the side of the road contemplating setting up my tent.

Somehow, by 7 p.m. I had eked out 40 miles. I only made it that distance thanks to a saying I've been muttering aloud to myself almost every day: "one pedal at a time." I just keep on turning my pedals and it always gets me farther along. Today I counted the number of pedals it took to get me between the mile markers and counted between 625 and 775 per marker. Mile after mile I counted the pedals this afternoon and it really helped me make it through the day. All I had to do was count around 700 pedals and I knew I would be one mile closer to my goal. There was no sun today, which meant almost no communication with the outside world since my phone was nearly dead and no listening to music or making voice memos.

Around 11 p.m. I set up my tent outside in the corner of a bar hidden from the wind and finally went to bed at 1 a.m. The wind was howling through the trees and there was a chance of thunderstorms. I looked at a more detailed forecast, and it appeared the next 450 miles to Kansas City would be into the wind. This may end up being the most challenging leg of the trip.

DAY 35: HITTING MY LIMITS

The Kansas border is 20 miles east and the wind is coming from the south at 29 mph. Severe thunderstorms are in the forecast but again, for some reason, I am very excited for the day. The weatherman is telling me it's supposed to be hot, maybe 85 degrees, but I'm not sure if I will notice that with the wind blasting. Every pedal will get me a little bit farther. Every 700 or so pedals will get me another mile.

The afternoon was quite pleasant. I pedaled 30 miles with the 30-mph winds coming at me from the south and all was going well. I was steadily cruising along at about 13 mph. In St. Francis I found a shady creek to cool off my heated body and it was absolutely wonderful. I realized I needed to start taking more time to relax and give my body and mind a chance to recuperate. I looked for some local food in town and had zero success, so I dug through the trash and found cinnamon candy popcorn and some pizza. It went down just fine at the time but leaving town I could tell it wasn't settling right.

When I left town the wind had picked up and the road headed a bit south, putting me right into the wind. On top of that I was climbing hills. My stomach ached with pain and within just a few miles of this I was on the side of the road puking up everything inside of me. If I didn't know that I'd just eaten fake food died

with red #40 I would have been very scared at the brightly colored fluids spewing out of me. I don't think I was puking because the food was tainted though. My body was already overheating as I fought the wind, the hills and the heat; and the cinnamon, which is a warming food, was the tipping point that overwhelmed my system. I was being heated from the inside, and the outside and my body needed to cool off. I knew the cinnamon popcorn was a bad idea from the start, but in my craving for carbs, I scarfed down the entire bag anyway. As I sat there on the roadside feeling miserable, the severe thunderstorms that had been forecasted seemed to be drawing closer. Luckily I had passed a farm just a few hundred yards back and I coasted back to ask if I could take shelter and recover.

I knocked on the door and a real nice lady named Jo answered the door. She welcomed us in and we sat down and got to talking. She is part of a co-op with 37 farms in a network that do food deliveries from here to Denver. It was a wonderful experience talking to her and I learned all about the food they produce. I purchased a bunch of her homemade jams and jellies. The rain didn't come but it was getting late so I decided to call it a night and crash out under her carport. They have a well that pumps ground water via a windmill so I had no shortage of water for the night.

A few of the thousands of road kill birds I found throughout the summer. Cars kill millions of birds each year. Bikes kill next to none.

DAY 36: TAKE A RIGHT AT THE TREES, AND HEAD FOR THE BARN

It was a pretty long night. I was too exhausted to sleep well. The 30-mph winds were relentless, blowing through the trees and shaking the shed. The noise from that along with all the turkeys, guinea fowl and chickens, cawing, yelping and shrieking made it difficult to sleep.

I lay around and took it pretty easy for the morning, and it was quite the beautiful morning. I stretched my muscles out a bit and ate some bread and jams. Jo gave me a tour of her farm, Prairie House Herbs, and I learned she is able to live out here very sustainably. Everything on the land has multiple purposes and coexists. Cats eat the rats. Goats eat the thorn-producing plants, keep the property groomed, provide wool and eat food that would have gone to waste. Chickens eat insects and lay eggs. Everything seemed to mostly take care of itself so the place was not high maintenance. Nothing went to waste on the six and a half acres. Pure water came from the water table 60 feet below, and they even had a windmill to pump it up without the use of electricity. The house was heated with geothermal.

The High Plains Food Co-op Jo's a part of is just exquisite. Between their 37 farms they offer fresh vegetables and fruit, fresh and dried herbs and herbal seasonings, grains, artisan breads, free-range eggs and organic meats including pork, yak, lamb, chicken, turkey and buffalo. Everything they produce is natural, organic and local. A few people eat 100 percent of their diet from the co-op. You can pick everything up at one location each week. This food is good, fresh, nutritious, free of chemicals and good for all the people involved, the animals and the planet. It has minimal-to-no dependence on fossil fuels, and the money stays in the community.

At 10 a.m. I hit the road and the southern wind was not too bad. The road from Bird City to Atwood was fairly smooth, and I was able to make good distance without exerting too much energy but the hot sun beat down on me the entire ride. The southern breeze made the sun more bearable but it was still hot. For much of the ride my eyes were half-closed and, if I let myself, I would have fallen asleep while riding. When I reached Atwood a calm lake with cool water welcomed me. I rested under the shade of an oak tree and then cooled off in the lake. As I floated in the water I realized that yesterday's rock bottom might be a blessing for the rest of the trip. It's time to start enjoying my days more, I thought. The purpose of this ride is to create positive change rather than to have fun and enjoy myself, but if I can do both I might as well. I took it all in and created a fresh start for the trip.

I headed to the local grocery store and found one locally grown item, lettuce grown in a hydroponics system. It was very cool to see this in Kansas, but I didn't buy it since it was in a very large plastic container. Instead I picked up oranges, apples and peanut butter, none of which was locally produced or organic, but at least they were all products of the USA. I was extremely reluctant to purchase this food but felt that I should to recover from my fatigue.

I left Atwood just after 4 p.m. and large hills and stronger winds greeted me. Even though I'd been guzzling water today I still had not been able to hydrate myself. I continued on exhausted, eyes still wanting to close but very appreciative of the fruits and peanut butter I had with me. I peeked over my shoulder every minute to check out the massive storm brewing behind. Lightning was bolting in every direction across the sky and heavy rain fell in the distance. With no shelter in sight I pushed on. I knew it was futile to try to outrun the storm so I scanned the eastern horizon for shelter. I found an old abandoned homestead, and as I stood in the road assessing the situation an old brown Chevy slowed down and stopped in front of me. A dark weathered man in overalls mumbled something to the effect of, "Are you looking for shelter for the night?" At my response he told me to take a right at the trees ahead and there would be a barn where we could take shelter. He was extremely vague and hard to understand, and most anyone from outside of the state of Kansas would have seen this as the beginning of a horror movie. But I took him up on his offer, not knowing exactly what the offer was. I took the right on the road lined with trees, and in front of me a home surrounded by a few sheds unfolded.

The man in the truck had beat me there and was unloading some mulch that he had picked up in Atwood. He introduced himself as Brad and seemed happy to have company. He offered us a Mickey's malt beverage, which I declined but Brent happily accepted. Boomer, a white 14-year-old golden retriever that was beyond excited to see us, also greeted us. Brad entertained us the entire night. He yelled out, "Kitty, kitty, kitty, kitty" and cats emerged from every bush, ledge and shed. This place was flooded with animals and they all wanted to play. We spent an hour sitting outside, Brad in his rocking chair smoking cigarettes

Booger the cat enjoying some of my attention.

and drinking his Mickey's. Boomer got his fair share of beer, too. When I first met Boomer I thought he might have been the stupidest dog I ever met, but now I realized maybe he was just drunk.

It's a different way of life out here. As Brad put it, a place where you can shoot guns from your porch and, as his wife Marsha put it, a place where your kids miss 30 days of school in a year from impassable muddy roads. This country is more diverse than most anyone can imagine. The 50 states all have their own character, and many I've learned are as different from each other as are some countries. The way of life, people, terrain, creatures and climate all vary so much. We are truly blessed to live in a country with so much variety to offer, and we should never take that for granted.

Brent (left) and Brad (right) playing with guns.

Brent doing what he does best.

DAY 37: YESTERDAY'S TOMORROW IS TODAY

I've been doing exceptionally well both physically and mentally through the last 37 days. I've had a few low points but each time I have bounced back in day or two. My body, mind and spirit are in prime condition and can handle these periods of struggle as they come. It's important to remember that hard times always come to an end, even when it seems they may not. I have learned in my time on this planet that to be at my highest levels of happiness my body must be in good physical condition. I sometimes forget this but I'll take this as another reminder. I've made it past this difficult time, and now that my body has recovered I should be able to handle the elements with more grace.

Day after day, no matter the circumstances, I am excited to be on the road on my bike. It was a leisurely, restful morning, and I didn't get a move on until close to noon. I said goodbye to the 20 cats, to Boomer, the stupidest dog I've ever met, to Booger, the little kitten that chased me down the road, and to Marsha and Brad, the most real Kansas folk I have had the pleasure of knowing. I was beyond grateful for their hospitality; their farmhouse on the prairie gave me rest and the ability to ride today in comfort. Open Kansas roads awaited and the winds were blowing. I was up for the challenge both physically and mentally.

My front bag was full of frozen cherries that Marsha had picked from a tree in Atwood and saved over the winter. They're like eating sweet soft ice cubes. My water bottle is also partially filled with these cherries, which will be a treat with every sip throughout the day.

Later in the afternoon I spotted a windmill off the side of the road pulling cool ground water into large aluminum troughs for cows. I pulled over and took shelter from the heat inside the cold water. It was so cold it nearly shocked my system but not cold enough to keep me out. I drank water straight from the pipe that was pulling it up from 60 feet below. These windmill-powered wells that use only energy from the wind are one of the most enjoyable parts of Kansas. The cold water brought power back into my legs and determination into my mind. I set a goal of pedaling over 10 mph for the next six miles. Even over the hills I managed 8 to 10 mph, while on the flat land my legs pumped at 13 mph. This was just another example of mind over matter. It's all about having a positive attitude. Positivity creates greatness. It's just that simple. Some of the same classic rock I've been listening to for the last ten-plus years kept my pedals moving along at a steady pace. It reminded me of the time when my main worry was getting girls to dance with me at high school dances.

Around 6 p.m. I reached Norton, Kansas, and as I sat resting, a new idea dawned on me. Why not use this southern wind to my advantage? If I cut northeast now this powerful southern wind could become a friend rather than a foe. I analyzed the weather for a dozen or so cities in Kansas, Nebraska and Iowa ,and the ten-day forecast called for southern winds north, south and east of me on all of my possible routes. Rather than continue on through Kansas in a SE direction to Kansas City and then through Missouri to St. Louis as planned, I could cut NE through Nebraska and visit Lincoln and Omaha and then go into Iowa, where I could visit Des Moines and Iowa City. Besides battling less wind I could also shave off a couple hundred miles. It just made sense to go with the wind and use what Mother Nature was giving me.

The idea excited me, but at first I was hesitant to change my plans since I'd told people along the planned route that I'd be there. So I decided to spend the night in Norton and leave the decision to the morning. As I rode south to a park in town my mind was already made up. I'd be heading north to Nebraska.

DAY 38: MEMORIAL DAY FEAST

When I woke up the winds were already gusting from the south, which would be much less of a menace with my newly planned route. The forecast called for southern winds for the next ten days and I was feeling relieved about that. Off I went at 8 a.m. I explored the cobblestoned streets of Norton a bit before getting back onto Highway 36 heading east.

"Not so fast," said Kansas. "I'm not finished trying to destroy your positive attitude and cheery ways. Here are some 25-mph winds from the EAST right at your face. HAHAHA Rob, I hate you." This was a huge hit to my stomach, but I slowly battled the wind head on for six miles knowing that I would be heading northeast onto Highway 383 shortly, which would make it a tad easier. Once onto 383, though, the winds continued to blow from the east at gusty speeds of around 25 mph, and the slight northern turn of the road made little difference. Kansas yelled out, "Rob, I FREAKING HATE YOU. I will not make this easy on you."

I let the winds eat away at my insides. "How is this possible?" I exclaimed furiously. Five consecutive days of strong southern winds and they vanish within hours of my deciding to take advantage of them. I laid on the side of the road in despair.

I got up and waged war against the Kansas winds for two and a half hours knowing that when I hit Highway 183 North they would at the least be coming from my side. I set four mini-goals of knocking out five miles in 30 minutes. I pedaled furiously and knocked out the first five miles in exactly 30 minutes. The second leg I missed by less than a minute. Then I blasted through the third leg, beating my goal by five minutes while still pedaling into side winds strong enough to knock a wee one or an old man over. Going into the fourth mini-goal my derailleur malfunctioned, but I managed to get it working in no time. Despite that hiccup I cruised into the intersection of 383 and 183 just ten minutes beyond my two-hour goal.

The tides turned at Highway 183. Tailwinds, favorable slopes in the terrain and determination allowed me to crush out the next 24 miles in one hour and 40 minutes. I found myself in Holdrege just before 5 p.m. after a 65-mile day and decided to make this town my home for the night.

I went to the local grocery store and found no food that was local but was surprised to find a small organic section, so I caved and bought some bananas and oranges. Then I took a trip around back to the dumpster and wished I hadn't bought that fruit. I found a Memorial Day feast large enough to feed 50 families for the entire weekend: a dozen types of fruits, including the same oranges and bananas I had just bought plus full boxes of apples, watermelons, avocados, potatoes, grapes and pre-cut fruits from the deli, all with my name written on them. A giant bag full of sandwiches from the deli, heads of lettuce, bags of chips, bottles of pomegranate juice and loads of half-gallon jugs of orange juice all screamed "eat me, I'm still good" from the dumpster. I loaded up three boxes, carried them across the street and set them under a pine tree.

This dumpster held enough good food to feed me for the rest of the summer, though I knew I could only take so much and it would only stay good so long. I wished I could have shared it with the people in need in Holdrege, but I just didn't have a way.

One thing I've learned on this trip is we have no shortage of food in America, but we do have a distribution problem. Imagine the life of this banana. Time, energy and resources are put into it in the country of Colombia. It is then shipped thousands of miles to America using fossil fuels and more time, energy and money. Then it's shipped around the USA using more fossil fuels and more time, energy and money. It then sits on the grocery store shelf and is then put in the dumpster. That's not the best use of time, energy and money I've seen.

I contacted a Warm Showers host via the app, and they said I could stay the night in their home. I pedaled over there very slowly with a bag of food in my right hand weighing 25 pounds. Bev and Timothy welcomed me into their wonderful home and the next few hours were spent happily chatting away in their living room. Amazingly, Tim had already heard about my journey online, and when I pulled up barefoot on a bamboo bike he knew exactly who I was. Just after nightfall I took a stroll and sat in a park next to a pond where I cleaned my dirty hands, feet and face and changed into some clean clothes. I felt incredible and was so happy to be in this quaint little Nebraska town on this fine summer's night.

Kansas had a talk with its neighbor to the north, Nebraska. It went something like this:

Kansas: "Hey Nebraska, did you get a little earthy fella on a bamboo bike ridin' in from the south yesterday?"

Nebraska: "I sure did, partner. Whatcha need?"

Kansas: "Well he snuck outta here when I was tryin' to shake up his feathers. I was just gettin' started with him. Would you mind roughin' 'em up for me a bit?"

Nebraska: "It would be my pleasure, partner. I'll blast some winds from the north at the kid. He won't know what hit 'im."

Kansas: "Give it to 'im good, Nebraska. That boy just smiles way too much for my likin'."

DAY 39: WIND, NEWS, AND NEBRASKA

I woke up in a bed of my own. I think that's the first time I've been able to say that in 40 days. I took advantage of the alone time to lounge in bed for an hour or two. My stomach was in pain so Bev suggested some baking soda with a glass of water to settle it down, and by golly it worked. It was such a wonderful experience staying with them. They are real fine folk and gave me an experience that will paint happy pictures of Nebraska in my head for some time to come.

Nebraska was true to the words it spoke to Kansas, sending winds straight at me from the northeast. They started out slow at around 10 mph but picked up throughout the day until they reached 25. I handled it well, consistently pedaling all day long. It was very hard to believe that after so many consecutive days of southern winds they would change to the northeast when I headed in that very direction. I could have taken this very bitterly and at times it got to me, but I just kept pumping away. Heck, the more challenging the ride, the more solid my legs will become, and I can't complain about that.

At Tim's suggestion I stopped into the NTV news station, just a stone's throw off of Highway 36, to see if they wanted to do a piece on my trip, and sure enough they did. Reporter Alissa Willard interviewed me and planned to air the clip on the morning and afternoon shows the next day. She was an awesome girl, and I had a really fun time hanging out with her at the station.

After the news it was back on the wind-beaten road for another 30 miles to Hastings. The wind ate away at my strength but it didn't harm my spirits. The power in my legs faded with each mile, and I counted down the hours until I would reach my destination for the night and could relax. I say hours because I knew exactly how long it would take me to get there if I just kept on pedaling.

I arrived in Hastings around 7 p.m. and headed straight to a pleasant park where I stripped down to my shorts and basked in the end-of-the-day sun. I felt better instantly as I lay there, allowing my body and mind to rest. I spent the rest of the evening in the park stretching, lying and walking around. It was just what I needed.

DAY 40: SEVERE THUNDERSTORMS

The severe thunderstorms that were predicted to slam my tent with rain and hail during the night never came. When I awoke at 6 a.m. I was surprised I hadn't been woken up during the night to a good pummeling by Mother Nature. Still tired, I was glad to be up early to go online and catch my story on the news. First I checked my phone, and I had a text from Alissa saying that the recording had malfunctioned, but she'd like to drive over to Hastings to do the piece again. I was glad she was coming to re-shoot because I think it will be an interesting piece for the people here in Nebraska. I don't think they get overly exposed to content about making the earth a happier, healthier place. Plus Alissa is absolutely gorgeous and I was excited to see her again.

Brent was in a restaurant across the street so I went over there to join him and connected to the free Wi-Fi. Here I learned that some serious storms were forecast for the area; I could also see them through the shiny windows. I plugged away at my e-mail inbox and was happy I did when the Nebraska sky dumped an Olympic-swimming-pool worth of water onto every square mile of Hastings (I actually calculated this statistic and it's fairly accurate). I would not have wanted to be out biking in that. I checked the weather forecast, and although it was calling for more severe storms later in the day I decided to hit the road. It looked like I would be safe until late afternoon, but tornados were looking like a possibility.

Off I went into the east and the southern winds had returned. The 20-mph steady winds at my side did not push me backwards, but they did take a toll on my fatigued legs. The last two days of intense pedaling have worn these bad boys out. I pushed on and for the first ten miles saw no immediate signs of inclement weather. As I passed by all the freshly planted cornfields it began to sprinkle on me. The rains picked up a bit at Mile 20 and the skies to the south and west were holding some heavy gray clouds. I continued on until the rain was coming down just hard enough to force me to tighten up my gear to keep it dry. I stepped out into the road from the shelter of a pine tree and had a clear view of the coming storm. It was a big one, and the weather app on my phone confirmed it was coming straight for me. Lightning lit up the sky and told me it was time to make a choice.

A home with a barn sat in front of me, and I could either ask for refuge within or race on eastwards and try to outrun the storm. The next town, Sutton, was ten miles ahead, and the radar made it appear as if the storm would not quite make it that far east. The heavy part was heading right at me but in a northerly direction, so I thought I could miss it if I scurried on east. Lightning and possible tornados worried me, but my gut told me I could dodge the storm. I stepped towards the barn to take refuge and stopped to look east. Again I stepped forward and stopped in my tracks, and then again a third time. Finally I decided, I'm going for it. I hopped on my bike and pedaled hard, knowing I only had ten miles to reach safety and would then likely be forced to call it a day.

The storm lurked behind me, and I kept a close eye in every direction for lightning or tornados. Sure enough I was making good time and the worst of the storm was still behind me. Then the edge caught up with me and I found myself in a downpour. This I could enjoy though — some good pure rainwater does the body good. On I pedaled through the rain, sometimes just a drizzle and other times a drenching.

The water tower of Sutton grew closer. As I got to the edge of town I could see a gas station ahead. It looked like I had made the right call. A car pulled over and the driver got out to take photos in my direction. I wondered if he thought a biker with a storm in the background was a good photo, but when I turned around I realized that he wasn't shooting me — he was shooting the tornado behind me. I approximated it was five miles to the west and right along the path I had just cycled. I was in a safe spot so I stood there calmly next to my bike and watched the twister travel north for a minute before sucking itself back into the clouds. It wasn't large, but it was the first tornado I'd ever seen. I felt no danger where I stood and took the opportunity to soak in the storms brewing around me. This is the earth at its finest. I exposed myself to the elements and let the raw life soak into me.

Not wanting to get stuck in the middle of the storm I pedaled the last half-mile into Sutton (population 1,500) and pulled up to a restaurant at the gas station. Within minutes the skies opened up, and hail the size of dimes and nickels came barreling down at around 40 mph. A few pieces ricocheted off the ground into my legs and one caught me in the ear as I stood under cover. Had I been out there exposed I would have taken quite the beating. I imagine hail this large can cause some pretty good bruises.

The forecast called for an evening of huge storms, and all the locals coming through the gas station told me to stay off the road. I took their advice and sat there in the restaurant letting the weather do its thing. I'd been invited to call into the University of Arizona radio show "Sex and Drugs and Stuff", and spent some time chatting on air with them. We talked about other stuff than sex or drugs, but there was a little of that in there too, or the lack thereof. I am not using alcohol or drugs for the entire 104 days of this trip — not even a drop of beer, a sip of wine, or a drag off a joint. I've also been abstinent from sex on this trip, including masturbation, which takes some dedication. I've always found myself much more successful without these distractions in my life. Sex and alcohol both serve a great purpose, and there is a time and a place for both, but I like to take breaks from them at times. It's a very good way to practice self-control and delayed gratification, and I find I have been extremely productive during these times.

Coincidentally, Kris Moody, the news editor for the Clay County News, happened into the restaurant, and we spoke for close to an hour about my trip and my time here in Nebraska and Kansas. He published an article in their paper. The meeting brought me another piece of good fortune as he connected me with the pastor of a church down the street who opened the doors for me to stay the night safe from the storms. I wandered over there at 7 p.m. and had a very pleasant evening in the church filled with coffins. I found a comfy couch where I spent some time writing and finally made it an early night when my computer ran out of juice.

DAY 41: WIND AT MY BACK

My body isn't used to getting a lot of sleep right now so I woke up before the sun. I went outside and was very appreciative of the warm, damp air. I took advantage of having the quiet church to myself and prepared a simple breakfast and ate it sitting at a table. Since I have been eating mostly food from dumpsters I have not been taking the time to appreciate it or give thanks to the earth for giving it to me. I usually say something along the lines of, "Thank you Earth for this delicious and nutritious food in front of me. Please let it nourish my body. I will use this energy today from this food to create a happier, healthier planet." I like to take time to eat my food and appreciate it as it goes down. It's better for digestion, and it helps me appreciate the simple things that give me life.

The forecast called for a clear afternoon, and I overheard talk between Kansas and Nebraska again.

Kansas: "Hey Nebraska, did you give heck to that little granola boy on the bamboo bike yesterday like you said you would?"

Nebraska: "You betcha I did, Kansas. I gave it to him good and even scared 'im a bit with a tornado."

Kansas: "Good stuff, good stuff. You know, I've been thinking. That kid ain't too bad. He's only trying to protect our land. Maybe we should take it easy on him."

Nebraska: "You're right, Kansas. I'll give him a little push today and put some southwestern winds at his back."

Kansas: "That's what I was thinking. While you're at it, move them clouds out of the way so he can charge up his solar panel. He'll need juice in his computer if he's gonna keep spreading the good word of the planet."

So just like that Nebraska sent southwestern winds my way, and I had an easy day of pedaling. Nebraska didn't take all of the clouds from the sky but enough to burn the skin on my nose and keep my cell phone charged all day. The forecast called for a clear day but a good chance of severe storms in the evening, so I set my sights on getting to Lincoln as early as I could. I stopped in the little town of Friend about 30 miles into the ride and didn't find any local organic food. A few towns over in Milford I really scored. The dumpster outside the local market was filled with jugs of milk, half gallons of orange juice, ears of corn and, best of all, Blue Machine juice. I grabbed some of each and was set for the entire day. All of it was perfectly good and in sealed containers. As a matter of fact it was still cold so it must have been freshly removed from the fridge.

I arrived in Lincoln, Nebraska, the state capital, at 3:30 p.m., having squeezed in 75 miles in under six and a half hours. The west side of the city was extremely unfriendly for a cyclist — I had another five miles to pedal to my WarmShowers host and that took me nearly an hour. I arrived at her house and was happy to be there with plenty of sunshine left in the day. I took this time to go through my gear and lighten my load. I took unnecessary stuff out of the trailer and will send some home or give it away.

I also weighed my trash and recycling and found that I had accumulated 0.5 pound over the last 12 days. I now have created a grand total of 4.5 pounds of trash and recycling in 41 days (4 pounds of recycling and 0.5 pounds of trash). The average American creates 4.5 pounds of trash per day — the same amount I have made in 40 days. The average American also recycles about 30 percent of their trash, compared to my 90 percent.

A big storm came in with hail and I took the opportunity to bathe in the rain. I grabbed my bottle of Dr. Bronner's soap and went for a run in just my shorts. I lathered up and let the rain rinse me off; the hail just bounced right off me. Talk about an eco-friendly way of showering. No water wasted there. I put my clothes out to wash in the rain as well. I've been drinking rainwater the last few days as well as water from bottles I find on the side of the road. I think it's safe to say I haven't wasted any water yet on this trip. I still have not turned on a faucet, except at a farm that had its own well back in Napa, California. I had a

My clothes hanging out to dry after washing them in a summer rainstorm.

tough evening with my host. She really wanted to provide for me by cooking, making tea, offering me a shower and being a really good host. But even simple things like her wanting to turn the lights on for me are an issue. I kept explaining to her that she was giving me everything I desired and more — a bed, a roof over my head, friendship — but she was having a hard time seeing herself a good host without presenting me with resource-consuming processes and items. She actually seemed annoyed with my

106

lack of need and mocked me for not wanting to use the water or the refrigerator. I've been able to avoid aggravating people so far, but on this occasion my self-imposed morals created steam in a relationship. I'm OK with that though — I'm refusing what I don't need for the sake of the earth and all the other beings that share it.

DAY 42: ASHLAND, NEBRASKA, NOT ASHLAND, WISCONSIN

For the first time in a while I made a fire to prepare breakfast and cooked up a dish of potatoes that I got way back in Steamboat Springs along with some mushrooms and corn. It kept my hunger, which is back in full force, satisfied for a few hours. On the road at 10:30 a.m. and it was a hot one.

Highway 6 took me to Ashland, Nebraska, which I just had to explore since I am from Ashland, Wisconsin. Just after Ashland I got the idea of testing out my next campaign: Stand up for Sustainability. I'm removing the seat from my bike and trekking across the state of Iowa standing up. The combination of my bare feet and the lack of a seat was exhausting, and most of the muscles in my body were burning all day. It appears to be more of an upper body and core workout than a leg workout, though my calves were burning pretty bad, too.

The trail led me all the way into Omaha for 40 miles of barefoot, standing-up riding, but not before I stopped at a grocery store dumpster in Gretna and scored about 20 good apples and enough bread to last me a few days. I found enough food — much of it not even past the sell-by date yet — to feed about 50 families for the day. I filled up a box full of bread and brought it across the street to an apartment complex, where I gave it to a lady who said she'd put it out for the residents. I imagine what I found in that dumpster was a very common occurrence.

Navigating Omaha was pretty miserable. The streets were in horrible condition for a bike, with potholes and bumps everywhere and shoulders nonexistent. I was happy to reach the apartment of our Couchsurfing host where I collapsed onto the couch exhausted after the 60-mile, hill-filled day.

Today ended the Barefootin' for Sustainability campaign. I pedaled 653 barefoot miles over the past 11 days, from Denver, Colorado, to Omaha, Nebraska. A total of $1.19 per mile was pledged between 19 people, which means I raised $777 from my barefoot riding.

DAY 43: JUNE 1ST IN OMAHA

Holy Macaroly, it's June. June! What happened to April and May? Yesterday I had decided to take today as a rest day so I spent the morning being productive while not riding a bike, which is my version of resting.

Before noon I headed down to the farmers' market and was excited to score some fresh, local food. It is still early in the season so it was somewhat slim pickings, but I managed to get some spinach, mustard greens, radishes, rhubarb, honey and tomatoes. All of it was exquisite. The juicy ripe tomatoes were from Graddy's farm in Carroll, Iowa, where they have 9,000 tomato plants in greenhouses and grow lettuce via aquaponics. It sounds like they run a very productive and sustainable organic operation. Then I popped over to Greenstreet Cycles to get some work done on my bike. They tuned it up, put on a new chain, fixed the derailleur and sold me a water bottle holder for the back of the trailer, where I will keep my sprouting jar. Now I have a convenient spot to always be sprouting wheat berries, an excellent source of nutrition. Greenstreet is an excellent bike shop, and I spent three hours hanging out with the five staff members. They run their business extremely responsibly when it comes to the environment and are doing their part to create a happier, healthier planet.

They don't have a free residential recycling program in Omaha, a city of nearly a half-million people, which boggles my mind. This is America, and we don't even have it together enough to have a recycling program in one of our 50 largest cities. I can understand that in a tiny town way out in the middle of nowhere, but it's amazing that we haven't managed to implement recycling nationwide. At Greenstreet Cycles they are doing their part to make Omaha a healthy city. Until recently they hauled 300 - 400 pounds of recyclables to the recycling plant five miles away via bicycle. That is dedication. Now it's only a five- to ten-minute ride, but you still have to pay to get the city to take the recyclables, even as a resident.

They are excellent at reusing material here at Greenstreet and donate most old parts to a community bike project that works with neighborhood kids and provides free bike maintenance training. Employees commute to work via bike; they estimate the average employee bikes 50 miles per week for commuting purposes. All the lights in the building are LED, which typically use ten times less electricity than incandescent bulbs. They reuse materials — turning old bike handlebar tape into handle grips for tools, for example — and hold clinics to advocate bicycle commuting for large corporations. They hold competitions between corporations here in Omaha to see whose employees can commute the most via bicycle, and apparently it's quite competitive. One guy commutes 65 miles per day for work. More important than his individual impact is the inspiration he provides to hundreds of people to bike their couple of miles each way, if he can do 65. Be amazing and you'll help to create more amazing people.

DAY 44: FACEBOOK FRIENDED BY THE LOCAL POLICE

I awoke to a cold and gloomy morning and I felt the same way on the inside. I got close to 12 hours of sleep but was still exhausted when I finally got out of bed at nine. I was feeling depressed, and the lack of sun to charge my cell phone and laptop had me feeling extra down. I spent some time in the morning stretching and took a short walk around the neighborhood to give my mind some time to wake up. I found a breakfast of yogurt and bagels in residential trash cans while I was out and about. I find it quite amazing that I can wake up any morning and go outside and find myself a good free breakfast from the waste of other human beings.

I was on the road at eleven and after 15 minutes of riding through Omaha found myself on a bridge crossing the Missouri River into Iowa. Here I took off my bike seat as I am pedaling across the entire state of Iowa without a seat to "Stand up for Sustainability." This is my way of making a statement that we as individuals need to take a stand for a cleaner, happier and healthier planet. The actions of every individual counts, and the easiest, simplest way to make this world a better place to live on is to clean up our own acts first. Let's stop talking and start doing!

My planned route across Iowa is 350 miles and I intended to do every last mile standing up. I was asking anyone who felt up to it to pledge a penny, a nickel, a dime, a quarter or whatever they wanted per mile. The money will be donated to One Percent for the Planet nonprofits that are doing their part to create a planet that we can be proud to live on.

More important than donating though is to stand up for what you believe and let your actions speak louder than your words.

- If you don't support oil, then don't drive a car. Bike or walk.
- If you don't support pesticides and GMOs than buy organic food.
- If you don't support wasting electricity, then switch to CFL or LED bulbs and pay attention to your usage.
- If you don't support landfills, then start recycling and composting and don't use one-time-use items.
- If you don't support horrible treatment of animals, then start eating a plant-based diet.
- If you don't support wasting water, then take shorter showers, do less laundry and pay attention to how much water you're dumping down the drain.

These are just a few simple suggestions of how you can start leading by example, but it's up to you to do what is right in your life.

I pedaled through Council Bluffs up steep hills and before noon I was into the countryside. I was tired but still managing the standing-up pedaling very well. It was a cold day for June, and I was surprised at the lack of warmth and sun. It kept the depressed feelings inside me, but with each hour and each mile my spirits rose. By mid-afternoon the sun had come out and the bounty of green surrounding me had me feeling happy again. This land is so pleasant and manageable, especially compared to some of the harsh lands I've just come from. This is the pleasant Midwest I've been eagerly awaiting for so long. It's similar to the land where I spent my college years and brings warmth to my heart.

In the late afternoon I stopped behind a grocery store to check out the goods and found about 1,000 pounds of good food thrown out. I took bananas, grapes, apples, pears, grapefruits, cherries, whole-wheat bagels and loaves of whole-wheat bread. The bread had a suggested sell-by date of June 4 (two days from now), and the fruit was in near-perfect condition. In the bags of about 100 cherries a few were mushy or smashed. It was an astonishing amount of food that would have taken hours to unload from the dumpsters. As I sat in the parking lot with Brent filming, company arrived. Two squad cars pulled up and two officers walked over to me as Brent continued filming. I greeted the police officers and told them about the incredible amount of food waste in our country and what I was doing to raise awareness about it. The two men in uniform were about my age and were very calm and cool. They told me that the store manager had called and said he wanted his garbage back. They told me to hold tight and went inside to talk to the manager. Upon their return the officers told me that the manager said he was okay with us filming the food and that I just had to put the food back when I was done.

So the good news is that I wasn't in trouble. But this was a great dumpster score and I wanted to eat it. So I asked the officers if I could keep some bananas and they said yes. I stuffed them into my bag and then said, "I'm going to keep these bagels too." They looked at me and said alright. I could see they were lenient with me so I just started to stuff food into my trailer, to which they responded, "Just make it look like you're putting it all back."

Stuffing food rescued from the dumpster into my trailer as Officer Hogue looks on.

I did just that and only lost about half my bounty. The officers weren't in a hurry and stuck around chatting. As my run-ins with the police usually go, we spent more time talking about the joys of life than what I had "done wrong." I knew it had gone really well when I checked Facebook a few hours later and one of the officers had sent me a friend request.

Here I am standing up for sustainability. Notice the missing bike seat?

DAY 45: AN EXCELLENT WORKOUT

I spent the morning admiring the lush green land around me and a beautiful lake that gave life to so many creatures. I watched a pair of geese on the shore of the lake grazing with their five young ones. They were like cute baby ducks, only five times the size. They brought joy to my morning as I ate my bounty of fruit, greens and whole-wheat bread. I filled up my jug from the lake and was on my way into the green land that awaited.

113

Today was an excellent workout. With each standing-up pedal I could feel the muscles in my body flex. My core contracted with each pedal, and my shoulder, back and arms flexed as I used these muscles for leverage. My triceps and shoulders were in a state of constant exertion, and every muscle in my legs flexed thousands of times throughout the day. Riding standing up has been a challenge but one that I'm overcoming with grace.

Fifteen miles from Des Moines I veered onto a beautiful bike path that appeared along the north side of the highway. I was happy to be off the busy six-lane highway. Shortly into the trail my body crashed. I ran out of energy and found myself on the side of the road cramming down every last morsel of food I had in my trailer. I had felt my body losing energy from pushing so hard into the wind for the last five or ten miles and suddenly I just couldn't go on. I pounded down a few raw eggs, bunches of spinach and mustard greens, the last of the honey, some water and a few sticks of rhubarb. It didn't take long for the natural goodness to soak into my body and I was back on my way.

On the outskirts of Des Moines I found a grocery store and rode around back to take a look inside the treasure chests. And treasures I found. Fresh pineapples, strawberries, grapes, green beans, beets and kale greeted me with a smile. I grabbed a shopping bag worth of this still-cold and very fresh produce and rode across the street to relocate the nourishment into my body. My energy levels rose instantly.

The last six miles were relative easy. Des Moines is surprisingly beautiful and full of bike trails and cyclists. I rode on a trail alongside a beautiful river surrounded by a blossoming canopy for a handful of enjoyable miles. I spent the end of a wonderful day in my host Kristin's living room, sitting on her comfy couch with her and her husband, Keith. It was great to be there and our conversation was enjoyable. They had many questions about my journey and I was happy to answer them. The company of human beings is something we should not take for granted.

DAY 46: COLD AND DREARY

I woke to a dreary, cold, rainy day and was not excited about it. This wasn't a warm, enjoyable shower — it was cold, depressing, bone-chilling rain, and there was no way I was going to bike in it. I washed my clothes in a pond as I stood out in the rain getting some of my only dry clothes wet as well. I was tempted to use the clothes drier in Kristin's apartment but fended off the temptation.

Around noon the sun peeked out for just enough time to juice up my cell phone, which put a little cheer back in me. Still feeling pretty low, I pedaled for 30 miles on miserable roads through East Des Moines. There was no shoulder and I was forced to ride side-by-side with trucks blowing exhaust at me. The cruddy roads continued after the industrial area; once I reached the countryside I was still riding on a highway with no shoulder fighting for space with cars and trucks.

After about 40 miles of riding the clouds opened up onto me. I enjoyed the rain this time as I was feeling dehydrated and the moisture soothed my body. Just after 7 p.m. I arrived in Newton, Iowa, where I would be spending the night. Sussane from Warm Showers greeted me at her door with a huge smile and invited me right inside. She had prepared all sorts of wonderful food, but I could not eat it since it was not local. However, she did have some local organic blue cheese that I was able to enjoy very much. I yearned to have a glass of red wine with her but couldn't. My excellent self-control made it easy to resist any and all temptations, and I was just happy to be in her wonderful home out of the rain and in good company. We hung out around the dinner table for a while and then spent the rest of the evening playing around in the living room doing headstands, giving massages and laughing. The day's depression lifted in this warm home. Around midnight I retired to one of the six bedrooms; Sussane had raised five children and now has this huge home to herself.

DAY 47: NEVER GIVE UP

I left the house with tears streaming down my cheeks. I wasn't sure exactly why I was crying.

Maybe it was the cold, rainy day.

Maybe it was the 90 miles of hill climbing in the rain that lay in front of me.

Maybe it was the thought of an arduous day of pedaling with no seat.

Maybe it was the voicemail I had just listened to letting me know my grandfather had finally passed.

Maybe it was the yearning for conveniences and comforts in life, like a warm shower, a washing machine, or time to relax.

Maybe I was missing the touch of a woman in my life.

Maybe it was the despair I felt, wondering, Who am I to think I can make a difference? It didn't feel like all my hard work was amounting to the change I desire to see in this world.

I pedaled out of the driveway nonetheless, knowing the only thing I could do was go forward. As I climbed hill after hill after hill, raindrops falling on my face, the tears continued to stream down my cheeks. I listened to the Avett Brothers station on Pandora, my first time listening to Internet radio on this trip, having not had the luxury of much battery life. I had heard many of these songs before, and they brought memories into my mind that added to the emotional morning. A ball of despair sat inside my chest but it had company. Next to it I felt a mountain of determination and excitement for what was to come. Knowing the sun would eventually shine upon me once again, I continued on down the road.

In the town of Grinnell I stopped at a grocery store to see if I could find some local organic food. All their dairy items were from Iowa but none were organic so I didn't make that purchase. I spent about 20 minutes learning about the products, and it was obvious that nobody knew where any of this food came from. This has been a typical experience — nobody in the store has any clue where the food they are selling comes from. Empty-handed,

I returned to my bike to find that my phone was no longer in the holder where I'd left it. The earphones dangled from the handlebars and everything in my bag was untouched, but my phone had surely been stolen. I spent a moment thinking about what to do and decided I was going to give it my all to get my phone back. I rushed back to meet Brent so I could use his phone to call mine. This was a moment where it was worth breaking my rule of using only solar-powered devices (although Goal Zero did give Brent a solar panel as well, so his phone was often charged by the sun). I called my phone multiple times with no success; it appeared the thief had turned it off. I texted the thief hoping he would read the message when he turned it on.

"Please give me my phone back. I'll pay you for it. I have photos and notes that mean a lot to me. Please, please, please. Text or call this number."

I ran back to the store to see if they had security cameras in the parking lot but they did not. I sat for a moment and realized I could use the "Find My iPhone" app. It showed my phone was active and just three blocks south of the grocery store. I called it and it was indeed back on. My text said it had been delivered as well, so I knew the thief was using the phone. I hopped on my bike and followed the GPS to where it said the phone was being used.

The phone was back off again, but the GPS showed it at the corner of Hampton and Western near a furniture shop. I searched around the shop and looked for signs. Nothing. I went inside and asked the employees if they had seen anything strange. I asked the owner if any of the nearby houses had shady people living in them and he wasn't sure, so I just walked across the street and knocked on the nearest door. A woman came out and pointed to a house two doors south, saying that the residents are known for stealing things and that she knew they had gone to the grocery store about an hour ago.

As I stood there ready to go to the house the GPS showed that the phone had moved one block south. I sprinted the one block south while hitting the "play sound" button on Brent's phone, which makes a loud beeping sound on a stolen phone. As I came around the corner I heard a loud "beep, beep, beep." I looked down and could barely believe my eyes. There was my phone placed neatly on a pile of rocks next to a bush. An hour of hard searching and barraging the phone with texts and calls and here it lay in front of me. I had imagined the battle ending with another human in front of me but certainly not by finding the phone ditched on the side of a house. I can only assume that my perseverance and determination scared the thief.

Adrenaline was rushing through my body and I shouted in joy for the next hour. I was so happy with my success and proud of my detective skills. All I could think was that my determination had paid off. Some would call it luck, but I would call it pure determination, perseverance and belief in my abilities. This is why time and time again I blow people's minds because I never give up. I try my hardest and I never give up. One out of a million people would have gotten that phone back, and the only reason I did is because I believed in myself and I did not give up. I encourage everyone reading this to go about life in the same manner, and I bet you will find out that the seemingly impossible is often quite possible.

On the way out of town I stopped at McNally's Foods, a wonderful little local market, and picked up local organic cheese, yogurt, honey and jam. I spent close to an hour talking to the owner and learned all about the wonderful things she is doing. After food has reached the suggested sell-by date they mark it down and give people the opportunity to buy it. This act of avoiding waste excited me so much. Finally a grocery store that cares about more than just money. Finally a grocery store that cares about the environment and cares about the people who shop there. They had dozens of local products and hundreds of organic foods. I could tell this store did what it took to keep food from going to the landfill and made choices based on so much more than profit.

While I was inside the store the rain started to come down. After the long afternoon in Grinnell I had no choice but to bike in the rain. I rode hard and the rain came down all the while. The rain was a bummer but I appreciated the moisture. The hard part was the lack of sun, which meant I would not be able to use my computer at the end of the day. My nerves were still running on adrenaline and the half-jar of honey coursing through my veins kept me pumping the miles out.

Just a few miles outside of Williamsburg a man greeted me on the road. He turned out to be the Warm Showers host I had arranged online, who had come to meet me. We pedaled to his home in the small Iowa town and made it there to see the sun come out from the clouds as it fell behind the tree line. It was quite the pleasant night. He took some locally caught Walleye out of the freezer and cooked it over a wood fire outside for me while his wife cooked for them on the stove indoors. I was impressed and happy for his generous effort and enjoyed sitting down with them at the dinner table. After dinner I stoked up the fire and put the PowerPot on to charge my phone. While I was at it I figured I might as well make some food for tomorrow so I threw some eggs, quinoa and beets in the water to cook. Then I spent some time hanging out with my hosts and retired to the basement just after 10 p.m.

Lesson from today: Never give up. Take breaks, take time to think, modify your methods of achieving your goals as needed, but NEVER GIVE UP.

DAY 48: BREAKING RULES FOR GOOD COMPANY

I woke up at 6 a.m., exhausted. I definitely did not want to get out of bed, but I had no choice as Dan wanted us to go before he locked up the house to leave for work. This was an unusual experience as most hosts are super chill about this. I was out at 6:30 a.m. and it was a bit chilly, but the sun was shining and I felt really good about that. I went for a morning stroll to the dumpsters and hit the road at eight.

My next stop was World of Bikes, and they were nice enough to do a quick tune-up on Brent's bike. Then I stopped at the

New Pioneer Food Co-op and filled up my honey jar with local honey and grabbed some local organic vegetables. I sat outside and nourished my body with the good food and soaked up the ambiance of Iowa City.

The afternoon was wearing on so I headed north on Highway 1 with Mount Vernon as my destination. I stopped at a grocery store right at the beginning of town. Before going inside I made a quick stop at the free outdoor section and loaded up on Naked pomegranate acai juice that had not even reached the suggested sell-by date, peaches, grapes, strawberries, yogurt, loads of wheat bread and bottles of fitness water. Thousands of pounds of food was going to waste in their dumpster, which is becoming a common find. There were around 150 watermelons alone and they were all perfect. I think they probably got a new shipment in and decided to just toss out the ones they had.

It started to rain as I sat under a tree eating my dumpster score so I called up a WarmShowers host who told me I could come on over. It turned out that my hosts, Richard Peterson and Shannon Reed, were professors at Cornell College, which my brother Levi attended. I reached their house at 5 p.m. and decided to take it easy and enjoy their company for the night and disregard any other things I had on my to-do list.

They were absolutely pleasant people to spend the evening with. They were big into local organic food and living an earth-friendly life and had all sorts of delicious and nutritious offerings for me. For the first time on this trip I allowed someone to cook me a meal. This broke the off-the-grid rules as they used water, gas and electricity: water and a paper towel to wash and dry the lettuce, gas to cook the food and electricity to ignite the gas stove. The food was all local and organic including a salad of greens, radishes and onions, a hamburger from a cow that had been raised just down the street on grass, and asparagus. I used some bread and tomato from the dumpster to make the burger into a sandwich. They did an excellent job of preparing this meal in an environmentally friendly manner, but it still used some resources.

The real key to a sustainable world isn't to forgo the usage of all resources but to use our resources wisely and in moderation. That's my message to you. Thus I felt it okay having this meal with them tonight. It was so wonderful to sit and eat with these fantastic people. I don't know what I enjoyed more, the interesting intellectual conversation or the pure local food. They were two of the most enjoyable people I have spoken to on the trip, and it may have been the most enjoyable night yet. Good conversation, good food, fun and knowledge gained on various topics.

DAY 49: FAMILY TIME

I woke up feeling refreshed and enjoyed the sound of Shannon and Richard in the kitchen talking about whether or not I could eat their local organic eggs. Even as environmentally conscious people, my simple actions were making them think. I spent the morning in their lovely house taking my time as I prepared for the day of biking. It was a very pleasant morning and the meaningful conversations from yesterday continued. They showed me all the wonderful food they are growing in their yard including lemons, strawberries, blueberries and a handful of different herbs. They really live a life to admire here in Mount Vernon.

Around 3 p.m. the clouds became sparse and the sun shined down upon me. I took some time to walk out through the tall grass as I ate a lunch I had prepared. The heat of the sun on my back and the brightness of the blue sky instantly cheered me up. The sun is such a powerful force and I have learned to appreciate it so much, for it is the source of my happiness. The sun gave me the motivation to pedal about 30 percent faster than earlier in the day and made the riding so much more enjoyable. I pushed on and just after 5 p.m. pulled into the busy city of Dubuque, Iowa.

My aunts, Louise and Myrna, who had driven over from Chicago to spend the evening with me, greeted me at the edge of town. It was such a wonderful feeling to be in the presence of people I know and love. We went into a grocery store and searched the shelves for local organic food, their gift to me.

Searching for local, organic food on the grocery store shelves with my aunts Myrna (left) and Louise (right).

I got two blocks of organic Iowa cheese that I managed to finish off in less than 24 hours. If you put food in front of me on this trip it won't last long. My body is constantly craving calories. Ideally I don't want to be eating so much dairy, or really any, but it is one of the few local foods that I can consistently find across America. We went to a restaurant for dinner, and my friends Grant and Vanessa drove down from Boscobel, Wisconsin, to join us. I got a salad with completely local and organic ingredients. This was my first time eating in a restaurant on the trip; I've avoided doing so because of the electricity they use to prepare food and the water they use to wash dishes. So I was definitely

on the grid tonight but my choice of food was about as eco-friendly as it gets.

Around Dubuque and at the restaurant I barely had a chance to rest my mind as people approached me about my bamboo bike and the solar panels on the trailer. The people in this city seem beyond excited about living an earth-friendly lifestyle. A man named Rob approached me at the dinner table and told me about a bike program he started in Dubuque, and with that short conversation he ended up hosting me at his apartment just a few blocks away. He had a sweet loft in downtown Dubuque filled with bicycles, and it was an absolute pleasure to sleep on his couch.

PART 3

THE MIDWEST

DAY 50: HELLO WISCONSIN!

I woke up to another morning of being overly exhausted but was quite excited for what was to come. It was 6:30 a.m., and the sky was not completely covered with clouds although it wasn't quite sunny. I was amazed to see the streets covered with booths selling local food, crafts and goods. Dubuque amazed me again today with its excitement for local culture and creating a healthy planet. My host, Rob from Dubuque Bike Coop, was set up at the market, and I learned about some of the great stuff they are doing. They make it easy for anyone to own a bike. For around $75 you can get a solid used bicycle. You can even use a bike for three months with a deposit you get back when you return the bike.

My goal was to be at Keith's Organic Valley farm at 10 a.m. and it was 23 miles away so I had to get out of the market rather quickly. I soon found myself crossing the Mississippi River into my homeland of Wisconsin. I was still quite exhausted so I wasn't jumping for joy, but I was quite excited on the inside. The ride to Cuba City was pretty easy on the body and the eyes with all the beautiful rolling hills full of lush green vegetation. I arrived at the farm around 10:45 a.m. and the sun was out in nearly full force. Keith welcomed me to his organic farm that had been there since 1848, and I spent three hours learning as much as I could. He owns and milks about 360 dairy cows. Here are some of the great things about this farm.

The cows are almost completely grass-fed. They eat about 70 pounds of food per day, all grass from the pasture except for seven pounds of grain supplement. Each cow also drinks about 50 pounds of water per day. This 120 pounds of input creates about seven or eight gallons (60 pounds) of milk. They produce all of the grain right here on the farm; they have 1,000 acres where they grow corn, alfalfa, oats, and sorghum. All of the grains are organically produced, and if all goes right with the weather, no feed has to be shipped in.

The cows spend the whole day out on the pasture except a few hours in the morning and a few hours in the evening when they are inside being milked. The cows are very well cared for and no hormones are used.

All the manure and pee is moved to a holding pond using a gravity feed and is then spread on the crops as organic fertilizer. This is a closed-loop system. The cows live for seven or eight years on this farm.

All of the water they use is well water, which means they are not diverting it from rivers or lakes, unlike many of the huge farms around the country.

These farmers also grow food for themselves, compared to industrial farmers who rarely eat anything they produce. The Wilsons drink the milk they harvest and eat meat from cows they raise. They also grow fruits and vegetables on the farm including apples, strawberries, garlic, pears and greens. A lot of the other food they eat is from the network of Organic Valley farms in the area including eggs from Ihm's farm in Lancaster.

This was a wonderful educational experience for me. I learned all about pasteurization, milk fat percentages, milking, diet and so much more. This information is so valuable and I urge everyone reading this to start learning about where your food comes from. We need food to live — it is one of the most important aspects of our lives, along with water, shelter, fresh air and exercise. We eat food multiple times per day, every day. Doesn't it make sense to have an invested interest in it?

I grew up in Wisconsin, the dairy state, and lived there for 23 years without ever visiting a dairy farm, except for maybe on a school field trip. I too am guilty of not knowing where much of my food comes from but I am changing that. It was an amazing feeling to drink milk that had come from the cow's udders that morning. It was unpasteurized but had already been cooled in the holding tank, and since I was there in the afternoon I did not get to milk a cow myself. I will do that on this trip, and I will be able to tell you firsthand that milk comes out of the cow at about 98 degrees, not cold like I had dreamed earlier in the trip.

I am very excited about Organic Valley's acts of sustainability and very excited to continue learning about their co-op of organic farms run in a way that is less draining on the earth's resources than industrial farms. Keith is a farmer through and through. He grew up on that land that was homesteaded by his family in 1848. He was happy to be living off the land producing food that he could be proud to feed his family and the American consumer. I don't think the man stopped smiling for a minute, and I know he was excited every day to be a farmer doing good for the earth, his community, and his country. This is the kind of family I want producing the food I eat.

When I parted ways with the Wilsons I also parted ways with Brent. We had decided to take some time apart from each other, so he headed east to Madison and I headed north to visit my Wisconsin friends from my time in university. It was freeing to pedal solo, and I imagined lying in a green pasture for part of the afternoon taking the sun in. Instead I headed to Platteville barefoot with the idea of relaxing in a park but ended up at the Driftless Market, which was an absolute gem of a store. My ten-minute stop ended up being a joyous and knowledge-filled three hours. The store and the people inside filled my heart with happiness. I learned of all the amazing things they are doing for their community and their customers. A few things that stuck out are:

- Thirty percent of the food they purchase is from the local region.
- The jams on their shelves are made in the store from fruits they pull from the shelf because of aesthetic imperfections or because they are too ripe to sell. So rather than throw this fruit away like 98 out of 100 stores I've been to, they turn it into a desirable product.
- The soups they prepare are partially made from vegetables that are past perfect, just like the fruits. They treated me to a bowl and it was exquisite.

- They have a very large and diverse bulk food section. Buying in bulk makes sense because there is no packaging, and you can buy just what you need, resulting in less waste.
- Produce that cannot be used to make jams or soup is composted. They produce about ten gallons of food waste per day from the store and café. Standard grocery stores would throw this in the dumpster, but they compost it, turning it into organic fertilizer, which they then use on the food they grow at home, some of which even ends up back on the shelves. They are so good at reducing and reusing that they don't even have a dumpster.
- They have bulk soap and laundry detergent, which means no wasting plastic bottles every time you need more soap. You bring your own container and fill it up.
- They put ten cents into a jar every time a customer does not use a plastic bag and that money goes to a local good cause.

I had to get going so that I would make it to Lancaster in time to get a good night's rest. I was very excited to be spending the night with the Carrolls, the parents of Abby, a girl I dated in college. The Carrolls are family to me and told me to make myself at home; they weren't going to be home until late so I had the house to myself for a while. I hadn't been there for three years and in the past I would visit with Abby, so it was going to be quite funny to be in their house by myself. I arrived at the house around 7 p.m., sat around and relaxed for a bit and then curled up in the guest bedroom before nine. I was absolutely exhausted and so thankful to have this night to rest up and spend some time alone.

DAY 51: LESSONS FROM THE PLUMBERS

I woke up in my comfortable bed after 12 hours of sleep, sweating under the warm blankets and vividly dreaming. Both my body and mind felt well rested. The basement bedroom was dimly lit and I walked up the stairs to start my day off with a hug from Patti, which I hadn't had in nearly three years.

We sat around the kitchen table catching up on the last few years of life. Before long Tom walked in. It was such a bright way to start my day spending time with family. We sat around in the kitchen and I explained the premise of my journey. It was an extremely pleasant morning, so enjoyable to relax in a Midwestern fashion with good people. A few hours later Mike and Allison showed up with their two children. We just hung out as Wisconsinites know how to do as good as anyone else on a Sunday. Mike and Tom had a beer in hand as usual, as did a great many of the men in the state of Wisconsin that afternoon. They own Carroll's Plumbing and Heating so I took this opportunity to learn about water efficiency and plumbing.

Modern toilets use between 1.2 and 1.6 gallons per flush; federal regulations say 1.6 is the maximum a newly installed toilet can use. Toilets used to use three gallons a flush and before that five gallons. So we have improved a lot in the last few decades but we still have a long way to go. An easy way to save water is to only flush when you need to: "If it's yellow let it mellow; if it's brown flush it down." Also you can put something in the tank such as a brick or a bottle filled with sand to displace water, which saves you an equivalent volume of water with each flush.

Faucets have a maximum flow rate of 2.2 gallons per minute or gpm (restrictors built into the plumbing keep water from being able to flow any faster). The kitchen faucet is the most commonly used faucet in the house. You can easily change to a more efficient faucet aerator that runs at 0.35, 0.5, 1.0, or 1.5 gpm. By switching from 2.2 to 0.5 gpm you can reduce your water usage by over 75 percent, for an investment of about $3 Talk about an easy way to save a ton of water. When I get home I'll definitely be changing out my faucets. Always turn off your faucet when not in use, for example while brushing your teeth. In general, just pay attention to water usage and try to cut back.

Showers have a maximum flow rate of 2.5 gallons per minute; again, restrictors in the showerhead keep the flow from exceeding this. However many older showers use three to four gpm. You can pick up a water-efficient showerhead for under $20, and you will make your investment back in a short time. The Carrolls estimated that 30 percent of the homes they service still have old showerheads, so make sure your showerhead is an efficient one. The average American is in the shower for 8.2 minutes and has a shower that puts out 2.1 gallons/minute. This means they use 17.2 gallons per shower to clean their body. That is 34 days' worth of drinking water down the drain in one shower. Most of us are not that dirty that we need to shower every single day. We could also spend less time in the shower. Put a timer in your shower if you'd like to become aware of how long your showers are and then make a goal to shorten them.

I also learned about the different types of water heaters and their efficiencies. When you are using hot water you are also using electricity or gas. So even if you don't think that water can be wasted, the EPA says that running the hot water faucet for five minutes uses about the same amount of energy as burning a 60-watt bulb for 22 hours. Try to minimize your hot water usage when possible.

It was awesome to catch up with people I love and at the same time increase my knowledge on water consumption in America from a family that is very knowledgeable on the subject.

Mike and Allison brought over a whole bunch of food from their CSA including spinach, lettuce, radishes and asparagus, plus a gallon of Organic Valley milk they had bought. The Ihm family farm was right on the front of the jug, which was a funny coincidence as I was going to visit the farm that day. Any feelings I had yesterday of loneliness were completely washed away when I woke up in the Carrolls' house this morning. My heart was warmed by their welcoming and generous nature. This is a common trait among Midwest people, but they exceed the average.

The Ihm farm was just 15 minutes north. John Ihm greeted me at the front door to the chicken house. It was quite the experience to be in a barn amongst 3,500 chickens that were all popping out eggs. I spent two hours with John, who lives on the

These chickens are considered free-range and produce organic eggs. If you think this is a packed shed you should see a factory farm.

farm with his wife and five children. His brother's family and his mom also live on the farm, and they all work the land to produce food. They are an Organic Valley farm and produce free-range eggs as well as milk. I learned how they produce the organic eggs on our shelves at the grocery store.

The chicks are hatched and raised at a different local Organic Valley farm and transferred here at 4.5 months. They lay eggs here on the farm for 11 months before being sold locally at about 18 months of age. Last year 2,700 of the 3,500 chickens were sold to local farmers who used them to lay eggs for another three-six months and then butchered them for meat. The other 800 were butchered immediately and used to make chicken soup. So these chickens have a life span of 1.5 to 2 years.

At their peak, the chickens here have an 88–95 percent laying rate. This means that each chicken lays one egg nine days out of ten; the 3,500 chickens lay about 3,150 eggs per day. With age the chickens slow down and produce fewer eggs, which is why they are only used for laying for about a year. The size of the eggs also increases with age, which for some reason is not as desirable for the market. Apparently the American consumer does not like large eggs.

These chickens are considered free-range. During the summer they spend about seven hours outside each day. The doors are opened at 11 a.m., and the chickens rush out to peck away at the ground for the day. At nightfall the doors are opened again and the chickens rush inside to roost for the night. The first month they live on the farm they are kept inside to train them to lay inside, and in the winter they are kept inside 24/7.

The chickens are fed a combination of corn, alfalfa, wheat, barley, oats, soybeans, lime, grit, B complex, oyster shells and a premix with 25 minerals. All of the grains are grown on the farm and the soybeans are grown at another farm nearby in Wisconsin, which saves a lot of fuel and packaging. 6,000 pounds of food feeds the 3,500 chickens for seven or eight days, as each chicken eats about a quarter pound (4 ounces) of food per day. All of the chicken poop is scooped out once a year and used to fertilize the crops grown to feed the chickens.

Most eggs weigh from 1.75 to 3 ounces. The craziest egg Joe and his children have ever found was 5 ounces, almost three times the average. They cracked it open and found another whole egg inside and two yolks — they cracked that egg and found it had two developing yolks inside it. Boy, would I have loved to find that egg! Crazy stuff like this happens in nature sometimes; irregularities are regular. We desire consistency and regularity but that is not the way the planet works. Part of permaculture is embracing nature's unpredictability and enjoying all the odd-shaped things that come with it.

The Ihms sell all the eggs that are not the right shape and size for the supermarket locally. They have never used a new egg carton — they get them all used from customers and local grocery stores. They also donate over 400 dozen eggs per year to the food pantry. Organic Valley picks up the eggs about once a week and transports them in reusable crates that create no trash. The eggs come out of the chicken very clean and usually don't have to be cleaned at the farm. This is done at the processing facilities, which are in the area.

John's brother Joe came by with his daughter, and we talked about their lives here in southwestern Wisconsin. They grow potatoes, apples, peppers, onions, beans, lettuce, squash, cucumbers, melons, strawberries and much more. They can beans and jar foods such as jams, applesauce and tomatoes, and make juices and pies. They eat eggs for breakfast almost every day and eat their own beef as well. Typically they get their meat when a cow gets injured and can no longer be milked. One cow produces about 800 pounds of beef, enough to feed the three families for a year. Joe quoted his father who used to say, "We're farmers so we're going to eat like farmers." About 75 percent of the food they eat they produce themselves. Another thing Joe said that stuck out was, "Most factory farmers don't eat a thing they produce because they know what's in it." He meant all the chemicals and hormones that go into factory farming. Organic Valley farmers practice what they preach.

Purchasing organic eggs at the grocery store is drastically more humane than purchasing factory-farmed eggs. In factory farms chickens are packed into windowless sheds, often so tight they barely have room to move. Many factory farms use "battery cages," stacked wire frames that are home to up to ten hens in an area the size of a file-cabinet drawer. If you saw this you would get nightmares knowing this is where your eggs are coming from.

At 4 p.m. I pedaled north to Boscobel to stay at my friend Grant's house. He had invited a bunch of my best friends from university over for an evening of fun. The 20 miles to Boscobel was very easy and enjoyable, and I did it in about an hour and a half. A few hills slowed me down, but I had about twice as many downhills to make the pedaling easy. As of yesterday my knees have started to be quite sore, but it has not been unbearable. I got to the house at 5:30 p.m. and was greeted by Kyle, Grant and Miranda, some of my best friends since 2005. Over the fire I cooked a present from Grant's dad, a piece of venison, with some trimmings from some other friends: fresh asparagus and radishes. Wow, that's a lot of giving. I also cooked a big pot of wheat and quinoa.

Even after this massive meal my body was still craving calories so the whole group of us took a walk down to the grocery store together to peek in the old treasure chest out back. Here I found a perfectly good Green Bay Packers' birthday cake. We headed back to the house and everyone had a piece of the fresh trash cake. I was surprised everyone took part and had fun doing it together. We hung out in the living room for a while and I answered all sorts of questions and told all sorts of stories.

DAY 52: FISHING AND CATCHING TURTLES

I woke up to the sun after another comfortable night in bed. Wow, the pleasure of sleeping in a bed in a room to myself. I decided to take the day off and stay in Boscobel rather than ride up to the Organic Valley headquarters in La Farge. I was torn, but I knew it was important to rest my sore legs and to catch up online.

My solar panel has only been working sporadically the last couple days. I don't know if it is the battery or the panel, but it's been very frustrating as I am dependent on it to communicate with everyone. I decided to plug into the wall today, for only the second time on this trip. I figured the positive impact I could make by being online was far greater than the little bit of electricity I would be using to run my laptop. It was so nice not to have to pay constant attention to every drop in percentage of my battery life. Over the course of the day I plugged in for about four hours. It was fun to be freely on the computer. I love using social media to spread inspiration for a healthier planet. It rarely gets old for me.

It was a beautiful day in Boscobel and I got a lot done. At 3 p.m. Grant and I biked over to his dad's house to pick up some fishing poles and headed over to the quarry. I am so glad I didn't miss this opportunity to spend some time on the lake. From our perch above it I could see more turtles in one spot than I have ever seen in my life — upwards of 50 — and I've been a turtle catcher since I could get out into nature by myself. The two of us walked along the edge of the clear lake spotting bass and bluegill and casting our jigs at them. We caught more than 50 bass; in many cases I watched them swim over to my lure and suck it up into their mouths. It is so exciting to watch fish in their natural environment feeding on prey, or what they thought was prey.

I also spent time trying to catch turtles with my bare hands, swimming through weeds so thick they looked like they would wrap me up and drown me. I did not succeed in actually catching one but succeeded hugely at enjoying myself. The water was a very pleasurable temperature and was so refreshing to be in. The last week of rain had muddied up all the rivers and had them flowing at dangerous levels and speeds, keeping me out of them. I hadn't bathed in over a week but was confident I wasn't smelly since everyone I'd hugged over the last few days had told me so. The water refreshed my body and mind as it always does. Water, along with the sun, is the source of my happiness. In an instant my day can be refreshed and rejuvenated by jumping into a natural body of water.

We released all of the bass except three that I took home for dinner. Riding without the trailer was joyous and I realized just how fast I could go on this bike. Grant and I raced through town, him in his car and me on my bike, and I was able to cruise at the speed limit of 25 miles per hour. He beat me home but I was just behind him the whole way. This is life in rural Wisconsin. It is simple and easy here. I understand why people choose to take this path, and I could easily be happy spending the rest of my life living simply, fishing and walking through nature. However, I know to create the world I want to see I have to be out there experiencing it firsthand and expanding my knowledge so I can pass it on to others.

DAY 53: THIS IS MY HOMELAND

Whether we realize it or not, every day we choose to be a part of the solution or a part of the problem.

I left Grant's house at 3:30 p.m. as the clouds rolled in, partially covering the sun. It had been a hot day, 85+ degrees, and this cooled it off a bit. A few sprinkles fell from the sky and the humid air was full of vigor and life. Leaving town I was tremendously grateful to have spent time with great friends and rested my drained body. I stopped behind the grocery store on the way out and loaded my bag full of blackberries, apples, nectarines, spinach and melons. These ten pounds of fruit would last me for about 24 hours. The dumpsters in the Midwest have been extremely abundant with quality food.

The terrain outside of Boscobel was stunningly beautiful and brought excitement to my mind and body. The road took me along the flooded Wisconsin River, which flowed through the forest in a river wonderland. The green land enthralled me and was full of magical scents from blooming trees and wildflowers. The temperature was ideal for riding in just shorts, and my hairy body trapped hundreds of little insects all over it. Insects bounced off my forehead and flew into my eyes, but I enjoyed this knowing all this life had been created by the river. I pedaled along feeling inspired by the beauty surrounding me. It was so grand that it brought sadness to me, as nature often does.

This is Wisconsin. This is my homeland. This is where my roots spread into the ground as a young boy and soaked up knowledge, experiences, friendships, love and memories. This land molded me into the man I am today. As far away as I travel and as long as I stay away it will always be the land that made me who I am.

On this journey I have created and solidified my mission in life and have dedicated myself to being the change we need in this world, the inspiration that people need to take action. To lead by example, to demonstrate what can be done and what anyone can attain. To teach simple ways to live a happier, healthier life that will create a happier, healthier planet. That is who I am and who I will be. The path I took in my younger years in Wisconsin did not always have an obvious arrow pointing in this direction, but I am thankful for every moment I have spent on this earth because it has brought me to where I am today and led me to this mission. It has created a desire deep inside me to be the change I wish to see. I gave thanks as I rode today through the Wisconsin wilderness for the shivers it sent down my spine and for being a source for the greatness inside me.

I passed familiar places in an unfamiliar way, on a bicycle. When I lived in Madison just 50 miles from where I was pedaling today, it would have been quite the task to pedal out here. Now it was just another 50- to 75-mile day on the road. I can cycle these distances now without thinking twice about it. Growing up in Wisconsin I drove everywhere and used a credit card to pump the gas. This credit card detached me from the fact that I was pumping money into my tank. For many years I never thought about reducing the amount of fuel I used. If I wanted to go somewhere I just thought, Hey, I'll put gas in the car to get me there. I did not think about saving myself money or not contributing to climate change. Now that I realize what this mindset does to the planet and how much more financially free I am without pouring my money into my car, I cringe at the thought of pumping gas into a vehicle. Life is just a matter of perspective and how we shape the world around us. Every day we have choices to make, and each one of us as individuals makes the decision to be a part of the problem or a part of the solution. In May of 2012 I chose to sell my car and go pedal powered.

DAY 54: RAIN WON'T STOP US

It was cloudy all morning but the air was warm and humid. Rain was in the forecast but not until after 5 p.m., which is exactly when I had an outdoor gathering planned. I mulled over the idea of moving it indoors but waited until the last minute to make the call.

I pedaled over to The North Face Madison. The staff had heard about my trip and wanted me to stop in for a visit. I was excited to meet them and learn about what environmental actions they're taking at their store and companywide. Laura, Laurie and Jeff were all working, and I hung out with them for about two hours. Here are some actions they're taking:

Reducing packaging. Last year was the first year they stopped offering gift boxes and packaging. Over the holiday season a few people raised a stink but TNF held their ground. They also ask customers if they'd like a bag rather than just give one to everyone. This gets people thinking; often they respond with, "No, I guess I don't need one." Simple actions like these have an instant impact and, if a great number of people do them, can have a massive impact.

At this store they are big time advocates of volunteering in the community, commuting to work, reducing, recycling and using eco-friendly cleaning products. All of the employees get involved in the community and the store puts together days to give back to the earth in ways such as invasive species removal from the parks and cleaning up trash. They keep track of miles commuting by bicycling and walking. In Wisconsin the weather can make it hard to bike or walk to work, especially in the cold winters. Laurie commutes about eight miles per day via bike, and Laura lives close enough to walk every day. Being better to the planet often means changing the way you do things. Sure it takes an effort at first, but usually it makes your life more enjoyable and healthy. Laura moved close to work, which means less time and money spent getting there, and days that are simpler, more enjoyable and movement-oriented. The North Face also pays employees to volunteer in the outdoors for eight hours per year.

Some of their products, including their sandals, are partially made of recycled materials. They're also removing petroleum from some of their products. The rain jacket they gave me to get through the stormy days is coated in castor oil, a plant-based oil, rather than petroleum-based waterproofing material. Many of their clothing items are composed of Bluesign-approved fabric, which means the raw materials are sustainably sourced, the chemicals in the fabrics are monitored to be less destructive to the environment, and the working conditions in the factories are above par. Knowing a product from source to consumer is an intricate task that takes a lot of time. Most businesses, like most individuals, have no idea where their products are coming from. This has to change and many businesses are making the effort to change. Bluesign is just one tool, but a very powerful tool, in this change.

I'm not promoting the North Face as a sustainable company — they could be doing a ton more— but I do think this particular store is making a solid effort to reduce their impact. Sometimes large companies take note from the little guys and the little changes at the bottom can trickle all the way to the top. Remember this if you are an employee and aim to lead by example to create change from within.

Laurie, the assistant store manager, biked with me to the restaurant where I had relocated the gathering, which served local food, beer and ice cream. About 15 of my friends came to spend the night together and many of them brought me good organic Wisconsin food. Abby brought me Organic Valley cheese, Claire brought lettuce and tomatoes from her CSA, Todd brought raw milk from a farm near his house and jarred venison from a deer he shot last year, and Miranda brought a zucchini and a sweet potato from a store in Madison. It's not easy to find stuff for a dude biking off the grid across America but they did, and it warmed my heart.

DAY 55: I LIKE TURTLES

I was up at 4:30 a.m. and started my day with a stunning sunrise as I pedaled over to the Monona Terrace. ABC Channel 27 was meeting me there to do a story for the Wake Up Wisconsin morning show, organized by my friend Sherry Czarnecki, a producer at the station. I wasn't exactly excited to be up at that time, but it was worth it to spread some inspiration to the Madison area. We were shooting live with the capitol in the backdrop but the camera equipment wasn't getting a signal so we missed the first segment at 5:50 a.m. We moved closer to the lake for the 6:25 a.m. show and had more technical difficulties. At the third attempt the signal was working, but we were in a much less ideal spot with noisy traffic. Despite this I was happy with the story that aired.

By 8 a.m. I was on the road. It was a gorgeous day and an easy morning of pedaling. Green land, blue sky and an orange sun guided me eastward. I was surprised at just how beautiful eastern Wisconsin was. I had lived in this state for 23 years, but in this short week biking through it I saw a lot of new places and gained new experiences in my homeland. I rode over bridges spanning beautiful rivers and was tempted to swim in every single one of them. Turtles were out and about looking for good spots to drop their eggs; I found one, a pig-nosed softshell turtle I think, laying her eggs on the side of the road. They like the soft gravel on the shoulders and often use them as nests. This is not an ideal, safe place for slow-moving animals and results in a lot of dead turtles. I also came upon a cool snapping turtle that I spent time playing with in someone's yard. There were also cottonwood seeds in their big fluffy seedpods drifting through the air like snow in December. It was magical, to say the least.

A snapping turtle going about his business in Wisconsin. This is one of the many turtles I came across while riding across America.

Fifteen miles west of Milwaukee I picked up a bike path that led me through beautiful green forests all the way to Waukesha. Once I hit the populated area it was almost another two hours of maneuvering through traffic and bumpy roads to get into Milwaukee. Three great friends greeted me, and even though I was exhausted after a long day I managed to spend some quality time with them.

DAY 56: GROWING POWER

Today I finally visited Growing Power, which I've wanted to do for years, ever since I first saw them featured on the documentary *Fresh*. My visit to their three-acre organic urban garden was more productive, educational and inspirational than I had ever imagined. Every corner I turned there was something interesting and exciting to see. The interns, volunteers and staff were all stoked to learn about my bamboo bike and solar panel-covered trailer as well.

The vision of Growing Power is to inspire communities to build sustainable food systems that are equitable and ecologically sound and create a just world, one food-secure community at a time. They thoroughly impressed me, and I truly believe this organization knows how to change the world for the better. They're already doing it, and if we just replicated their system around America we could be on our way to a healthier, happier nation tomorrow.

Here are some of the spectacular things they are doing at Growing Power:

- Growing quality food in large quantities. They grow food for more than 10,000 people per year, including more than one million pounds of vegetables. A large portion of their veggies are grown via aquaponics, and they also raise over 35,000 tilapia and yellow perch per year in tanks. Aquaponics is a sustainable food production system that combines raising aquatic animals such as fish (aquaculture) with cultivating plants in water (hydroponics) in a symbiotic environment. The fish poop in the water, and the poop is broken down by nitrogen-fixing bacteria into nutrients that are taken in by the plants. The water is circulated through the system via pumps so nutrient-rich water is always being delivered to the plant roots. There is no soil in an aquaponics system because the roots are submerged in water, where they can access nutrients. This highly productive system of farming can produce high-quality food in large quantities year round, even in cold environments.
- Keeping food from the landfill. Growing Power composts 43 million pounds of waste per year — and 21 million of that is wasted food they pick up from stores, distributors, restaurants, school cafeterias, etc. Instead of letting it go to the landfill, Growing Power turns

DUDE

this wasted food into valuable fertilizer used to create more food. They also feed some of the wasted food to their goats and chickens, which creates fertilizer as well.

- Growing Power has a vision of a world where everybody has access to good food. They transform communities by providing healthy and affordable food to lower-income communities. They teach people what real food is and what they need to eat to have a healthy body. I've been learning that some parents feed their children nothing but potato chips and sugary drinks for lunch, and many people know close to nothing about food. Growing Power is doing their part and more to change that. They grow food, grow minds and grow the community.

- Their Farm-to-City Market Basket Program is a cross between a mobile grocery store and a CSA program. Not all the food is local food — they don't grow bananas or oranges in Wisconsin — but it is all healthy. This is an excellent way to provide good, healthy food at a good price in a convenient way. If there is one thing Americans love, it's convenience, so if we're going to get people eating healthy, it likely can't be too complicated or challenging.

- Growing Power also offers all sorts of workshops, outreach projects and youth education programs. A nonprofit, they have multiple streams of income to raise the funds they need to keep creating a better world. I respect this greatly as many nonprofits don't understand how to generate revenue. Growing Power seems to be doing a very good job of it so far.

To quote Will Allen, Growing Power's founder: "If people can grow safe, healthy, affordable food, if they have access to land and clean water, this is transformative on every level in a community. I believe we cannot have healthy communities without a healthy food system."

Growing Power is passionately working to end food deserts in America.

DAY 57: THE MILWAUKEE TO CHICAGO 100-MILE RIDE FOR SUSTAINABILITY

I woke up to the sound of rain. I thought I had left my bag open on the deck and it was getting soaked but then realized it was right next to the couch I was sleeping on. It was a gloomy and cold morning but it could have been worse. A few weeks earlier I had planned a ride called "The Milwaukee to Chicago 100-Mile Ride for Sustainability" and invited the public to join. It wasn't anything fancy, just people getting together to ride bicycles in the name of sustainability. My friends Mitch Hunter and Casey Hubner joined in and helped plan it, and we hoped for a big turnout this morning. But I figured the rain would probably stop most people from joining us and I was okay with that, as I desired a relaxing day with close friends. By the time we got over to the meeting point the rain had let up, and although it wasn't warm it was still pleasant. Just after ten a guy from Milwaukee named Bruno, who learned about the ride from Reddit, joined us, too. So it was the five of us riding to Chicago.

It was an absolute joy to be pedaling alongside some of my best friends. It made the pedaling extremely easy — the 50 miles we had to do today were a joy and not a task at all. We took our time and made many little stops. Each mile was pleasurable as I talked with the guys. Mitch has been a best friend since 2006, and Casey is becoming a better friend every time I see him. Bruno turned out to be a really cool dude, too. For all three of them these 100 miles would be the longest trip they'd ever been on and the first time doing a multi-day bike trip, and I was very excited for them.

The first 15 miles or so were along Lake Michigan, and I saw all sorts of new neighborhoods and sights even though I had previously lived here for more than a year. The day gradually warmed, the rains held off, and the sun even shined a tiny bit. Casey was excited to watch me find good food from dumpsters so part of the day was spent peeking into treasure chests, which turned into a fun game. He had been reading my stories over the last month and just couldn't fathom there being this abundance of free food — he was having a really hard time believing it without seeing it. Before too long I found a bounty of boxed crackers and a whole fresh pizza, and we all had trash lunch together. It was really fun to share this with friends.

Later in the day Brent was trying to switch gears on his bicycle as he looked at his phone and took a serious fall, finding himself on the ground in the middle of the road. Bruno was riding close behind him and wound up running over Brent and falling hard to the concrete. When I looked back at the commotion, Bruno was holding his shoulder and seemed to be in excruciating pain. It was a rush for both of them but they turned out fine. So on we pedaled through Racine and Kenosha, sometimes along the lake and sometimes on the city roads. The guys stopped for ice cream in the afternoon and by then the sun was out and the skies were blue.

That night Casey and I went to an Aldi grocery store and scored 45 pounds of food that we brought back for dinner for everyone — but first we wolfed down a still-frozen half-gallon of moose tracks ice cream. We got strawberries, blueberries, grapes, melons, apples, avocados, bananas, zucchini, grapefruits and a load of donuts and muffins. Everybody ate some of it for dinner and for breakfast the next day. My good friend Scott Stipetich happened to be driving through to Ashland from New York and spent the night camping with us also. We all sat around the picnic table together having a happy time just hanging out after a day of biking. The air was warm and the night was pleasant. There was lightning on the horizon, and then suddenly it really started to downpour. I threw all of my stuff into Scott's trunk, and we sat in the car catching up until I passed out in the passenger seat and him in the driver's seat for a good night's sleep. This was my first time sitting in a car since San Francisco, and I felt like I was doing something wrong just being in there, even though we weren't burning any gas.

DAY 58: BIKE HEAVEN

The sun was shining when I woke up in the car. I was excited to see the sun and feel its warmth on my skin. It was a beautiful morning, a world away from yesterday's rain, and I spent it relaxing, playing with friends and eating loads of fruit. Before hitting the road we stopped at the beach for the most enjoyable swim of the trip. The water was cold and it took a bit of enticing. Man was it fun to have my friends around, after two months all on my own. It's a heck of a lot more fun. My body and mind were both so refreshed playing and cleaning up in the fresh cold water.

Then we were back on the road for an enjoyable day of riding in the sun. Today was much more biking-oriented than yesterday, as we wanted to get to Millennium Park at a reasonable time. The first part of the trip took us mostly on surface roads through the cities, but the next 30 miles was mostly joyous riding on bike paths and smooth roads in upscale neighborhoods. I felt happy, healthy, and excited to be alive in the presence of good people. Bike paths bring substantially more joy than busy roads with cars, which is what we hit once we got to Chicago. This can be a bit nerve-wracking at times but I enjoy racing the cars and cruising through when they are stuck in traffic.

We caught the Lake Shore Path and found ourselves in bike heaven. Good-looking gals were all over the place, and cyclists, rollerbladers and runners were all as happy as we were to be out on this gorgeous day. It was the type of weather I'd been dreaming of since I left San Diego. My heart belongs to the Midwest summer, and the Chicago lakefront is one of my favorite places to spend a summer afternoon. The lake is cold and refreshing, the sand is pristine, the beautiful women are plentiful, and the great city of Chicago with its impressive skyline hangs over it all. Man can create beauty after all. We were all in high spirits at the accomplishment of arriving in this city wonderland.

Me and the guys arriving in Chicago after 100 miles of riding together. Bruno, me, Casey, Mitch (left to right).

We stopped to take in the skyline and then pedaled on until we had to get off the lake path to go to Millennium Park. I took us off a half-mile too early and wound up navigating us the wrong way down some bustling one-way roads. It was a zoo of people and cars, and we were a group of five dudes on bikes trying to make it the last half-mile. I led us down sidewalks and at one point up a two-story flight of stairs to Michigan Avenue. That last half-mile took 40 minutes, but we finally arrived at the Bean, where we were greeted by my family and friends after our 100 miles of riding.

DAY 59: SUMMER DAYS OF REST

Today was a simple day. I slept in and spent the morning at my grandpa's house relaxing and resting. I've considered this place a home for a long time and take great comfort in being here. I had a lot on my list of things to do, but I made sure to also have a relaxing day.

The most important thing on my agenda was washing my clothes, some of which I hadn't washed since Boulder, Colorado, over a month ago. I rode my bike five miles to Lake Michigan where I waded into the clear cold water and scrubbed my clothes by hand with a Dr. Bronner's bar of soap. I learned after this journey that you should not use soap in a natural body of water, even if the soap is biodegradable. Soap should be used at least 200 yards from the body of water so that the soil can absorb the soap, and microorganisms can break it down. It took me about an hour and a half to wash everything but I enjoyed soaking up the natural water of Lake Michigan and the rays from the sun at the same time.

On my way home I stopped in at a large chain grocery store dumpster and stocked up on food for the rest of my stay in Chicago. I picked up 12 Naked juice drinks, two loaves of top-quality wheat bread, a half-dozen organic salads full of walnuts and cranberries, and fresh produce such as apples, nectarines, peaches, plums, and bananas. That, along with the local organic food that my aunt had bought me at the farmers' market, would provide plenty of nutrients and calories for my rapid metabolism. A security guy approached me at the dumpster as I was packing the food into my trailer and told me that it was cool if I took the food but that I shouldn't come back. He explained that the store got a citation for rats, and they think it's because homeless take stuff out of the dumpster and scatter it all over the place. If you ever dumpster dive, leave the place cleaner than you found it so the stores don't have a reason to prevent it.

My dumpster score in the foreground and my freshly washed clothes air-drying in the background.

Back at the house I squeezed my dripping-wet clothes over the tomato plants to reuse the water and then hung them all out to dry on the power line that runs through my grandpa' s yard. As I did this I looked up and saw a plane flying overhead, and for the first time in a long time I imagined what it would be like to be on one. I thought about getting on a plane and crossing the country in a matter of hours instead of 100 days. This brought feelings of excitement to me for the day when I will return to a somewhat normal lifestyle. It also excited me because I have fond memories of flying to Chicago in the summer, and now I was in Chicago with no need to get on a plane. I have everything I need: a warm Midwest summer, food to eat, family and friends to laugh with, clean air to breathe and a bike to get me where I need to be. I don't need money, electricity, showers, or any of those daily things we take for granted. I am complete.

DAY 60: BIKING WITH AUNT LOUISE

Today I planned to rest and recuperate, get caught up on things I've been trying to do for weeks, spend time with my aunt and visit friends in the city.

I woke up around 7:30 a.m. and spent the entire morning and afternoon at the house. I alternated between the comfortable couch and the soft grassy yard that I've been enjoying since I was in elementary school. Much of my time was spent on the computer, and I also went through my gear to get rid of weight and bulk. The more possessions I have, the less freedom I have. It takes time to maintain, clean, organize, and keep track of all of my stuff. I have a lot of stuff on this trip in order to demonstrate the usage of different products to reduce consumption, but much of it just consumes my time. So I consolidated and packed a box full of stuff to send back to San Diego. My trailer is substantially lighter and less full — that excites me.

Aunt Louise came home at three and we went for a bike ride together on the nearby trails. This was her first bike ride in over ten years, and I was very happy to be on it with her. She used a bike I had purchased when I was here last summer and left behind for either one of us to use. It was a fun six-mile ride through the Harms Woods trails, and I was very happy to be riding side-by-side with my aunt.

Then I pedaled into the city to visit some friends in Rogers Park. I left the trailer at home and enjoyed riding my bike without lugging it behind me. I rode down Devon Street, the Little India of Chicago. If I wasn't living mostly off the grid I would have stopped into a restaurant and gotten some of my favorite ethnic food, but I was content to just take in my surroundings.

I arrived at Maggie and Katie Scrantom's house just before nine and the two of them and their roommates warmed my heart as they always do. I spend a night at their house nearly every time I visit Chicago, and it's always joyous. We sat around in the living room catching up over the last couple of months. It was just a wonderful night with people I love. Both Maggie and Katie are beaming rays of sunshine, full of talent and intelligence. Maggie cut my beard and hair with a pair of scissors. This was without a doubt the most enjoyable haircut I've ever received in my life. I often think of it as a chore but this was quite the opposite.

DAY 61: FOR THE LOVE OF A GOOD WOMAN

I awoke in the brightly lit living room after seven hours of sleep. A yoga mat lay on the floor so I took some time to stretch out as the rays of sunshine beamed into the house and reflected off the hardwood floor. Another beautiful day in Chicago lay before me.

I walked a block down Devon and spent part of the morning in a café typing up my blog. It was very pleasant to take my time sitting in the coffee shop surrounded by the daily activities of fellow humans. Then I had to meet up with Brent and was happy to be cycling the streets of Chicago. Next I was off to the beach near Loyola Park, where I spent a few hours in the sun stretching, swimming and relaxing. It was blissful to be soaking in the sun and giving my body the attention it needed, which I have not been doing enough on this trip.

As I lay in the sun feeling content I thought about Maggie and what a wonderful human being she is. I've been drawn to her since the moment I laid my eyes on her in the summer of 2007. She's a ray of sunshine and every time I see her my heart flutters. It has been so amazing to see her growth between the occasions we spend together. Last night she told me she recently sold her car and now rides her bike and takes public transportation everywhere. She has incorporated exercise into her daily routine the way it should be, not going to a gym to run on a treadmill but making physical activity a part of her daily routine. Her diet has become much healthier as well, with much more whole, unprocessed foods, less animal product, and more fresh produce. Hearing all of this put a grin on my face from ear to ear.

Thinking of my love for Maggie brought forward memories all of my past loves. I thought of the experiences I had had with them and how each has led me to where I am today. All of my past loves were at one time my future loves, and this stirred my imagination about who I'll meet and who I'll love next. I imagine a strong woman, a woman who will challenge me to be my best, both mentally and physically. A woman who makes things happen and has a cheery, positive outlook on life. She'd be a woman with intelligence that could complement mine so we could create great things together. She'd have similar interests but different areas of expertise so we could grow together. I imagined a thin, dark-skinned woman with long, flowing, brown hair, but this was trivial compared to who she'd be on the inside. Wonderful images flowed through my head as I wondered where and when I'd meet this woman and whether I would know it when I did. Life is unpredictable, and this excited me because I have no idea when or in what fashion this woman will appear.

DAY 62: EMBRACE LIFE

It was a hot morning and I was happy to be a part of it. I spent it writing as I sat on my grandpa's familiar and comfortable couch and enjoyed my last few hours at home.

I met up with Brent at North Avenue Beach. It was good to see him again after a few days apart; he'd spent the four nights with a friend in the city. The skyline was beautiful and I sat in front of it, legs dangling over the side of the concrete pier eating a sandwich I had prepared from the fresh organic veggies and local cheeses my Aunt Louise had packed for me. I soaked in the border where concrete jungle meets raw open water and wished I could spend the day lounging right here. Alas, after some much needed stretching I was on my way south, heading into uncharted territories.

The lakeshore path continued south for nearly 20 miles along the beautiful lake and through a dozen parks. Then my surroundings slowly turned into an inner-city neighborhood. It's always exciting for me to be in inner-city neighborhoods and experience another diverse part of America. The more I see the more I learn and the more I am exposed to, the stronger I become. Exploring these communities helps me to understand perspectives different from my own. I believe this helps me to be a more understanding, compassionate human being and gives me the ability to relate to a wider range of people.

The neighborhoods continued on and led me into the state of Indiana and eventually into the city of Gary. I'd been through Gary before in a car but I'd always done my best to get out as fast as I could and had never soaked it in. In my mind the city was synonymous with pollution and huge factories. I can't say I would want to live here but I was happy to be experiencing it. The roads were terrible, and many of the cars gave very little room for error as they passed by at alarmingly close distances. In the heart of the steel mills and oil refineries I found it difficult to take in full breaths due to the poor air quality. That along with the heat of the sun made for an uncomfortable physical situation yet I was still happy to be experiencing one of the filthiest cities in America.

An eerie squeaking noise beckoned me to follow, and I found myself pedaling through a residential neighborhood of Gary. I assume it was slow-moving trains but I never did discover what was creating this noise that drew me to it like insects to a light at night. I stopped and watched a handful of people playing basketball as I soaked in the uniqueness of Gary. From what I can tell the vast majority of the residents of this town are black people, which is not something I am often exposed to. Where I grew up there was very little diversity and those 18 years surrounded mostly by white people are still partially engrained in me. I imagine this is the case for most Midwest youth. Most white people tend to avoid the completely black neighborhoods, as do I at times. They're just not places I end up going very often. I find the differences between me, a small-town white guy, and an inner-city black guy so interesting, even if they are very subtle compared to our similarities. We have such a different perspective on life having been raised in such different environments, and I have so much to learn from this way of life. I would love to spend a few weeks in Gary, Indiana, for the sake of education, but I don't know if I will ever make it happen.

I made my way out of this city, past the many abandoned and rundown houses and businesses, and found myself surrounded by trees again as I entered Indiana Dunes State Park. I contacted a host on Warm Showers and he accepted my request to spend the night at his home. I arrived shortly after five after 58 miles of riding. I left my bike there and walked a couple of minutes down to Lake Michigan to refresh and rejuvenate. Before going for a swim I gave my service to the earth and picked up about 20 pieces of trash from the shores of the lake. I decided I would pick up at least one piece of trash every day for the rest of the trip. Hopefully by then it will become a habit that I continue for as long as I live. If every American picked up a piece of trash tomorrow that would be over 300 million pieces of trash. If we all did that every day we would pick up over one trillion pieces of trash per year. It would take almost no effort by anyone. Will you pick up a piece of trash tomorrow?

I swam, I stretched, and I lay in the sand. It was just what my body needed. Back at the house I conversed with my hosts, Ed and Monica, and it was fun to learn about Indiana and the Gary area from two people who were born and raised there. It was a good night but I didn't feel like my off-the-grid adventure sat too well in their mind. I felt Monica had a desire to prove me wrong and dismiss my self-imposed rules. She offered me some local organic strawberries that I gladly accepted but she was not happy when I asked her to please not wash them. It was a very simple request but she felt her way was the right way. I feel for all the people out there who live with a family who just doesn't understand them. I spent a few hours on the computer and then set my bed up in their backyard.

Embrace life, no matter what it sends your way. Embrace the weather, be it rain or shine. Rain, snow, sleet, fog, sunbeams, gray clouds or white fluffy clouds; they're all beautiful and all serve a purpose on this earth and for us, the humans that populate it. Without this diversity the earth, magnificent and beautiful, would not exist in the splendid form that it does. Remember to embrace all of the earth's offerings and every day will be more enjoyable.

- If it's raining down on you, if you're sweating your balls off, if your teeth are chattering from the cold, if you're uncomfortable, it means you are blessed with life.
- If you see things you don't like, your eyes are still working.
- If your neighbors are too loud and keep you up at night, it means your ears are functioning properly.
- If you smell nasty cigarettes at a bar or a rotting animal on the side of the road, it means your nose is doing its job.
- If you feel those mosquito bites itching on your legs or your body aching from a long day of work, at least you still have your sense of touch.
- If that slice of pizza wasn't the tastiest you've ever had, just be thankful you have a tongue to taste it at all.
- If your heart is crushed, it means you still have the ability to feel emotions.
- Life is a matter of perspective. Change your perspective today and you'll be living in a new world tomorrow.

DAY 63: THE SUMMER SOLSTICE

Today is the first day of summer, and I intend to honor it by spending nearly the entire 24 hours in the outdoors. I spent a bit of time in the backyard stretching and packing and hit the road at 9:30 a.m. Highway 12 was an enjoyable ride and much of the morning I found myself pedaling under the shade of trees through Indiana Dunes State Park. I ate the remaining bit of my food last night so I awoke with an empty stomach and had to pedal until I could find a grocery store. Those 20 miles of pedaling were beautiful but very fatiguing as my stomach ached for food to energize my body. In Michigan City, Indiana, I found a grocery store and loaded up on breads, cheeses and pre-made salads from the treasure chest. The cheese had been shipped all the way from Spain, over 4,000 miles away, just to end up in the dumpster. It was certainly enough food to last me the day. I also had one and a half gallons of water with me from the leaky hose in Ed's backyard.

The riding was smooth and I was making good time when a wheat field presented itself before me. I walked through this beautiful golden field of wheat, arms spread wide, feeling the grains in my hands. This glory only lasted as long as I stayed oblivious to the massive rain clouds bellowing towards me at a rapid speed. I watched them for a while knowing that I was asking for it but was willing to take the risk of them opening up their wrath upon me. Once it was just about too late I bolted east to outrun the storm. I scanned my surroundings for cover but was unsure if I would take it if I found it. I welcomed the rain. The winds swooped in from the west pushing me along at a swift pace, keeping me just barely ahead of the storm. I watched the clouds speeding along above me, and it was a fantastic sight to be seen. Even pedaling at 15 mph I could see how rapidly the clouds were moving. This is what makes summer in the Midwest great: hot sunny days interrupted by boisterous thunderstorms that send water flooding through the streets.

When the storm caught up and released its fury upon me I took cover in an old garage at the end of a driveway. It appeared the owners might be home but I ducked in anyway. The couch inside enticed me to rest, but instead I prepared myself a sandwich

and enjoyed it in the rain. I embraced the weather and soaked it all in as I watched the cars zoom by on the highway. You could consider rain like this a burden but with the right mindset it's a blessing. I waited out the storm in the garage for another 30 minutes and was back on my way around 5 p.m., but not before a man in a truck pulled in and said, "My wife called and said there is a crazy guy in his underwear in our driveway." I was in fact in my underwear, but I assured him I was not crazy. I gave him my website, and he headed back to work, after saying, "You can stay in there for as long as you need. Just don't steal anything."

As I pedaled on, ideas for future adventures revved my engine and inspired me to pedal faster into the unknown. I flew down the road with my legs taking the bike as fast as it could go. This excitement only inspired me more, and the ideas kept on budding inside my brain. I find that my bicycle on the open road is often the best place to find great levels of inspiration. I arrived in the small town of Edwardsburg, Michigan, where I scanned the streets for a church or abandoned building to take shelter for the night. I was tired and ready to call it a night. As I sat down on the curb I decided to see if I could find a WarmShowers host and I found one in Elkhart, Indiana, just ten miles southeast, directly on the route. His name was Neil, and he answered the phone and told me to come on down. He told me he's going to a solstice party tonight and that I was welcome to join or just stay at his house and rest. The idea of the party enticed me but I had to ask, "How far is it from your house?" He replied, "Oh, you are a purist. I love that." He said it was only three miles and at this I knew it was going to be a good night amongst good people, and it was.

DAY 64: A NATURAL BODY OF WATER... EVERY DAY

I awoke in a living room full of toys to the sound of a little boy yelling, "Dad, Dad, Daaaaaaad, Dad, Dad, Dad, Daaaaaaad," which I found amusing. Neil already had a fire going for me, which he even started using flint and cattail fluff. He presented me with an unlimited supply of local duck eggs to cook for breakfast over the fire. But first I had to bike to the river to collect some water and while I was there I took a refreshing dip in the picturesque river. What a peaceful way to start my morning.

Back on the road, I craved for rain to fall down upon me and cool off the surrounding earth and me. Instead I settled for a quart of fresh local strawberries from Sweet Corn Charlie's, a roadside food stand where a humorous Amish woman and another woman worked. I also picked up a cucumber, a zucchini, a red beet and a few sticks of rhubarb. It was all good, all local and all organic. I finished off half the strawberries as I answered a gamut of questions from the ladies and polished the rest of them off just down the road.

Throughout the day I found myself riding side-by-side with a horse pulling along a buggy loaded with Amish people. How diverse America is! A few days ago I was in the rich suburbs of northern Chicago surrounded by million-dollar homes and shiny toy cars and then I was riding through the brick projects of Chicago's South Side. Then I was in the nasty industrial section of Gary, Indiana, and now, just a day later, here I am riding amongst the Amish in horse-drawn carriages. I spoke to some Amish people today and learned that their way of life is changing. Most of them no longer live off the land, and in this area a large percentage of them work at the motorhome factories, as this is the motorhome capital of the world. I was quite surprised to hear this and to see the driver of one of the carriages drinking a Mountain Dew. I'm not very knowledgeable on their beliefs, but they don't seem to be holding to them as strictly as they once did.

Late that afternoon a monstrous storm was threatening from the south. Brent had a flat tire to fix so we ducked under an over-hang of an elementary school. I sat and patiently waited for the rain to come so I could play in it, soak it in and drink it. I waited for those clouds to open up onto me like a kid waiting to open presents at Christmas, but they never did. I even set up my rain jacket and pot to collect rainwater but the storm just missed us and headed to the northeast. I pedaled on to the town of Angola, and after loading up on oranges and bananas from an Aldi dumpster I found a beautiful lake to camp on. I arrived just after 7 p.m.

My bathing time became a time to connect to my surroundings and immerse myself in nature.

I spent many hours on this computer,
powered by the large solar panel to the left of me.

with plenty of time to bask in the water, stretch and take care of my body on the land as the sun went down. I was elated to be on the shores of this lake with easy access to cool water to freshen my body. I've decided that I will swim in a natural body of water every day this summer. The summer of 2013 will be one to remember.

DAY 65: THE ICE CREAM CRAVING

The night had been a long one with the full moon shining down upon me. Early in my attempts to sleep I was sweating profusely under the blanket, but I had to keep covered from head to toe to protect myself from the sky full of mosquitoes. Then as the night wore on my body temperature dropped and I was quite cold. Considering the challenges, the night passed fairly quickly and the sun rose as it always does.

At 10 a.m. I was off and by eleven I was through the town of Angola and on the open road. The sun beat down on me with fury but I sped along at 15 to 20 mph all morning long. The heat forced me to take a couple of long breaks, and all day I craved ice cream. I've been desiring ice cream nearly every day for the last month but usually I can overcome it. Today was a whole different

story. Every bone, muscle and organ in my body was screaming, "GIVE ME SOME FREAKIN' ICE CREAM, ROB." It
was Brent's birthday today, and my brain conjured up images of a
Dairy Queen ice cream cake as a celebration. Of course I was eating half of the cake in these mental images. All day my thoughts
lead me back to ice cream. I doubted I could find local, organic
ice cream and was pretty certain that even if I did, it would be
in a package that I would have to carry all the way to Vermont
with me. So my morals and self-enforced rules stood between me
and my much-desired ice cream. All day I went back and forth
between ending my day with ice cream or holding to my com-
mitments for this journey. One minute I was certain I'd be diving
into an ice cream cake to cool off from the heat of the day and
then a minute later I'd decide against it.

The thought of arriving at a destination where I could
put something cold into my body kept me speeding down the
roads through the 90-degree weather without a problem. On
this trip I have not really been able to experience the simple
pleasure of cooling off with a cold drink. There aren't really
many options that have no negative environmental impact. No
bottled beverages from the fridge, no buying ice, no fountain
beverage machines, no bottled water, no cold water from the
tap and no putting things in the fridge or freezer. All of these
options use electricity, create waste and/or come in packaging. To cool off I have been bathing in lakes and rivers, eating
fruit and occasionally finding something in the garbage that
is still cold, like a bottle of water or even the occasional ice
cream. Today I came up with a new trick.

The only physical things that stood between me and ice
cream now was the southern headwind and ten miles of road.
The question still lay in my head, would I give in to the
temptation or would I hold my moral stance? The headwinds
slowed me down a bit but did not keep me from making good
time, and I pedaled that ten miles in just over 40 minutes.
The Dairy Queen presented itself on the outskirts of town,

and as I walked in to buy Brent his birthday ice cream, only one obstacle stood between my ice cream and me, my morals. I highly doubt DQ has fair practices for the cows that produce their milk, and I'm certain that their food is full of chemical ingredients that are not good for the earth or the people eating the stuff. At the last second I saw a man throw a full cup of ice into the garbage, and I made my move. I grabbed the cup of ice and emptied it into my mouth cube by cube as I rested on a bench in the air-conditioning. I was being cooled off from the inside and out and I decided this would suffice. I sat in the restaurant for a half-hour occasionally grabbing another cup of ice that was thrown away. I left the building feeling cooled off, and when I stepped outside I realized just how hot it was. My body had adjusted to the cool interior of the building, and now the outside world felt like a boiler room. This was another great example of life being a matter of perspective.

As I rode away from DQ I thought, I will not look at life the same way after this trip. You may not look at life the same way after reading about it, either. You may decide to lead a simpler lifestyle. You may put less of a priority on money. You may realize that humans are not the only important creatures that walk the planet. You may begin the transition into living freely. You may even start living the life you want. But beware: there may be no going back to the easy conveniences you take comfort in now once you've started to think about life this way.

I am weak. I am inferior. No, not compared to the average human. Compared to the average human I am strong, brave and courageous. However, I am a human; therefore, I am weak and inferior. I have learned in my years of exploring the world and countless hours observing creatures that we humans are far inferior to most of the creatures that walk this planet. Yes, we are intelligent, likely the most intelligent creatures on earth. But where we excel in intelligence we lack the ability to coexist with the earth, the elements, nature and our surroundings. Like no other creature on this planet we have evolved into needing an accessory or tool for everything we do. We've complicated the simplest of tasks. The daily activities we carry out just to survive have become impossibly complicated.

To sleep, we need a bed full of blankets and a roof over our head.

To eat, we need cabinets and drawers full of utensils, dishes, pots and pans. We need refrigerators and ovens that use electricity and gas. Most of us no longer eat food whole and simple as it comes from the earth.

To drink water, we need it to pass through specialized pipes and systems.

To wash ourselves, we need showers, soaps, gels and scrubbing pads.

To cover our bodies, we need closets and dressers full of fashionable clothing.

We can't figure out where we are going without computer screens telling us. Most humans can't even tell you which way is north or south in their own city, let alone walk through a forest without being completely lost. A deer or wolf can get where it's going without the help of any accessory.

To move our bodies, we need cars and bikes and boats and shoes and special inserts for our shoes. We need a 2,000-plus-pound accessory that runs on petroleum to get us to the store that's a ten-minute walk away.

To get simple exercise, we run on a treadmill or ride a stationary bike indoors, both of which take us nowhere and consume energy rather than create it. We have weights to lift and machines to push and pull on to shape our bodies into admirable forms.

We can't even poop without the help of a special seat and paper that comes from chopped-down trees.

All of the simplest things in life, we have turned into complicated tasks we can't accomplish without accessories. Most humans never think twice about how convenient our lives are with all of these accessories. The sad thing is that as they create convenience for us, these accessories create inconvenience for the earth, our environment, the people around us and even ourselves. You don't see the inconvenience being created because it's outsourced. It is outsourced to the air around that was once pure, to the water that used to be pristine, to the humans who slave away in misery in enclosed buildings, to the huge holes in our earth filled with trash, to the forests that are disappearing, and to the death of millions of creatures each day from pollution and destruction. To get the toilet paper we need, we destroy forests. To get the petroleum we need to run our cars, which pollute our air and water, we kill innocent people in far-off countries. To get the plastic, one-time, use items we need, we destroy lives and our planet.

All of these things are supposed to make our lives simpler, but just make them more complicated and intricate. We have to work long hours to afford all of this stuff. We are constantly trying to keep up with the times and buy the same stuff, just slightly updated, year after year. We need space to store it all and insurance to protect it. We need people to take care of it. We need more money to manage our stuff. Most accessories reduce simplicity and time to live and add stress and complication to our lives. We are so busy taking care of our stuff. The other creatures on this earth get to live freely. Most of the humans I know have very little freedom and are always tied down by something.

Simplify your world and you will find yourself living a happier, healthier life. You will have time to do the things you actually want to do. You won't have to work as much because you won't need as much money. You won't have to clean as much because you won't have stuff to clean. Spend your time living, loving, eating, learning, exploring, breathing, exercising and being outside. Spend your time with friends and family. Spend your time helping others and helping create a better world. Spend your time living out your dreams. Do what you really want to do. Do it for yourself and do it for the people around you and the earth you live on. You only live this life once so make it the life you want.

PART 4
ENTERING THE EAST

DAY 66: WHAT ARE THE CHANCES OF THAT?

I started the day early, fully stocked up on water from last night's rain. The clouds had been generous and I had harvested lots of rainwater using my rain jacket and rainfly laid out on the grass. I filled my one-gallon jug along with my 32-ounce water bottle, my pot and my bowl. I super hydrated and could feel the water being delivered throughout my whole body. Water has been scarce for me at times on this trip, and most days I have rationed my supply and paid close attention to how much was left in my jug. Today it was a joy to drink water freely without the fear of running out lingering in the back of my head.

I was excited to be on the road early and hoped that would mean I would finish pedaling for the day at a decent hour. I could tell it was going to be a hot day, and I welcomed it but also felt some dread. On the way out of town I passed a Subway and saw them taking a huge bag of fresh bread to the dumpster so I stopped and stocked up on carbohydrates. I took about a dozen loaves from the 100 in the bag, all wheat bread and all as fresh as the bread you have in your home right now. It's Subway so it's not the highest quality, but it would power me through the day. I cruised out of town and pedaled 30 miles before noon.

A cyclist pedaled up by my side on the open road and in a very excited English accent blurted out, "I f***en know you, man." Turns out this young dude, Wreford Steward, had seen me at the Earth Day Celebration when I left San Francisco on April 20, nearly two months earlier. He had intended to talk to me that day but had been busy preparing his own trip. Then here, 66 days and 3,000 miles later, we run into each other in the middle of Ohio. The crazy part is that he too had embarked on a cycling adventure from San Francisco, only one day after me. Our routes had taken us through different states and past different landmarks but somehow we had wound up in the exact same spot at the exact same time 3,000 miles after we started. America is such a huge, magnificent land. You could explore it for a lifetime of 80 years and never see it all. We have the option in this country of living in community or living in nearly complete solitude. This is a land of choices, where in a matter of a few days you can be thousands of miles away in a nearly different world. Sure, America has its problems, but I am grateful every day for being fortunate enough to be born in this splendid country.

After a day of riding with Wreford I decided to stop just after 5 p.m. on the banks of a cool shallow river. I lay in the water fully submerged and let the fish nibble on my body. It felt good and they were keeping me clean. Life is best for me when I am immersed in the life of other creatures. I bathed, skipped rocks and washed my clothes in the tranquil setting of the river surrounded by forest.

I didn't have my tent with me as I'd left it behind in Wisconsin, thinking I wouldn't be doing much camping on this populated side of the country. I couldn't have been more wrong, so I've been sleeping under the stars almost every night since I left Chicago. It's been a challenge with all the mosquitoes and the rain, but I am still excited to sleep under the stars. I have a strong desire to be able to sleep without accessories like blankets, a tent, or a bed. I want to be able to sleep in the grass. I want to be able to sleep on a branch in a tall oak tree. I want to sleep in the sand by the ocean. I have a strong desire to lay my body down wherever I become tired and sleep through the night until daybreak. I know this is possible but not without a lot of practice. I have become accustomed to the comforts of sheets, blankets and pillows, and a roof or a covering over my head. I yearn to live simply and freely like the other creatures that roam this earth.

This was not easy to practice here in mosquito land. I think maybe it is something I could practice in southern California though, where rain is infrequent, the climate is mild and insects are few and far between. The mosquitoes were horrible here so I sucked up my pride and asked Brent if I could sleep in his small tent with him. He turned me down so I brainstormed for other options. As I sat on my sleeping pad I became aware of little flashing lights coming from every direction. The forest appeared to be a night sky filled with millions of stars, only they were blowing up every instant. This explosive night sky was fireflies in numbers greater than I had ever seen before. But for every glowing firefly there was also a mosquito searching the forest for blood. I picked up my phone and reached out to Wreford, who had continued on to Norwalk to spend the night in a hotel. I sent him a message on Facebook, and to my surprise he answered immediately, inviting me to come take refuge in his hotel room. I packed up my gear and hit the trail for the six-mile ride east.

DAYS 67-70: THE AMERICAN DREAM FARM

I need sleep. I want sleep. I crave sleep. But my mind is so stimulated by this world and by this journey that I cannot sleep.

I felt gloomy and out of place waking up in the hotel room. It just didn't feel right to be inside a confined area and I felt very off. I probably should have gotten out of there right away but instead I sat in bed and wrote for a few hours. When I left at 10:30 a.m. the gloom held inside my chest, but it was lifted slightly by being on my bike and under the open sky. There was a fair amount of cloud cover so the morning was cool and pedaling south on Highway 250 was easy. The shoulder was almost non existent and covered by rumble strips, giving me close to no room to ride without being in the road. Every other vehicle that passed was a full-size semi blowing by with a very tiny margin of error. I only had 15 or 20 miles on this busy rural highway so I just pedaled along at a rapid pace to get off of it as quickly as I could.

A flat tire changed my game plan, and I found myself on the roadside with a problem-solving task ahead of me. I had put off getting spare inner tubes for the last few hundred miles and didn't have any extras, so my only option was to patch the pinch flat. I found two decent-sized holes in the tube and doubted my abilities to patch them. I remained calm, ate an apple and decided to just go with the flow and do my best. Every challenge I've had on this trip I've overcome, and it has made me a slightly more experienced and skilled human. With that thought I embraced the flat and the discouragement inside me transformed into excitement. I was curious to see if my resourcefulness would prevail.

The flat took me a long time to patch but it appeared to be holding, so I pedaled ahead a half-mile to the ice cream shop where Brent was waiting. The ice cream was homemade with Ohio milk, and they put it directly into my bowl, which meant they would not have to use water to wash dishes and there was no packaging for the landfill. It was not organic ice cream so I did break that rule. The woman behind the counter told me I could find a hardware store in New London, ten miles ahead, and I figured they would have spare tubes there.

I pedaled on with a slowly leaking tire that I pumped up every three miles. At the store I snagged the last tube they had in my size, put it in my bag and pushed on. I figured I'd just keep using the patched tube until the patch stopped holding. Five miles outside of town it blew, and I pulled under the shade of a tree to switch out the inner tube. As soon as I grabbed the box I realized I had screwed up. I'd grabbed a Schrader valve instead of a Presta valve, which meant the valve was too big for the hole in my rim.

If you haven't realized by now I'll put it out there: I'm a fairly inexperienced cyclist and haven't taken much time to learn bicycle maintenance or how this machine functions. This was not really a good idea considering my whole mission and life revolved around this bike. I'm barely capable of patching an inner tube, which is a very simple task. But what I lack in preparedness I make up in resourcefulness. This incompatible inner tube didn't deter me for a moment. I whipped out my pocketknife and carved the edges of the hole in my aluminum rim to enlarge it. I wondered if this would weaken the rim but was nearly certain this solution would be successful. It was a pleasant time under the tree and I began pedaling again in just under a half-hour.

The day was full of challenges but I was grateful and happy for them because they gave me a chance to test my skills. I pride myself on being resourceful and having excellent problem-solving skills so I find these tasks quite enjoyable. I am no mechanic but I can think and act on the spot. I believe being able to act spontaneously and solve problems is what makes me successful at life — in adventures, business, or personal life. I don't believe I was born with these skills but have honed them by challenging myself daily, heaving myself into the elements and exposing myself to situations where I have no choice but to be creative. If you picked up a basketball tomorrow for the first time in your life would you expect to be a talented dribbler and shooter? If you've never been exposed to mathematics would you expect to be able to solve complicated problems on your first day in class? I imagine you've said no to both of those questions. It's the same way with life. If you don't put yourself out there and give yourself challenges, it is unlikely you'll be able to overcome them when they're sent your way. At the age of 26 I've put myself through so many challenging situations that many of the daily challenges that most of us humans face are not problems for me at all. What is a mountain to cross to many is merely a speed bump to cruise over for me.

Put yourself out there. Challenge yourself. You will grow into a stronger, more confident human being.

Just before 7 p.m. I arrived at the Stoller's Organic Valley farm where one of the youngest boys, Clark, met me at the end of the driveway. Dinner was waiting at the table and Scott, Charlene and their children Doyle, Lynette, Nelson, Warren, Toby, Clark, Rosemary and Melody instantly warmed my heart. It was time to see what life is really like on an Organic Valley farm.

Close your eyes and imagine the picture-perfect organic dairy farm. If you drink milk or eat cheese, imagine where you'd like it to be coming from. Go on, close your eyes and take a moment.

- What did you see?
- Did you imagine children running happy and free all over the farm?
- Did you imagine chickens picking up the scraps and keeping the farm clean?

- Did you imagine a cheerful family sitting around the dinner table together holding hands and giving thanks for the food on their table?
- Did you imagine a dinner table full of food, grown right there on the farm?
- Did you imagine a place where the farmers eat the very same food they send to your table?
- Did you imagine vast fields of grains, wheat, barley, alfalfa and clover, where the cows are let out to graze each day?
- Did you imagine playful dogs keeping all the creatures on the farm in their place and the creatures out that don't belong?
- Did you imagine trees full of cherries, pears, plums and apples and bushes full of raspberries, blackberries and strawberries?
- Did you imagine a spring-fed pond hidden in the woods with a homemade wooden diving board sitting ten feet above it and a boat made out of a 55-gallon grain barrel?
- Did you imagine a hand-pump well sitting in the yard where fresh clean water comes from 30 feet below?
- Did you imagine a pleasant house full of love, education, laughter and fun?
- Did you imagine a lush green garden full of all sorts of vegetables, from spinach and kale and corn and potatoes to beets and lima beans, all surrounded by vines full of concord grapes?
- Did you imagine honeybees flying freely around the farm pollinating the flowers and creating honey to sweeten the farmer's meal?

If you imagined all of that you might be at the Stollers' Organic Valley dairy farm. At the Stollers', 80 percent of the food on their table is grown right there on their farm and everything they eat is organic.

This is the farm every company tries to depict on the milk carton. The farm where every American imagines their dairy comes from — in short, the American dream farm. Sadly, most of the dairy in American supermarkets today doesn't come from family farms like this, but from huge installations that look more like factories. The dairy they produce is often of inferior quality and full of growth hormones. Profit is the bottom line on these factory farms, and nutrition, health, environment and the animal's welfare typically take a backseat. But here at the Stollers', they consider themselves stewards of the land and take great pride in caring for the farm, the cows, the consumer and themselves. They understand we must coexist with our earth and when creating food we are at the mercy of the environment around us.

I came for one night intending to leave the next morning and found myself there still four nights later. It wasn't just one thing that kept me there but a combination of the food, the company, the nature and the opportunity to learn where good food comes from. I couldn't have dreamed up a better farm experience.

Spending a little time in the Stollers' personal garden on their dairy farm.

The kids were all superheroes. They amazed me with their physical strength and how each one was capable of any task they tried. They could climb anything, hang from the rafters in the barn and swing higher than any city boy I know. They all had a thirst for knowledge that at times could be quite exhausting. Each of the Stoller children are home schooled by their mom, Charlene, and each seemed to be very intelligent not only from the books they read but also in understanding the earth around them. Each of them had their chores to do on the farm, and they all had an invested interest in making sure things ran smoothly. The work of everyone made it possible to live a mostly self-dependent life at home. Together they made a family and a community.

Even with all the work these kids did they still got to be kids here on the farm. They had fun and enjoyed life as it should be enjoyed at that age. They had all sorts of time to play before, during and after chores. They had time to jump on the trampoline, go swimming in the pond, play board games, compete at everything there was to compete at and play any game they could make up. These were happy children, occasionally crying from rough play but never complaining.

I learned a lot while I was on the farm and helped out with some of the daily chores. Scott, the father, taught me all sorts of things. Most of the time when I was lending a hand I was actually slowing him down, but he was happy to have me helping out. He had his system and could have done it faster without me but I think he was excited to teach me. He went about milking the cows with ease, and everything was very smooth and convenient both for him and the cows. I pitchforked hay to the cows, which knew exactly where to go to get their food and get milked. They were in and out of the barn very quickly. The cows knew the system as well as the farmers and didn't cause a fuss. I learned how to put the milkers on and for the first time in my life I got to milk a cow by hand. I even drank milk that came straight from the cow. Earlier in this trip when I was riding through the desert I had dreamed of cold milk straight from the cow and someone pointed out to me that it comes out at body temperature. I found out firsthand that it is indeed 101 degrees when it comes out of the udder. What I like most about the cows at this place is that 100 percent of the food they eat is grown organically right here on the farm, which means it doesn't have to be trucked in and it's not that GMO junk that a lot of farms are feeding their cows.

I spent time in the kitchen with Charlene helping to prepare some of the meals. Breakfast was at 9:30 a.m. each day and supper was at 3:30 p.m. They only eat two meals a day, but there was plenty of snacking on healthy homegrown and homemade foods in between and after meals. Some of my favorites were the granola bars, ice cream, popcorn, raspberry cobbler and popsicles made of raspberries, strawberries, grape juice and maple syrup. Imagine a popsicle that is delicious, super nutritious and made completely from food from outside your door. There was no shortage of healthy food on this farm, and I stuffed myself at every opportunity. Every meal we had was made from scratch, delicious as food can be and even healthier. I would have imagined huge servings on the plates of each of the kids but that was not the case at all. I assume it's because the food is so nutrient dense that a little goes a long way, unlike the fast and processed food that most Americans are eating today that only leaves them craving more of the chemically synthesized flavors. They also had meat at most meals, but it made up a small portion of the meal compared to the grains and vegetables.

It felt amazing to be on this farm, and know I could eat anything here and feel good about it. Even the delicious cake, pie and ice cream were full of health and nutrition. They don't buy much in packages, which means they produce very little garbage and don't waste food. Any waste goes to the chickens that turn the nutrients into eggs to eat or manure to spread on the crops, which the cows eat and then turn into milk. It's all a circle of life here, and everything has its place and purpose. The farmers understand nature and let nature do its thing. They use their knowledge to help nature along in certain places. For example, they favor purple martin birds, which eat up to 2,000 mosquitoes per day each. They use hybrid seeds, not GMO seeds, in order to produce higher yields. They provide water from the ground below for the plants and help to create healthy soil. Everything stays pretty natural, and they depend on the earth to create the bountiful yields they receive.

Obviously not everyone can grow their own food and not everyone should; we need people in cities making other things happen. What we can all do is pay attention to where our food is coming from and only support food we can be confident in and proud to eat. We can buy food that has ingredients we can pronounce. We can buy foods that have only a handful of ingredients or less and not a list so long our attention span doesn't allow us to make it to the bottom. We should know our farmer and support local farms and companies that are transparent and sustainable.

On some of the Organic Valley products such as the soy milk, you can even follow the label to see exactly what farm the food came from. On their website you can "Meet your Farmer" — just type in your zip code and you will see a profile of the OV farmers near your home. Organic Valley doesn't have secrets and has a transparent business model. Their co-op of 1,800 farms across the country are all family farms like the Stollers' and they all own a part of Organic Valley.

I should explain my relationship with Organic Valley. Before the trip I wanted to find a sustainable nationwide food producer that I could incorporate into my journey. I wanted to visit their farms across the country, learn about the organic food in America's grocery stores and eat their food while I was at the farms. Ideally I wanted a company that deals with fruit and vegetables but I couldn't find that; what I did find was Organic Valley. I told them about my adventure, and they agreed to work with me by sending me to farms along my route where I could meet farmers, see their sustainable practices firsthand and get a taste of their lives, their lands and their food.

If all the large-scale dairy and egg farms produced food the way Organic Valley farms do we would be living in a drastically more humane and clean country. I wanted to show a good option that you can get at most grocery stores across America, and these guys fit the bill. However, the best thing a person can do if they want to drastically cut back on their environmental impact is not to change to organic animal products but to switch to a plant-based diet and give up meat, dairy and eggs all together. Or at least reduce meat and dairy consumption to a few times per week or a few times per month. Even organic meat, dairy and egg farming uses a ton more water, fossil fuels and space than vegetable and grain farming. The huge amount of land used on these farms to grow grains for animals would be much more wisely used to grow food for people to eat directly. Large-scale animal agriculture is the single largest contributor to many of our environmental problems, and switching to a plant-based diet is the single greatest change a person can make to live a more earth-friendly life. But if you are going to continue eating eggs, dairy and meat, then switching to organic and locally raised is a huge step forward!

The Stollers are stewards of their land, working with the earth, not against it, to grow food.

DAY 71: THIS FARM JUST DOESN'T WANT ME TO GO

I awoke early after a wonderful night's rest in a bunk bed. The last two nights I've slept for ten hours and it's made all the difference. My body was exhausted from my rigorous schedule and the energy I've put into writing.

After four nights in the same place I was ready to be on the road early today. My body and mind yearned for the freedom the open road provides. Charlene insisted on preparing a meal to send me off, and it was a delicious baked oatmeal dish along with yogurt and milk. After all, this was a dairy farm, so of course there was milk. I chowed down as much as I could to energize myself for a long day of riding and then headed to the garage. As I pumped up my tire, a large psssssst of air gave way and the tire flattened.

This farm just doesn't want me to go. Yesterday I was about to leave in the mid-afternoon and it started to pour down rain. I waited and the rain continued, then supper was ready, which I couldn't resist, and then the day was gone and I was too full to get on the bike. Now this, another pull from the farm to keep me there. I was yearning for the road though and had miles to cover.

I was able to scrounge up a patched tube and pedaled to Orville, just ten miles to the south, where it took two hours to get my bike fixed. The children had screwed it up while playing with the gears. At the same time I did some maintenance to the bike and switched out the patched tube for a new tube. I also stocked up on spare tubes to avoid getting stuck again.

The Stollers had loaded me up on cornbread, waffles, wheat bread and cherries from the garden. It was all homemade, home grown, delicious and nutritious, and best of all meant I wouldn't have to search for food at all today and likely tomorrow. On top of that I had enough water to last me a day and a half. What a blessing. It was a hot and sweaty day so 12 miles from Lisbon, Ohio, I stopped at a lake to cool off and freshen up. Man, did it feel good to get in there and get clean. The lake was just loaded with weeds but I didn't care at all. The last 12 miles went by in a breeze. I averaged 11.6 mph today and did 73 miles of riding. Not a bad day back on the bike.

DUDE

I pulled into Lisbon at about 7 p.m. to find a celebration taking place in the town square. A band was playing *Journey* and it was a fun "welcome" to the city hidden in a valley surrounded by lush green forests. I didn't know exactly where I was but I did know it felt like a whole new world and I was excited for it. It felt a bit like the South, a bit like the Midwest and a little bit like the East Coast. Just a short pedal from the town square were my Warm Showers hosts, who turned out to be an interesting couple in their 70s and 80s. I sat in the kitchen talking to Ruth Ann and her husband Clare for about an hour, but I was really exhausted and still had a story to write so I rushed off to my basement bed as soon as I could. It was dark and quiet and I was happy to be there.

DAY 72: PITTSBURGH, PENNSYLVANIA: GATEWAY TO THE EAST?

What a day. It was all around enjoyable but could have been miserable with a different mindset. I loved nearly every minute of it.

I woke up at 8 a.m. after a solid night's rest and was off at 9 a.m. I had intended to stop right away to have a little breakfast, but instead I pedaled 20 miles before taking a break. Pleasant country roads led me through beautiful green land. I was still loaded up on food from the farm, and I took a nice long break in the grass to finish off most ,of it when I began to feel fatigued.

At midday I found a beautiful river that ran along the roadside. As I played in the creek, rain started to sprinkle down on me. I was very happy to be surrounded by all of this water and content watching the raindrops drip from the leaves and splash down into the river. The rain grew stronger and poured down on me for most of the rest of the day. I pedaled on with my rain jacket and shorts and loved it. At times the shoulder was a small river and my only option was to pedal right through it. I took a few breaks to sit in the sun when the clouds momentarily parted and biked when it was pouring. Highway 51 was just a miserable road for a biker and often there was no shoulder, leaving me in the same lane as cars going 65+ miles per hour. I really didn't mind as I was just happy to be playing in the rain. I don't see much rain in sunny San Diego so I'm excited to be in it while I'm here.

I expected to have friends in Pittsburgh but I did a shout-out on Facebook to find that I do not. So I jumped on Warm Showers and with a fair amount of trouble eventually found someone that could host me for the night. He was two miles north and I headed his way around 7 p.m., up a huge hill with the air still hot and humid. I was doused in sweat by the time I got there. The guy was pretty drunk and pretty talkative. The story I needed to write took me a few hours, and with all the talking and the blaring TV it took me until close to midnight to finish it. He was chain-smoking cigarettes, so I had to keep going outside to breathe fresh air. He was a real nice guy, but this was not my best Warm Showers experience. However, he did have a spare room with the most comfortable bed I'd lain in since I left home. I slept like a king.

Today I ran out of cash and realized that my bank doesn't have any branches in the entire state of Pennsylvania. It will take me a week to cycle through Pennsylvania, and I've decided to take this opportunity to practice living without money. This will be the first time I've ever restricted myself completely from using money in the United States. I once flew one way to Cabo, Mexico, with just the clothes on my back, a passport, and a phone (no money, no credit card, no backpack) and hitchhiked 1,150 miles home, but about $30 went in and out of my hands during that time. I will be completely penniless in Pennsylvania, practicing a new way of living that just a short time ago I could have only imagined.

DUDE

DAY 73: THE GREAT ALLEGHENY PASSAGE

I started this trip in April. May and June are gone and a new season has begun. The days keep passing by and now it's July.

Today was quite the day. I woke up not feeling my finest mentally and didn't feel exceptional at any time throughout the day. The morning greeted me with a dreary gray sky and chilly rain, and although I was excited about the weather the day before I just wasn't in the mood for it this morning. It did give me the opportunity to take it slow for the morning since I wasn't going to start off in the rain. The bad news is it meant I had to go longer without food and water since I had finished up the last of everything I had before going to bed. My throat was sore from all the secondhand smoke and I could have really used the hydration. I was feeling depressed, though I knew I would be just fine and time would heal me.

My mind felt instantly clearer once I was out of the big city. By 3:30 p.m. I was very hungry and very dehydrated. I finally found a score of fruit (melon, tomatoes, bananas and nectarines) and an unopened bag of walnuts in a grocery store dumpster, which was just what I needed. I'm sure there was local organic food around somewhere but I wasn't able to find it with the minimal effort I put in. I was only 15 miles into the day and felt a bit in despair as I wanted to get into Philadelphia on the fifth and needed to put in some decent days of riding to do so.

The trail led me into rural Pennsylvania and followed the beautiful Youghiogheny River the entire way through small towns and forest. Just when I needed it most I found a hand-pump well on the trail and drank water to my heart's content. I hope that I will never take water for granted again. The trail was a good ride, dirt but very packed down and very flat even though most of the surrounding land was riddled with hills.

The sun and the distance traveled definitely helped me clear my foggy head. It was beautiful out and I stopped a few times to eat raspberries that were growing alongside the path. Towards evening a heavy rainstorm came down and soaked me pretty good, but I was cool with it and happy to ride in the rain. After five miles or so I found a campground and set up under a wooden shelter. I was really hungry and wanted to pedal ten more miles to the next town but I was just out of juice. There was a group of young Jewish guys from Pittsburgh camping there, and they let me use their fire to boil my wheat berries. Unfortunately I was too tired to stay up until they were soft enough to eat but they left the pot on for me until they went to bed so that I'd have breakfast waiting for me when I woke up.

DAY 74: 1000 BERRIES AND WATERFALL BRAIN FREEZES

Thunder roared and the skies poured down rain all night long while I slept safe and sound in my wooden shelter. I vaguely remember waking up a handful of times to the sounds of blasting thunder and roaring trains and being glad I was protected from the rain and mosquitoes. Starting at 7 a.m. I tried to get out of bed but my exhausted body

overruled my energized mind until just after 9 a.m. The wheat I put on the fire before retiring last night was soft and my stomach was happy to have it. Before hitting the trail I filled up my water jug at the hand-pump well and was grateful to have all the water I would need for the day.

I pedaled on through the lush, green, deciduous forest. The path followed the river for most of the way. After ten miles of riding I arrived in a small town and loaded up on pizza from the dumpster to keep my body fueled. It was just a quick stop and I pedaled on. Four miles later a washed-out path stopped me. A waterfall was just barely pounding the right side of the path, but the entire path was so washed out I assumed the water had been falling harder on the path during the night. It wasn't anything I couldn't easily walk my bike through, but it managed to stop me for nearly an hour to bask in its beauty. I stood underneath it and froze my brain under the hard pounding water. Just a few miles ahead some downed trees forced me to detach my trailer from my bike and carry each one individually through a maze of branches. It was just another small obstacle that made the trail a little more fun.

I'm a happy man in nature.

The dirt trail continued and so did the beauty. The river to my left was muddy but gradually cleared up as I continued upstream. To my right, crystal clear waterfalls fell from above and flowed underneath the path every few miles. When there wasn't a waterfall to look at there was a wooden bridge to cross that gave me a view of the forest and the river. The forest here is so thick with trees and vines that I almost feel like I am in a rainforest. There is so much clean water flowing and dripping that it reminds me of Maui, where I spent the month of February this year. I stopped at one creek, filled up my jug and drank right out of the swift cold stream. I wasn't sure that the water was safe to drink but was willing to take that risk. This was partly laziness, as I didn't feel like pulling out my pump to purify the water, but I also had this desire inside me to drink the water as it flowed from the earth uninterrupted.

The terrain remained flat for most of the day. At times the trail was smooth and at other times it was downright muddy. Around midday a cool guy from Lancaster, Pennsylvania, approached me and we ended up riding together for five or ten miles. We were cruising along at 13 mph as we spoke and the conversation energized me. He turned back to return to his family and I played Xavier Rudd through my earphones. This energized me even more and I found myself flying through the mud holes at 17 mph. This eco-warrior speaks my language, inspires me and has helped me pedal on many occasions when my body didn't feel like it.

I was covered in mud from head to toe and wheel to wheel and was very happy. I stopped on a wooden bridge perched high above the rocky river and watched a deer slowly and cautiously wade from one side to the other. Just a mile ahead I took a break to eat the last bit of wheat and was fortunate to find an abundance of black raspberries. I had been seeing small patches along the trail throughout the day but nothing compared in size to this. The mud that covered my body protected me from the thorns as I moved from bush to bush picking the berries and putting them into my mouth. In a matter of 45 minutes of picking through the bushes I ate 1,000 berries and by the end of the grazing I felt quite content. I had put my solar panels out in the sun and managed to juice up my batteries a fair amount. I didn't get any cell service on the trail, and it was great to be un-plugged from the outside world for a couple of days.

I've enjoyed embracing every element the earth has thrown my way on this trip. The last week has brought me an abundance of water, and it's filled my days with joy. The rain could have pro-vided misery had I not decided to embrace and appreciate it. My bamboo bike is holding up very well through this weather, but the disc brakes and the chain have been full of sand. It hasn't slowed me down much and I've been maintaining them as needed. Speaking of embracing the elements, with just two miles left on the path the rain began again. It was quite cold but I loved it. It rinsed some of the mud off me but not enough to keep me out of the river to wash up. The river was warm compared to the rain and I washed off my body, the bike and the trailer.

Rockwood turned out to be nothing but a tiny village, so after scrounging up a bit of food I pedaled seven miles on the pavement to Somerset. I managed to find a couple of unopened boxes of granola bars in a CVS dumpster and was set on food for the night. Then I found a church with open doors in the middle of the city just a few blocks away. Both the front and back doors were open with lights on so I went inside and called out "Is anyone here?" No response, so I pulled my bike through the back doors and rolled my sleeping pad out to sleep for the night. I figured if the place was open maybe they left it that way as a refuge for people. I was a little hesitant to be inside the building uninvited so I was on edge as I sat there writing a few pages. I finally lay down when the clock struck midnight but the adrenaline in my veins kept me up in the darkness.

DAY 75: BACK ON THE SLAB
AND FULL OF JUNK FOOD

Here's a quiz for you. Which of these did I not eat today?

- A box of granola bars from a CVS dumpster
- A microwaveable Thai noodle dish from a CVS dumpster
- A can of clam chowder soup (sell-by 2011) from a dumpster outside Subway
- Seven custard-filled donuts from a Dunkin' Donuts dumpster
- Handpicked black raspberries from the roadside
- A nutty bar found on the side of the road
- A jar of peanut butter found in an abandoned house with a 2008 sell-by date. That's five years past the sell-by date.

The answer: I did not eat the nutty bar found on the side of the road. That was actually yesterday.

This is a pretty strange list of food to eat, even for me, so you might have some questions.

Why did I eat all of this junk food? I ran out of cash in Pittsburgh so I couldn't buy any food. I could only eat what I could find without money.

Why don't I have money? My bank does not exist in Pennsylvania. Since I'm using only cash for the entire journey and not carrying a debit or credit card, I have no money until I get to New Jersey, where my bank is. Of course I could just transfer money from my bank account to someone I meet in exchange for cash, but I want to see if I can make it across the state without money.

So how am I getting food while I cross Pennsylvania? I'm eating any food I come across, whether it is on the roadside, in the trash or growing in the woods. I use good judgment with eating things that could be harmful. You might think from the selection above that I would get sick all the time, but I can tell when food is unsafe for consumption. Plus I'm enjoying testing my limits, testing my immune system and, most importantly, testing the preconceived notions that my head is filled with.

Is this challenging? It's not as challenging as I would have thought before this trip. We waste so much food in America that I have found I can rely on waste to not only survive, but thrive. In fact, we throw away nearly half of all the food we produce in America; meanwhile, one in seven are food insecure. Usually I can eat very healthy and nutritious food with no money and without taking anyone else's resources. If we continue our wasteful ways I am confident I could never buy food again and live a long, healthy life. The list above is a rarity — I can usually eat better in this manner than most do by purchasing food from the grocery store aisles.

Now about today...

I awoke abruptly throughout the night, but I guess that's the way it is when you are sleeping in fear that the janitor will stumble upon you at any minute. Noises kept startling me but it was always just the hot water heater kicking on or something outside in the alley. Just before 6 a.m. I woke again, and this time there was someone moving around in the church. I looked outside and saw a truck just outside the door. I heard the person shuffling around in a room around the corner so I packed my stuff up and in just a few minutes was headed for the door. My clumsy trailer made enough noise to surely get me caught, but I managed to sneak out to the park benches without being seen. Just one minute later, the person emerged from the door and it turned out to be the janitor. He drove off without even looking at me. He never went in to the room I was sleeping in so I could have slept through the morning, but I was happy to be up early even with just five hours of poor sleep.

Once on the road, the terrain got easier and I was cruising downhill for about seven miles. This was a surprise and reminded me yet again that you just never know what the future holds. The tough times always pass.

All day I searched for food and just didn't have a lot of luck. I stopped in the town of Bedford and didn't find anything to eat. There was a farmers' market but since I didn't have any money on me I couldn't buy anything.

Ten or so miles later I made it to Breezewood. By that point I was really hot and out of water. I scanned farms all morning for a hand pump, and even though I saw two I just didn't stop. That wasn't very sensible, but it's often the case when I'm in a groove on the bike. When I'm flying downhill I don't want to slow down and when I'm pumping up a hill I just want to make it to the top. I filled up my one-gallon jug from the rainwater barrel at the church this morning so I wasn't in any danger, but it wasn't tasty water and I wasn't going to drink it unless I had to. In Breezewood I stopped into a gas station and scooped up ice from the fountain soda tray that other people had wasted and found a few half-full bottles of water in the garbage cans to add to it. Ice-cold water that would have gone to waste, you can't beat that. I gulped it down as fast as the ice would melt, and at Dunkin' Donuts I found a whole bag of donuts and bagels in the dumpster to feed my body with quick energy.

From there it was a giant climb up in extreme heat and I was feeling it big time. I stopped at a small spring-fed creek and submerged as much of my body as I could while gulping down my ice water. When the water in my bottle ran out I filled it with water straight from the creek and chugged as much as my stomach could hold. As I cooled my body down from inside and out I sat and appreciated the water, the soil, the trees and the creatures around me.

The climbing continued for a while and eventually leveled off again high above the town I had just left. The highway went over the interstate at one point; I saw a sign that said, "Washington D.C. 128," and couldn't believe where I was. It started to set in that I was nearing the opposite side of the country. The East Coast was so near, but I was still in the beautiful Appalachian Mountains and happy to be there. Riding in the brutal heat through traffic is going to be a new experience for me.

DAY 76: THE GETTYSBURG NAP

I was looking at the map last night to see how much pedaling I had left until I arrived in the big city of Philadelphia. A huge part of me (my aching legs) wanted to get through the Appalachian Mountains as fast as possible, but another part of me (my heart and my soul) wanted to stay in the peaceful mountains for the rest of the summer. Looking at the map I realized I was about a 60-mile ride from Gettysburg, and then I remembered that today was the 4th of July. I thought Gettysburg would be a very fitting place to spend Independence Day so that's where I set my sights on for the night.

I woke in the big shed where I had taken shelter last night, still exhausted and not feeling my finest, physically. I could tell my body was not functioning at its highest level from a lack of

One of the many weird places that I called home for a night.

nutrition. It was a gorgeous day and I was excited to continue exploring the beauty of the Appalachians. I pedaled out of Hustontown early and continued on Route S on the small local highways that led me through lush green peaks and valleys. It was just me on the open road with the beautiful mountains surrounding me and the cool air of the morning to accompany me.

Ten miles into riding I stopped at a creek, and by then my body was already quite hot. The creek was cold and I soaked it all in. The water was full of hundreds of crayfish and I caught a few to test my skills. I wasn't hungry for crayfish but wanted to know that if I needed to eat them I'd be able to get them into my pot. I caught a few and put them back.

I continued on, much of the time downhill through forests, over creeks and through state parks. The forest here is more open and less thick than the forest in western Pennsylvania. As I pedaled along I watched deer gracefully sprint away upon my arrival and groundhogs scurry off the roadside. The sun came through the leaves, lighting up the forest floor.

I finally found some fruit in a dumpster today and gave my body the nourishment it needed so badly. Watermelon, honeydew, grapes, cherries, oranges and apples went into my body in one sitting, and about six pounds worth. Midday I found another creek in a state park and cooled myself off from the 90-degree day. I lay naked in the clear cold creek hidden by the thick foliage and then sat on the riverbank with my feet in the water, eating grapes and cherries. I soaked in the beauty of the forest and the summertime. I am so happy to be alive in this wonderful world I live in.

I pulled into Gettysburg around 5 p.m. and was excited to be surrounded by the commotion of the big celebration. I am not normally a fan of big crowds, but I embraced the 250,000 people who were wandering around the town with a normal population of about 9,000. I rode through town and found a nice open piece of grass to lie in just outside the national cemetery. I put my solar panels out to collect the energy of the sun and lay next to them on my back soaking it all in. When I flopped down on my sheet my mouth opened wide with a yawn and I realized I could take a nap. It was early in the day yet and I had time to kill. I fell asleep nearly instantly and enjoyed the absolutely beautiful evening. This was my first nap of the trip and it refreshed me like nothing else had before. What a nap it was. The relaxation didn't end when I woke up, and I continued lying on my sheet stretching out all of the muscles in my body.

I felt very energized leaving town. After a short burst of pedaling I found an abandoned building on the roadside that I could have slept inside, but instead just slept on the porch outside. A big fenced-in pond of some sort sat 30 feet from where I lay. It was home to a population of frogs that were croaking so loud I didn't know if I'd be able to sleep. Energy was still running strong through my veins, and the croaks were stimulating my ears, which kept me up for a while. As loud as it was I was happy to be lying in the heat of the summer night surrounded by these four-legged croaking friends.

DAY 77: PENNILESS IN PENNSYLVANIA

I've nearly crossed the entire state of Pennsylvania now and I've done it without using a penny. Was it really hard? No. In fact it was quite easy. Why was it easy? Because so many Americans are wasteful, and I am easily able to feed myself off of this waste. Because I ride a bike that uses my own free energy rather than drive a car that costs 10 to 20 cents per mile. Because the land provides for us and I use its provisions. Because I am resourceful and use what is available to me. Because I do good and so others want to do good for me. Because I understand money is not needed to live, and it is only something that has been created.

It has been a wonderful experience living penniless as I crossed the state of Pennsylvania. It is an enlightening feeling to know that I can survive in this great country without money. I firmly believe that if I gave away nearly everything I owned tomorrow and closed all of my bank accounts I could not only survive but thrive in America. Why? Because:

I've learned the power of the human body and that I can get by on my feet or a bike. The bicycle is an amazing machine that can get me just about anywhere I need to go.

Some 165 billion dollars worth of food is thrown away each year in America, much of which is still delicious and nutritious. All I've got to do is open up the dumpster. Also once I opened up my eyes I realized that food was growing free all around me.

Water existed long before money did and I believe it is a right, not a privilege. With a water purifier and a reusable bottle I can get water from just about anywhere, be it a natural body or a tap.

It turns out that my body needs so much less than I thought. If I carry a tent, sleeping bag and sleeping mat I can sleep just about anywhere. I've slept in campgrounds, parks, roadsides, abandoned buildings, churchyards, fire stations, baseball fields, backyards, even cemeteries. Plus there's websites like Couchsurfing and Warm Showers with millions of hosts that will have you in their home for free. There are also empty houses and empty rooms all over America and people that need help and have resources to exchange.

I've simplified my personal hygiene and learned that I don't need so many products to keep my body in tiptop condition. The only body-care products I carry now are toothpaste, Dr. Bronner's Soap, a toothbrush, floss, coconut oil and essential oil. I've learned that the more naturally I live, the more freely I live.

I've gotten back to exchange and barter. Money makes things very convenient, but I can almost always exchange for what I need without bringing it into the picture, especially now that I've simplified my needs. To a large extent I've made goodness my currency. When I do good for others, others do good for me. The great thing about this is, the more I give, the more I receive. There are so many people in need of help and all I have to do is go out there and help them.

I live with a purpose greater than myself. By traveling with a purpose to make the earth a better place I find that my needs are more easily met. People are always excited to be a part of a greater cause. By involving them they often receive as much from helping me as I receive from them.

I've found ways to entertain myself that don't cost a cent. I let nature provide me with smiles. A drop of rain or breath of fresh air can make my spirits soar. The clouds can make my heart sing. Watching the birds interact, the wide array of insects go about their day, or the plants blowing in the wind can captivate me day after day.

Friendship costs not a thing, and there are 300 million Americans and seven billion earth citizens for me to interact and pass the time with.

It's a totally new way of thinking. I used to think money was freedom, but today I've found my greatest freedom in stepping away from the monetary mindset. It takes resourcefulness and your brain. Sure, it's not always easy, but is sitting at a desk and hating life easy? Sure, it can be challenging at times, but don't you have plenty of challenges in your "normal" life at home, too?

Simplify your life and set yourself free. You only live once, maybe, so live a life you can be proud of.

Waking up in a playground

The fenced-in pond turned out to be a flooded batting cage — I realized I was sleeping at an abandoned play place with a mini-golf course. If someone were to tell me they woke up at an abandoned mini-golf course I would assume drinking was involved but that was not the case. It was just a convenient place to sleep for the night. I woke early, rolled up my sleeping pad and got on the road early. I had a 60-mile day ahead of me to get to Lancaster, Pennsylvania, and the morning flew by.

A few miles from my destination I found a beautiful creek with picnic tables under a pavilion not far from the bank. I put my solar panels out, sat in the shade of the pavilion and wrote stories. Every hour I got up and walked to the creek to cool off my body and immerse my soul in the refreshing water. I washed my clothes in the creek and hung them out to dry. The first time I walked down the bank of the river to swim, a large frog plopped into the water and burrowed himself into the mud to hide from me. I could see him holding his breath, partially covered in mud, and I think he could see me too. Each time I returned he was on the bank waiting for me, and each time he jumped back into the river with a splash. I love frogs. I always have and always will.

I arrived at Katie's house, my host from WarmShowers. We relaxed for a bit and she gave me fresh peas and mint from the garden out back. We walked downtown and wandered for a bit along with her friend Michelle. It was nothing too special but that's what made it great. It was nice to just walk around the city in the company of peers for a while. Lancaster is full of Amish and Mennonites and that created a pretty unique experience. Loads of religion in this city and loads of Jesus-preaching handouts to be found littering the sidewalks.

DAY 78: HOT DAYS

I slept in a bit and dragged myself out of bed at 8 a.m. It was very enjoyable to sleep in. I spent the morning at Katie's apartment writing, and she made me some local eggs from free-range chickens. This was one of the very few on-the-grid meals I've had, and for some reason this morning I didn't mind bending the rules a bit. Basil from the backyard complemented the delicious eggs.

It was downright hot after I left the house, and I was feeling the effects of the heat and dehydration. Eventually I found a couple of bottles of water in a gas station garbage and a whole tray of wasted ice in a fountain soda tray. That helped a lot but I was still quite dehydrated. I stopped in at a farm that was selling all sorts of fresh food and filled up my jugs of water from their cold well. I would have loved to purchase some of this fresh produce but as I am not using money that was not an option.

Once I had water, the day became much easier. I rode on through the heat. The country road was nice and hilly and often covered by the shade of trees. At 5 p.m. I stopped at a river and basked in it for a half-hour, just soaking in the cold water and nature around me. Experiences like this refresh my body and mind and keep me happy and healthy.

From the river it was a short ride into West Chester, where I stayed with a journalist and photographer who had found me on Facebook. Her name is Sarah and she was a wonderful human being. There were signs written in chalk on the sidewalks and sides of buildings that led me to her door, and on my arrival she had fresh kale, potatoes, raspberries, peaches, lettuce and zucchini from the market waiting for me. It was a beautiful evening of hanging out and speaking to this intelligent and like-minded individual.

DAY 79: THE POTTY STORY

The weather channel was forecasting a heat wave with temperatures upwards of 100 degrees. This is not ideal cycling weather in most people's minds but it didn't worry me much. I'm a man who loves a good hot day and receives joy from the rays of the sun beating down upon me. The goal for the day was 60 miles to Princeton, New Jersey, and I mapped out a route that took about 25 different roads through residential neighborhoods and small highways.

I worried that I would be pedaling on busy roads through congested traffic but that was barely the case at all. There were plenty of steep hills to climb but there were even more hills to coast down, creating a cool breeze to keep me smiling. After 25 miles of pedaling I stopped at a beautiful, wide river that Brent and I played in for about an hour. We had rock-skipping contests, rock-throwing contests and, most fun of all, screaming contests. We yelled at the top of our lungs as we heaved and skipped rocks while standing in the water up to our waists, laughing until our stomachs could take no more. My throat was hoarse from the yelling but it was so enjoyable I didn't care. I find I feel remarkably alive when I use my vocal cords to this extreme. It is such a simple, human act that many of us have forgotten about. Of course I'm not talking about yelling in anger but just releasing our inner human and inner animal.

On Highway 206 I saw a toilet on the curb, presumably that someone was throwing away. I thought this could make a funny photo opportunity since I haven't sat on a toilet since I left San Francisco 79 days ago. So Brent got in position for a good photo, and I pulled my pants down to my ankles and, without exposing myself much, sat on the toilet to pose.

At that moment a man walked out of his house and was quite unimpressed with what he saw. He took out his phone as I told him I wasn't actually pooping in the toilet, but when he put the phone up to his ear he said, "I've got two male Caucasians here..."

which clearly gave me the message that he was on the phone with the police. Not wanting to get in trouble for a harmless act, I jumped on my bike to speed off. I was taking the situation very seriously, pedaling as hard as I could, but Brent was already a block behind me apparently not realizing what could be coming. Assuming the man had told the officers I was heading north on 206, I turned right to zigzag through some neighborhoods and throw them off. Within just a few minutes Brent was nowhere in sight, but my phone rang and sure enough it was him. He told me that seven police cars were surrounding him, and the officers were requesting my presence.

I felt the best option was to grant their request so I began pedaling to meet Brent. Another squad car found me first though. I pulled off to the side of the road without him even motioning to me but he flipped on his lights on and treated me like a dangerous criminal anyway, yelling, "Get down on the sidewalk!" Within moments two more police cars showed up and I was surrounded. The leading policeman was a stern man who acted like he was going to throw the book at me. "So you pulled your pants down and exposed yourself to the whole world?" he asked. I responded, "Yes, I did pull my shorts down. I did so as I sat on the toilet and kept myself pretty well covered up." Considering there are seven billion people on this world, and I suspect no more than five of them saw me naked, I thought his statement to be fairly inaccurate, but I bit my tongue.

The other officers standing around me were a lot more interested in what I was up to and didn't seem upset by my minor offense. While the tough guy was in his squad car they asked me all sorts of questions about my bike trip and my off-the-grid mission. One officer asked where I was planning to stay tonight and I told him Princeton. He responded by saying, "I was f**king a girl in Princeton once and got caught by the police while I did it." Many of my minor run-ins with the police have involved vulgar language and incidents of them not coming off as very respectful to the people they are supposed to be serving. They are usually very nice people, and I always have a good time with the police who stop me for whatever harmless thing I was doing. But I expect police to hold themselves to a little higher standard than speaking like that. Often they stoop down to the same level as the person who has "done something wrong," and I just don't find that to make much sense. The insane inefficiency of our police force and the insanity of their excessive force and inflated egos could make an entire book.

After speaking to the "cool cops" who didn't seem to care a bit about what I did, the stern cop came out of his car and told me to, "Keep your pants on in the future." A lady cop pulled up and asked me, "Do you smell as bad as your friend?" I said, "No, I don't," and she responded by saying something to the effect of, "You did get some great photos. I looked at them." I gave her my website and told her where she could see them later.

So I was off with another story to tell and was happy for the way everything ended. I thought I might walk away with a public indecency ticket, but I would have been okay with that. Every time I have a run-in with the cops I come out with a great story and nothing on my record, and I wouldn't change a thing.

Princeton was just six miles from there. As we rode in to town an out-of-this-world sunset led us to a really nice park with a lake in the middle that we decided to call home for the night. Strong winds were coming in with a huge thunderstorm on the horizon. We were hoping to find a pavilion to keep ourselves dry, but I welcomed the rain and hoped to harvest more than I could fit inside my stomach. We found a huge house by the lake with two people sitting outside that greatly confused me. What the heck is this house doing here and how do I access this lake without going on their property? Turned out it was actually there for receptions. This meant I had the shelter I was looking for and would get to spend the night on this lake in the beautiful woods. I couldn't have found a better situation. I swam in the lake in the dark with turtles all around me and when I returned to the house the couple was gone. I set up the tent fly to collect rain when it fell and pulled out my laptop to write. The only problem was I was too dehydrated to think about anything other than water, and I couldn't help but sit there and wait for the rain.

But as I sat waiting I thought about how all the people that have asked me, "How do you have the time to do all this?" I've answered in many different ways in the past, but as I was sitting there by the peaceful pond I realized I hadn't been giving an answer that was true to my feelings. Here is what I realized.

I have time to do everything I do because I am human and I am alive. Therefore, I have 24 hours in every day, which is 1,440 minutes, which is 86,400 seconds. I have seven of these days in each week, and I have 52 of these weeks in each year, as does every living human. No human being has more time or less time than any other. Time is not something we can buy or win. It is not something we can steal or borrow. All living humans have the exact same number of minutes in a day. There is no such thing as not "having" time for something. We choose not to devote our time to doing something so that we can spend our time doing something else instead. It's a choice. Life is a choice. The choice can be conscious or unconscious, but it is a choice either way.

Maybe a better question would be, "How do you manage to accomplish so much with your time?" My answer to that is simple but maybe unique. My answer is something you won't hear out of most people's mouths. I'm going to be blunt here, and I'm going to be realistic.

I choose not to waste the life I am privileged to be living. I choose to put the minutes I am fortunate to have to what I consider good use. I live on a marvelous and diverse planet, and I have made the conscious decision to make as much of my life as I can for myself and for the people around me.

I am human and every human is capable of being amazing if they choose to be. I have chosen to be amazing. I choose to spend my time doing things I can feel proud of, that award me with a fuller life and that create a better world. I choose not to spend my time watching TV and playing video games. I choose not to sit around the house or the bar drinking beer. I choose not to spend my time doing drugs or smoking pot. I don't spend a half-hour to an hour each day making myself look handsome in the mirror. I don't waste time working a job that I get nothing out of except money. I don't waste time buying stuff I don't need. I don't waste time sitting around doing nothing. I don't own a car that takes time to maintain and results in me sitting in traffic. I have done all of that in the past, but no longer. I don't own a house that has constant needs. I'm not attached to all sorts of material possessions that take time to organize and maintain and keep updated. I don't have a pet or a child to take care of, and I don't intend to have one. I don't cut grass that doesn't need to be cut and wastes fossil fuels and pollutes the planet. I don't spend my time catching up on celebrity gossip.

I don't need a lot of money, which means I don't need to work to make a lot of money. The less money a human needs, the less money they need to earn and in turn the less time they need to spend at work. Less time at work means more time for life. I don't waste my money on all sorts of things that I don't need. I put in my time at school and have finished my formal education.

I keep things simple, which allots me the time to make life grand.

Instead of spending my time doing useless and mundane things ,I seize each day, because I probably only have about 30,000 of them in this life. I seize each hour because I'm blessed to get around 1.8 million of them. I seize each second because I'm fortunate enough to breathe for just 43 million of them. I seize each moment to show others that life can be seized.

I spend my time cooking and eating healthy food. I spend my time traveling my country and my world. I spend my time outside breathing fresh air. I spend my time doing activities that are good for my body. I spend my time with friends and family. I spend my time laughing and loving. I spend my time going to new places, trying new things and meeting new people. I spend my time learning and expanding my knowledge. I spend my time helping others and spreading health and happiness. I spend my time giving back to this earth that I call home. This is what I think makes a good life, and this is how I choose to spend my time.

It might seem impossible to you to live a life like this — Yes, it is, if you have filled your life with all sorts of time-wasters. To live a life this simple yet enjoyable you have to simplify your life. Get rid of unnecessary possessions that bog you down. Don't measure your life success by money and possessions. Drop your ego and do what makes you happy, not what America tells you to do. Ride a bike instead of drive a car. Make conscious decisions and practice self control. Don't spend two hours in front of the TV each day and say you don't have time to eat healthy or exercise. Two hours is roughly 12 percent of your waking day. That's a lot of time.

You can do a lot can in one minute. You can do a lot can in one hour. You can accomplish a lot can in a day. Take advantage of the time you have on this incredible place we call earth. Be amazing. Create the world you want to see around you. Be marvelous. Live a life that is beyond just you. Be natural. Be you and be true to yourself. Live simple and you will live free.

If you sleep for eight hours that means you have 16 waking hours in your day.

Here's an example of what can be done in 16 hours:
- 60 minutes preparing and eating a healthy breakfast and preparing a lunch to go
- 30 minutes exercising, walking, or thinking positively to start the day off well
- 30 minutes riding your bike to work or school
- 480 minutes at work or school
- 30 minutes riding your bike home
- 30 minutes at the grocery store on your way home
- 60 minutes preparing and eating a healthy dinner. Having a friend over as a social event will double this time

- 30 minutes stretching, meditating, or caring for your body
- 60 minutes to lounge, read a book, or watch something educational.

That still leaves 2.5 hours in the day, and 2.5 hours is a lot of time.

This example fills many of the human needs. It also doesn't show that you probably have two days free from the 480 minute work / school day. It could be picked at endlessly and doesn't include everything you might need to do in a day. But the point is, there is a lot of time in a day and it's solely a matter of how we use it.

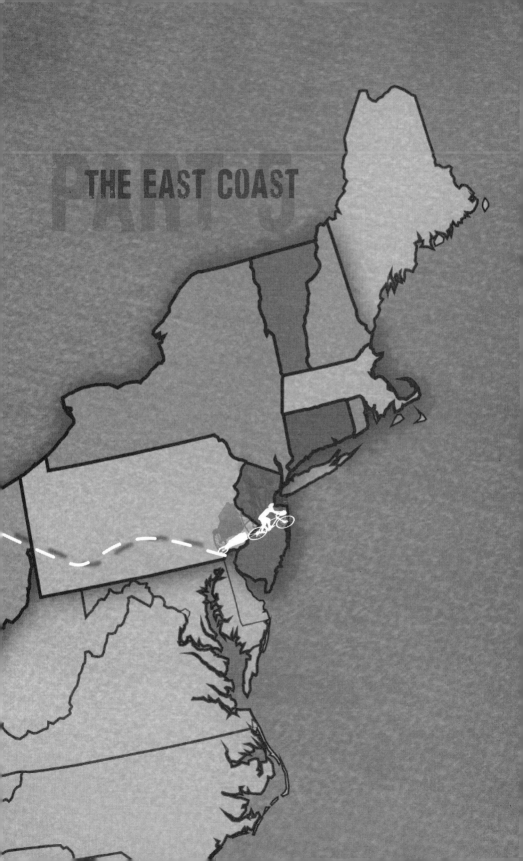

DUDE

DAY 80: HELLO NEW YORK CITY (I GUESS THAT MEANS I BIKED ACROSS THE COUNTRY)

I woke at 6 a.m. and knew I was up for good. I felt very inspired so I took the morning to sit on a bench with a beautiful view of the lake and write. I wrote for a couple hours and then went in the pond and played in the water and the weeds. I had no desire to get on the road early since it was a beautiful morning and there was no place I'd rather be. The only catch was it was going to be a hot day, and it would be more pleasant to ride in the morning hours than the hot afternoon.

Testing my limits, something I like to do to continue growing.

I got on the road at 10 a.m., thirsty and hungry as I had no food and minimal water. Now that I was in New Jersey and had successfully crossed Pennsylvania with no money, I was happy to go to the bank and take a couple hundred dollars out. I went straight from the bank to a health food store and bought good-quality honey and produce to feed my hungry body. I had a 55-mile ride to New York City ahead of me, and the first couple of hours were on some laidback county highways through good-looking terrain. The day went by pretty smoothly. These days, pedaling 50 miles in a day is second nature, and I don't even really have to think to do it. It doesn't take too much energy and sometimes at the end of the day I wouldn't be able to tell you if I had just relaxed at the beach all day or put in a full day of riding.

I crossed a bridge that provided the worst cycling conditions of the entire trip, by far. There was no shoulder so I rode on the sidewalk even when that was non existent. Much of the time it was a very narrow dirt walking path completely overgrown by weeds and littered with debris that could pop my tires. I made it over a second bridge, but there was a casualty: my ukulele got caught on the side of a pole and was ripped to pieces despite all the protective layers covering it. Bummer. I'll make good use of it somehow because I'm not trashing it.

Once in Jersey City I unwound for a bit. I swam in a pond that cooled me off, but it wasn't a clean-looking body of water. From the east side of the city I took in a beautiful view of Manhattan, and it suddenly set in that I had ridden my bike across America. The trip was not over and this was not my end destination, but I had indeed ridden my bike across the country. I acknowledged the accomplishment and then tried to figure out how to get to the island of Manhattan. The nearest bridge was more than ten miles north, which would have added at least 20 miles of riding through the city. So instead I took the public ferry across. It was a six-minute ride and cost $7, including the bike. It was the first time in 80 days that my body had moved by means other than my own power or forces of nature. I didn't want to do it, but I gave in. It was quite enjoyable to feel the wind on my body as we crossed the water.

So here I was in Manhattan. I was amazed how many people were riding bikes and how happy and friendly everyone was. The streets were flooded with bikes, pedestrians and cars, and everyone seemed to be getting along well. Smiles were everywhere. Everybody was doing their own thing, but they all seemed to be happy to be out and about on this summer day. Manhattan has a new bike share program that allows residents and tourists alike to rent bikes from kiosks on the street, and the bikes were all over the place. I really saw some great things going on. It took just 20 minutes to leisurely cross Manhattan, and I soon found myself at the Brooklyn Bridge. There is a beautiful path for cyclists and walkers to cross the bridge and it was also flooded with happy people. I spent a half-hour or so casually making my way over to Brooklyn and checking out the views.

I had four miles to go to Greg Radicone's house. Greg is one of my best friends, and I hadn't seen him in six months so I was very excited as I rode over to his place. Spending the evening with Greg was an amazing contrast to being alone or amongst unfamiliar people, as I had been for most of the trip. We sat on his couch and talked about the past, the present, love and life. Yael, another great friend, came home a few hours later and it was awesome to see her as well. At one time both of these friends were roommates of mine in San Diego. We carried on until we were exhausted.

DAY 81: RELAXING IN THE CITY

I slept like a rock on the couch and didn't wake up until nine. I arrived in New York a few days early so I have a week here and am in no hurry to do anything in particular. I do have some stuff going on here but it's a fairly leisurely week. So I hung out on the couch until noon, writing, using the Internet and going through my stuff to take out wasted space and weight from the trailer.

When I got out of the house around noon I had a list of simple things to do, including: find food and water, take a swim, cut my nails, trim my beard, stretch and lay in the sun. I accomplished many of these things right outside the door in Prospect Park, where I also watched a red-tailed hawk catch a pigeon in its talons. He pulled the feathers out with his beak and then shredded the meat bit by bit with his sharp beak, right there in Brooklyn. I got some food at a local market to tide me over for the day and found a dripping water fountain where I was able to collect over a half-gallon of water that would have evaporated on the sidewalk. In the park I lay on my sheet and checked more things off my to-do list as I watched a man pick berries from the trees and eat them. He said they were cherries and blackberries, and I was pretty interested in eating some myself. I asked if he did this often and he said he did, so I figured it was safe. What he called blackberries were mulberries, but the little things he called cherries looked just like cherries, except they were about the size of peas. They were very bitter and I didn't care to eat many of them. It seems just about everybody walks past these sources of food without ever realizing they are there. This includes myself, but since I've started to pay more attention I am learning that free food is growing all around us.

I met up with Greg back at the apartment and we went into Manhattan to meet with friends. He took public transportation and I biked the six miles through Brooklyn, over the Brooklyn Bridge and through Manhattan. I absolutely love flying through busy city streets, riding as fast as the cars and being much more maneuverable. It's like a real-life video game, a bit dangerous, but I keep my wits about me. It took me 41 minutes from Greg's to Giulia's door, and from there her boyfriend Joey and I went to a cafe to meet Greg. We watched two friends of theirs, a duo called Twiddlin' Thumbs, play incredible music, but I had so much energy coursing through me it was hard to be inside the building.

Then Giulia, Joey and I wandered the streets a bit and headed back to her house, where we intended to get to bed fairly early. Instead we stayed up past midnight talking. When we did finally get into bed the topic of astrology came up, and we wound up in a long discussion. It was good to converse and it's good to be in the big city.

DAY 82: HECTIC, HECTIC, HECTIC...

I don't even remember today starting. I guess this is life in the big city, where everything is hectic and everybody seems to know it. Where it takes so much time to get around and there's so much less time to do things you actually want to do. I've found myself muttering under my breath, annoyed with people that are slower than me, be they pedestrians, cyclists, motorists, or passengers on buses. It's me, the dude who's been trucking it slowly across the country for the last 81 days, and here I am muttering unnecessary words at the people moving slower than me on the street. That is completely ridiculous.

I've been here for less than 48 hours and I can see that it's changing me. My heart is beating faster and a whole lot of excess energy is speeding around inside my chest. It's all right for me because I'm only here for a week, but if I was to stay here I would be extremely anxious about what it was doing to me and would not be comfortable. I am grateful for this opportunity to see the contrast and experience life from the perspective of a city person.

Hectic, hectic, hectic. That's the word and the feeling flowing through me from toe to toe, from hand to hand and from ear to ear. Busy, busy, busy. I've got to be here and there and here right now and 15 minutes ago and in 20 minutes. This feeling doesn't exist in the country life. I had tentative plans with a handful of people, and the buzzing bees inside me rattled those plans out my ears and back in through my nose and then back out through the tiny little holes in the corner of my eyes.

Navigating the city was a freakin' ball. I love riding my bike through this concrete playground with all sorts of obstacles to dodge and speed past and all sorts of weird and beautiful humans to look at.

After I crossed the bridge for the third time the skies unleashed a load of pure water and the streets were soon running with it, probably not so pure anymore. It was exactly what I wanted. Rain to feed my dehydrated cells. Rain to nourish my brain so I could think straight. Rain to wash the sweat and dirt from my body. The timing wasn't right because I couldn't harvest the water in large quantities, but I took advantage of it as much as I could. It would have been blissful if I didn't have a backpack with my computer in it to protect. My human body can take all the rain the skies can throw at me and then dry off naturally when the rain ceases, but with material possessions to protect I don't feel free to bask in the glory of the rain. I still embraced it and even found a spout coming out from a church that was sending a waterfall down to the ground below. I filled my quart-sized water bottle twice and drank it all in. The flow even lasted long enough for me to shower underneath it and soap up with my Dr. Bronner's soap.

I walked away from that church squeaky clean, with a belly full of water and a full bottle for later. The rain died and I got back to Greg's house just a short while later. I sat on his comfortable couch and isolated myself from the world. There were just a few windows and I felt trapped in this cave. The air does not flow in, and I find myself breathing in the same stagnant air that sits in this apartment all day long. I don't like it. It's one thing to be in a house where I can easily walk outside or sit on the porch, but in this apartment building I have to walk through one, two, three doors to get outside. They lock behind me so I have to bring keys. It's not a free feeling.

Greg found me a leaky fire hydrant this morning, and I went over there and was happy to find it was still dripping water out into the streets. I expected a real slow leak, but it was wasting a lot more water than I had imagined. I was grateful for the leak because it meant I had drinking water but laughed at the irony since my work is to reduce waste. That is possibly one of the most interesting aspects of this adventure, my hope for waste to live off of when I am trying to stop waste from occurring. I filled my bottle up twice, chugging it both times as I sat on the fence nearby. I filled it up a third time as well as my one-gallon jug and cleaned up a bit before heading back to the apartment. I wished I had a five-gallon bucket to fill too so I could wash my clothes but figured it'd still be leaking tomorrow. Convenient waste for me.

Most people would walk by this leaky hydrant and not realize just how much water the "small" leak is wasting. I timed how long it took to fill a one-gallon jug and it was two minutes. That means 720 gallons of water is being wasted each day from this hydrant alone. A human needs eight cups or a half-gallon of water per day to live. That means this hydrant is wasting a one-day supply of drinking water for 1,440 people every day it leaks like this.

DAY 83: A DIFFERENT PERSPECTIVE

Here are some insights into my mind on Day 83 of living a minimal impact lifestyle...

I sat on the couch and tears fell from my eyes as I thought about the people who have inspired me throughout my life and who have shaped me into who I am today. I am very proud of the life I lead so I have a very deep level of appreciation for the people who helped me to get here. I also thought of all the amazing people who are out in the world making a better life for themselves, their communities and the earth. The people who are sacrificing their comforts and the luxuries they could have to instead live a humble life that is better for the people around them. The people that are making a conscious effort to start living a happier, healthier life. The people who are waking up and quitting jobs that are taking them nowhere and getting rid of all the crap that is bogging them down.

212

Part of me thinks I need to snap out of all this, ignore it and get out of here. The other part of me thinks I need to experience this. That is the part of me that I am choosing to follow today. If every new perspective from which I see life makes me a more understanding, knowledgeable human, then today was an important day in my life.

Ponder this for a moment....

Ever eaten a little bag of chips or drunk a bottle of soda? If so, how long did it take you to eat it? I'd finish one off in about five minutes. Five enjoyable minutes that is. But besides that, what did I really get out of it? There really isn't much nutrition in either of them. They are both really expensive on a per-weight basis. They are very processed. I am satisfied for a bit but nothing long-term comes from this transaction with food, compared to eating something healthy that gives my body vital nutrients and creates good energy for me to use.

Not much came from that transaction but a lot went into making it happen. That five minutes of comfort and enjoyment now means there is a plastic bag or bottle on this earth for con-servatively 450 years (if it doesn't get recycled). That means it will still be around when your kids', kids', kids', kids', kids' kids are walking this earth. Those five minutes of enjoyment don't really seem worth it to me. Eat an apple, compost the core, and your great, great, great, great grandchildren, let alone your kids, won't be burdened by it.

But I recycle, you may be saying ... and yet the plastic still had to be created, which took time, energy and resources. It has to be picked up by a truck that runs on fossil fuels, which takes time, energy and resources. A factory has to break it down into a raw material, which takes, you guessed it, time, energy and resources. Then they turn it back into another bottle or some-thing of the like to go through the same energy-intensive process all over again. Not to mention that most materials aren't truly recycled and are actually downgraded into lower-grade materi-als, meaning that they can only be recycled so many times. Then there's the fact that a substantial portion of our recyclables are shipped to countries such as China to do the dirty work, so we are polluting their countries in the process. It takes energy and resources to create all food, but when we use the earth's natural energy and resources, like soil and water, they are cycled through with minimal negative impacts.

But humans have to eat, right? Yes of course, but food doesn't need to be so resource and energy intensive. It grows from the earth naturally. What is a more earth-friendly choice? Natural, unpackaged, whole foods. Rather than potato chips, eat a potato. Rather than soda, drink water with a slice of lemon. Rather than applesauce eat an apple. It's just that simple. It takes a lot of energy and resources to pick the apples, transport them to a factory, process the apples in the factory, add preservative ingredients, package them, package the packages, ship them to the distributors and then distribute them to the stores. In our current system getting the apples to the store takes a fair bit of resources as well, but not compared to the applesauce.

DAY 84: WHAT'S IN YOUR TRASH?

Today I had the pleasure of visiting a couple of nonprofits that are making massive strides in the world of reusing. America is a throwaway society where many of us don't think twice about the useful stuff we throw in the garbage. Film Biz Recycling is changing that right here in Brooklyn. They are just amazing.

I hung out with Eva Radke, the founder, and she gave me a tour of the 11,000-square-foot facility and told me how this place came to be. It started with an idea entering her mind. She asked her friends in the reuse industry, "Am I crazy, or is this a good idea?" That was just five years ago and now they have diverted over 800,000 pounds (400 tons) of materials from the NYC waste stream.

So what exactly does Film Biz Recycling do? A lot, but I will tell you just a few of the things that impressed me the most. They divert stuff from the film industry that would likely have wound up in the landfill and instead give it a useful purpose. Eva explained how wasteful the film industry is. Since time is of the utmost importance and money is apparently quite abundant, they buy everything they need in volumes greater than they need plus a ton of stuff they probably won't need, so it is there if and when they need it while filming. When the filming is over they often just throw it away because that's the easiest thing to do. That is where FBR comes in. They take props, wardrobes and set materials from NYC's film, television, commercial and theatre companies and redistribute them through their network of charities and nonprofit partners around the city.

The stuff they do not redistribute sits in their huge retail store, prop shop and creative reuse center in Brooklyn. They have everything you've ever seen in your wildest dreams and more. Some of it is weird and wacky, like a lie detector, breakaway glass and Chinese cooked ducks from the *Men in Black* movie. You can also find everyday things like furniture, household goods and dog kennels here as well. If you like cool, reused stuff this is the place for you. If you are in the film industry you can rent, rather than buy, stuff like a bearskin rug, to cut costs and reduce the environmental impact of your production. All purchases support FBR's social and environmental mission to redistribute valuable, material donations to communities of need throughout New York City.

These guys eat, sleep and breathe some of the important R words: reduce, reuse, recycle, redistribute and repurpose. Even the food in the kitchen comes from movie sets, mostly (a lot of that ended up in my stomach today).

All of this happened because the idea of one woman, Eva Radke. It's just another example of how the actions of individuals do matter. I am very grateful she took that leap of faith and went for it. We need more people like her and the hundreds and thousands of people who have helped her since. I thank every single one of them as well.

After a short seven-mile ride through the rough roads in a diverse range of Brooklyn neighborhoods, I made it to another very inspirational place. The "Queens of Reuse" sums them up in my mind, but it goes so much further than that. Materials for the Arts is a division of the NYC Department of Cultural Affairs, and they are creating a cleaner, happier America day in and day out. I could write a series of books about all the great things that are happening in NYC because of them, but instead I'll sum up their incredible nonprofit in a few paragraphs.

MFTA specializes in "creative reuse." They collect unneeded materials from businesses and individuals and give them to nonprofits, schools and communities with art programs. Basically they take what might have become garbage and turn it into beauty. Their giant warehouse includes set props, fabric, paint, wardrobes, giant piles of rubber bands and wood, to name a few things. They take in over a million pounds of materials every year, and it is all there in their giant reuse center for thousands of programs to come pick up, completely free of charge.

Within the building they have classrooms full of magic. In the P-credit classes teachers "Learn how items from the recycling bin and free supplies from Materials for the Arts can be creatively reused to make projects for lessons in all content areas." I walked into a classroom of teachers that were making awesome educational things to incorporate reusing into their lesson plans. Musical instruments, board games and card games were a few of the things the teachers made, and they were all beautiful. There was so much energy in the classrooms, and everyone was so excited to be there. They also accept field trips where children can learn about the art of reuse in the 35,000-square-foot building of magic.

Artists explained that working with used materials opens up their creativity and saves them a ton of money. They call it reuse art and they do a lot of it around here. Just a few weeks ago they did a fashion show, and one of the dresses was made from an old lampshade. In another class they made flowerpots and learned about composting (which is something they do here at MFTA). Now that is walking the walk.

It's not just reusing ordinary stuff and turning it into art. It's about enjoyment. It's about education. It's about creativity. It's about giving opportunities and resources to kids that wouldn't have them otherwise. It's about saving people money. It's about inspiring people to be more resourceful. It's about making use of what you have rather than running to the store. It's all surrounded by love.

Harriet Taub, the Executive Director, and Rachel Kuo, the Communications Coordinator, were both extraordinary women and both clearly dedicated to and excited by this program. They are in it for the right reasons and have a genuine love for what they are doing. I hope more people out there start to do what they love, like these women do.

DAY 86: THE NOT-SO-OFF-THE-GRID PARTY

I woke up on the couch and spent most of the morning on the computer writing and using the Internet. I had a party to attend at noon or I probably would have sat on the computer for a few more hours. Having to be somewhere at a certain time stressed me out a bit, and of course I didn't leave the house until 11:30 to get there when it was a good four-mile bike ride away. I hadn't eaten yet, and since it was Sunday, it was a great day to spend time at a farmers' market. That's what I really wanted to do.

I found a market and it was just absolutely fantastic to be there. I bought gooseberries, currants, tomatoes, all sort of veggies and homemade yogurt, all of which were organic and local. I also bought some bread that was locally made, from 90 percent New York-state ingredients. It was some of the best bread I've ever had, and I had finished off the whole loaf by the end of the day.

I got to the party and at first it was awkward. I'd been invited by a nonprofit that had learned about my journey through Facebook and wanted to celebrate my arrival in NYC. I hadn't met them in person yet, and when I walked in the woman who had put the party together gave me an awkward hello and offered me a seat. Then we just sat there in silence and watched the really loud band play. There were just a handful of people there, and I think most of them were members of the band that was playing next. Between sets she didn't introduce me to anyone, and I kind of stood around not talking. It was awkward to the point that I wasn't even sure if the party was for my arrival in NYC after all — maybe it was just some trick to get me to come.

I had discussed my Off the Grid Across America mission with her in detail and explained that if there was to be a gathering for me it had to be extremely low impact. I could sense over the phone that she just wasn't getting it, but I went along with her anyway. When I showed up it quickly became apparent that she didn't understand anything I had told her. She called it the Off the Grid party, but the building was heavily air-conditioned. All the music was electric guitars and amplifiers and used a ton of electricity. They were cooking burgers and steaks over charcoal. They even had bottled water and single-serve applesauce in plastic squeeze containers, which goes against three environmental aspects of the trip: not local, not organic and packaged. It was an example of someone who talks about green but doesn't actually get it. If someone truly cares about and understands sustainability, they'd buy apples, not single-serve packaged applesauce. I was ready to just get the heck out of there and so much of me just wanted to walk out the door.

Instead I stayed, not wanting to hurt anyone's feelings. I started to talk to some of the people when the music was not so loud. After a while, more people started to show up, and it finally started to become fun. I was talking to a ton of people, and I could tell the wheels were turning in their heads. I was glad I stuck around because I think many of the people there were inspired enough by my adventure to actually take action. My different views on water and electricity opened up a new way of thinking to them. I strongly believe that some of them will be making real changes in their lives to start living a more earth-friendly lifestyle. I am very excited about that. I was very appreciative of everyone there and all the music they played. I had a lot of fun after the first awkward hour.

I got out of there around 6 p.m. and headed over the Manhattan Bridge into Manhattan to meet some friends. As I parked my bike I saw a goddess-like woman walking in my direction, her hair flowing away from her face into the wind. Her bronze skin radiated the last bits of light in the sky, and there was an aura surrounding her that brightened my eyes up like two huge globes. I hadn't seen a woman like her since I left California. Maybe she is naturally that way or maybe it's because she just flew here from the magical island of Maui, where many people are deeply connected with the earth and the people in their lives.

She was walking near the fountain to cool off from the heat of the day. The instant I saw her I knew it must be Chrissy Kapoor, a friend of a friend from Maui I had never met before. I had a heart-lifting evening hanging out with Chrissy and some other absolutely beautiful people. I was exhausted from a long day of talking when I got there, but I was instantly rejuvenated in the presence of these friends, new and old.

DAY 87: NERVOUS ENERGY

I woke up and I had a bit of anxiety at the idea of getting out of Brooklyn. Actually, I think I've had a little anxiety inside me since just before I got here. I had an incredible time in NYC, but the different energy messed with my calm body and mind quite a bit. I hadn't been on the road in nearly a week and was out of my routine of biking nearly every day. On top of that I was due in Northport at 5 p.m. for a meeting and that stressed me out. It was only a 40-mile ride and

Of all the difficult times on the trip I wouldn't have expected this to be the moment when tears would fall from my eyes. The more I thought about it the more I cried; I didn't know exactly why I was crying but it didn't matter. I'm a bit overwhelmed, and I was very glad to be shedding tears, as I know it is a good release. I would see something on the computer that would send excitement throughout my body and then more tears would come. A very mixed bag of emotions today.

I'm seeing life from such a different perspective right now. Being here in the city surrounded by all this technology is starting to close in on me. I am sitting here looking at the oven and seeing this everyday piece of technology in a different light. This thing is so huge and so beyond me. It's so complicated and I know close to nothing about it. How it was designed and how someone figured out to put this together are so beyond me. The giant factories that put it together are beyond me. All of this to do something very simple that I do with sticks and twigs that I find underneath trees. When I am done cooking all that's left is some ashes that I scatter. When the people who use this stove are done, there is still a giant thing that will likely one day end up in a landfill.

It's been so long since I sat in a building by myself secluded from Mother Nature. I feel very isolated. I am seeing how different of a life I am living compared to everyone around me. Without a lot of people around it's easy to perceive the weird things I do as the normal. They are as much a part of my life as turning on a light switch is for you. Now I see Greg going into a room and closing the door to use the toilet whereas I go outside. He and Yael can simply open up a fridge and use the stove when they want to cook whereas I have to go out and find food. For the first time in my life I sat in an apartment with white walls surrounding me and realized just how isolated I was from the world around me. I was starting to feel a little crazy and imagined what it would be like to seclude myself in this white-walled isolation tank for 24 or 48 hours without leaving and without distractions like my computer and phone.

wouldn't be a problem, but it still tied a small knot in my stomach. I knew the solution to this anxiety was to just get on the road and start pedaling, which I did but not until about 11 a.m., an hour later than planned.

Before leaving town I paid one last visit to the leaky fire hydrant. For five days I had lived solely off water from this one hydrant. I drank from it. I showered in it. I did my laundry in it. I brushed my teeth with it. In the last 87 days I have only used 105 gallons of water. The average American uses about 80 to 100 gallons of water per day. That is what I used in 87 days!

DAY 88-89: NORTHPORT, NEW YORK

My two days in Northport were some of the most enjoyable, heart-warming days of the trip. I pedaled there from Brooklyn, and Tina Davies and Mike (Mr. Smiles) were waiting for me, as they had been for the last 86 days. Tina has been an amazing supporter of my trip and I love her to death. Tina is a mom to me and of course she took care of me like a son. She even had locally grown, organic food waiting for me when I arrived.

It started with a police escort into town. That was embarrassing — I thought it drew too much attention to me and was a misuse of resources — but Tina had insisted. Then at the gazebo in town the mayor, George Doll, was waiting, along with my friends Greg, Melissa and Kevin. It was like I was riding into my own hometown. Then the news station came and did a story about my arrival in Northport. Oh yeah, there were also flyers in half the windows in Northport to let the whole town know about my arrival. Tina set up all that.

Once all that commotion was over I was excited to just hang out and relax in the presence of people I love. We bought ice cream at the local sweet shop and had dinner at their favorite restaurant that night. Tina set up a massage for me the next day, and it was a body-changing hour. After walking out of there I was not sore for the first time since I left San Francisco, 4,300 or so miles back. I spent two nights there and the whole time was so much fun. The second night Tina and I went over to Kenny's house and we caught up. The last time I was here was September 2012, and the funny thing is none of us knew that the next time I arrived it would be on a bicycle ridden from the other side of the country. Kenny showed me his photo book from his six-month hike on the Appalachian Trail, which he did at the age of 62. He is one tough dude and is always fun to be around. A lot of people use the excuse of age for not being able to do what I do, but Ken is proof that it can be done.

The most enjoyable part of my two days in Northport was going for a bike ride with Tina just before I left, just the two of us.

It was so nice to see her on a bike and it was even nicer to be by her side. I told her I'm not coming back unless she rides her bike at least once a week during the summer / fall.

AS POSTED ON FACEBOOK:

For the next week, I will be living off of drippy faucets as I cycle from New York City to Boston. That is 250 miles through a heat wave! The weather forecast is calling for temperatures in the 90s for the next four days, and there is a heat advisory in effect. I'm going to need your help!

Help me find dripping faucets along my route so that I can drink. Invite me to the leaky faucet, fill up a bottle and meet me on the road, or just leave it on the roadside for me. Look for leaky faucets, hoses, fire hydrants, or even ice from the catch trays of fountain soda machines. Be creative. I'll take any water that is still clean and was going to waste.

I'm leaving from Central Park at 5 EST on July 17th and will arrive in Boston on approximately July 24th. If you're looking for me I'll be the guy on a bamboo bike pulling a trailer covered with solar panels.

Here are some of the major cities I will pass through:

Manhattan, NY- 07/17	New Haven, CT- 07/18-07/19
Stamford, CT- 07/17	New London, CT- 07/20
Westport, CT- 07/17	Providence, RI- 07/21-07/22
Bridgeport, CT- 07/17	Boston, MA- 07/23 or 07/24

DAY 89: DRIP BY DRIP DAY 1

I left the official launch point of Central Park in Manhattan at 5 p.m. today but I actually biked there from Northport on Long Island, 40 miles east. We are in the middle of a heat wave that will be lasting through the week; I hear it's already the most extreme heat wave since the 1950s.

While I was in Central Park a guy named Patrick pedaled up beside me and ended up riding with me for a good chunk of the evening. We pedaled through Harlem where we met Skeletor, a bike messenger who knew the area well and led us into the Bronx. That is where I found my first water, a leaking fire hydrant, just 6.6 miles into the journey. I cooled off from the 90+ degree temperatures and drank in as much water as could fit in my belly. I filled up my jug and water bottle and was back on the road, hungry and in much need of rest. I counted nine leaking fire hydrants while I was in the Bronx. I think that as temperatures rise in the New York boroughs so do the number of busted-open hydrants. This is a blessing for me because it means I can easily find drinking water, but as the entire purpose of my work is to reduce water waste it is not what I am

hoping to see. I even saw a guy with a massive wrench trying to break a hydrant open to cool off from the heat wave. Talk about a huge waste of water!

After another ten miles of pedaling I was waiting at a red light thinking I should find a church to sleep in when I looked to my right and, sure enough, there it was. I found the pastor and he said it would be okay for me to camp out in the grass behind the church.

DAY 90: LEAKY FAUCET WATER FROM FACEBOOK

I awoke at 6 a.m. and heat was already in the air. I took some time to relax in the churchyard and talk to the groundskeeper before getting on my way before 7 a.m.

I rode on Highway 1 for the morning, and for the most part the heat didn't get to me. Pedaling along at 10 to 15 miles per hour created a nice breeze that kept me cool. At one point the sun was scorching down and the concrete was radiating the heat at me like a furnace. The creeks of sweat running down my back turned into flowing rivers. Each downhill ride cooled me off enough to pedal up the next hill though. About 20 miles into the day I found a brilliant creek and cooled off in it under the shade of the trees. I laid in the water to bring down my body temperature and got out when I had had enough. Lowering my body temperature in this manner keeps me cool on the road for close to an hour.

I stopped into a grocery store and got three massive locally grown cucumbers. They are 90 percent water and were probably close to a pound each. I figure I got over a quarter-gallon of water from eating those throughout the day. This allowed me to conserve the water I did have, which lasted until close to two, when I had pedaled 40 miles. I happened to pass the Connecticut Post so I popped in to see if they'd be interested in doing a story and sure enough they were. I spent an hour, with them and from there I had ten miles through the heat to get to a leaky faucet. I ate seven oranges and got some wasted ice from a fountain soda tray in a gas station, which tided me over a bit, but boy, was I thirsty. My mouth was stinging from too much citrus, and my hands were sticky with orange juice. I found a half-full bottle of boiling hot water on the side of the road and drank that, too. I would imagine it was 100+ degrees but I was happy to be drinking it.

I stopped in at Patagonia to say hello and tell them about my adventure. I am an ambassador for One Percent for the Planet and this 104-day journey is ending at their headquarters in Vermont. The founder of Patagonia, Yvon Chouinard, is also the founder of One Percent for the Planet, and I love everything they are doing. They hooked me up with an autographed copy of Yvon's book, *Let My People Surf.* I've wanted to read it for a solid year and now I'm excited to dive into it when this journey is over.

Fellow traveler, Rachel, collected water from a friend's leaky faucet to help me with my Drip by Drip campaign.

from my whole body. Everyone else had fans on them but since I am not using electricity I just opened the door next to my room. Bad idea. The room filled with mosquitoes, and in my deliriously tired state I woke up slapping myself for the better portion of the night.

The afternoon wore on and the sweat continued to pour out. I took breaks from the computer to drink water and eat oranges and bagels from the dumpster and occasionally some kale from the garden. My solar panels were soaking in the sun today and gave me enough battery life to last the whole day, and then some.

I met my host David just last night at a red light out front of a bagel shop. We were both looking at the shop because a car had just crashed into it. It was literally almost halfway through the front doors. While we were waiting for the light to turn green he asked me about my solar panel and then asked if I wanted to go swimming with him and his friends. Then he offered his place to crash without any hesitation. He is a senior in high school and lives in this big house with just his mom. We were complete strangers yesterday and now roommates for two days.

Later in the afternoon we went to a park down the street and went for a swim and also picked out a good spot to meet the news station that I was doing a story with later that day. Fox WTIC contacted me to do a story on my adventure and told me to pick a place to meet. I figured I might as well find somewhere beautiful so that the viewers could see some nature for a change.

I took a swim in the creek while I was waiting for the news team to come. I thought to myself that most people probably don't go for a swim to freshen up before their interview and that made me chuckle. The story went very well. Afterwards I hung out in the park and sat on a rock by the lake. A giant snapping turtle swam up to the shore, and we stared each other in the eyes for a solid three minutes. I don't know if I was in his spot or if he was just checking me out, but I was glad to be in the beast's presence. It was nice and cool by the lake, but when I headed back to the house the sweat started to pour out of my body again. It's hot but I like it.

I lay in the guest bedroom writing, in the dark of course since I can't use any electricity. Since I have now officially crossed the country off the grid I have lightened up a tiny bit on my rules. Only a tiny bit though. I plugged into an outlet at Greg's apartment in NYC to use my computer more than my solar panel could provide. I have purchased a small amount of food that has not fit the guidelines, such as peanut butter that wasn't local, bread in a plastic bag and nuts that weren't organic. I used a toilet today for the first time since the adventure began. I think I will allow myself one toilet usage per day. Every time I flush a toilet I use 1.6 gallons of water, which is well beyond a day's worth of drinking water. I have a hard time doing it and have decided I am going to build a compost toilet when I get back to San Diego to conserve water. And I haven't even thought about getting into a car.

Back on the road tomorrow. Supposed to be another hot one. I wouldn't have it any other way.

DAY 92: ROADSIDE WATER BOTTLES

I woke up at 7 a.m. feeling disturbed from a night of bad dreams. I went to the bathroom and then crawled back into bed only for the painful dreams to continue until I woke again at 8:45. I didn't remember much of the dreams but my heart was feeling very heavy. I went downstairs, and David's mom offered to make me some eggs, which I gladly accepted. Then she went out to water the garden, and I filled up my jug from the leaky hose connection. I managed to get almost a gallon in a few minutes. Those leaks really add up quickly.

I packed up my stuff and was on the road again. I stopped at the farmers' market where I picked up a bunch of veggies, some blueberries and a solid loaf of bread. As I poured the blueberries out of the basket into my own container the lady next to me said she'd take the other half that I couldn't fit and paid for mine. Thanks so much, lady. That was awesome. I met some really cool people and had a fun time as I always do at farmers' markets. I wasn't that talkative as I was still feeling down and tired.

I decided to ride separate from Brent today, as I feel much freer on days when I am on my own. So he headed to New London, and I headed back to the waterfall in hopes of finding a shirt I left there yesterday. The 2.5 miles up there went quickly, and I was happy to be going for a swim in the falls, whether I found my shirt or not. When I got there I stood on the rocks looking around and was let down when it was nowhere to be seen. I really wanted to find it. Then I looked down at my feet and there it was. My eyes lit up and sent a happy little chipmunk running around in my stomach. I felt rewarded for making an effort even when I thought finding the lost shirt was unlikely. A reminder to never give up.

As I rode on I was thinking about how most of my friends have been telling me to take it easy and bend the rules of Off the Grid Across America. The way I figure it is I'm only doing this for 100 days, not a lifetime. I'm living in this extreme manner for just a little over three months to draw attention to things I feel are important that we all need to think about. I intend to be on this earth for at least 30,000 days so living full on by this rigorous set of rules for 100 of them is not that much in the grand scheme of a lifetime. I am a strong believer of everything in moderation, and although nothing in these days has been moderate, I am only doing them for a moderate amount of time: about one-third of one percent of my lifetime. This trip has been a deep practice of self-control, and I believe that if we all adapted such self-control we would quickly see improvements in health and happiness all around us. We'd also see vast improvements in our environment.

The 90+ degrees really has not been bothering me. I have exposed myself to a varied range of elements in my 26 years on this earth and have learned to adapt to whatever conditions the earth throws at me. I don't have to run to an air-conditioned apartment when it's too hot, and I don't depend on fans that run on electricity to keep my body cool. The earth is a marvelous place, and the extremes are one of the things that make it so marvelous. The extremes create the diversity that provides a sense of awe. I appreciate the earth for what it is, whether that reality makes me drip sweat from every pore or cuts off the circulation to my toes from the cold. I'm not strong enough to always feel this way but I do my best. This is what makes me human. When my body is being put to the test I know I am alive.

I passed a natural foods store and figured I'd check their dumpster to see if I could find anything good. Sure enough I did: four loaves of top-quality wheat bread, a few freshly made tofu and tempeh sandwiches, mouthwatering cookies and biscuits, and a slightly leaky bottle of premium-grade olive oil. It was probably 60,000 worth of food and would keep me fed for three days. The only thing I'd have to buy was some fresh fruits and veggies.

I found five bottles of water on the roadside that day and evening, totaling about 50 ounces (close to half a gallon). This and the gallon from the leaky hose kept me fairly hydrated. I also had blueberries on two separate occasions, which are full of water. Towards 8 p.m. I climbed a big hill and waiting on the other side was one of the largest street fairs I have ever seen. It was a half-mile long and completely packed with people.

I walked my bike through the massive crowd of people feeling like I was in a different world. I had just come from the beautiful and quiet road that followed along the ocean and was abruptly thrown into a mass of thousands of people. It was entertaining to watch. I asked a police officer what the festival was, and he said it was the town of Niantic's 4th of July festival (which was weird to me as the 4th of July was two weeks earlier) and there would be fireworks soon.

DAY 93: MY HAWK-LIKE SEARCH FOR WATER

At no point today did I know where my next drip, sip, or gulp of water was going to come from. My tongue searched the desert-like terrain of my mouth, hoping it would find water. I knew I was controlling that tongue and that it would find no moisture, but it seemed to have a mind of its own, searching every corner of my mouth for liquid. As I rode along, my eyes constantly scanned my surroundings for potable water. I felt like a hawk soaring through the sky searching out prey, only my eyes were scanning for half-full water bottles on the side of the road, drips from spigots on the sides of houses and any sign of leaking water.

My hawk eyes brought me success many times through-out the day. My first water came from a bowl sitting in the kitchen sink of my host, Chris. Just in case he intended to use that water to wash the dishes I left enough to get the job done. When I hit the road at 11 a.m. I found my next water inside of two huge cucumbers. I've learned on this trip just how hydrating fruits are. Many times I have peed bright yellow from dehydration and then found my pee to be clear after eating a half dozen apples or oranges. A cup of discarded ice that I found in a garbage can supplied me with about 10 ounces of water around noon. A bit later I found an unopened 17-ounce bottle of water to quench my thirst. The day was moving along slowly and so were the miles.

Midday I stopped at a state park where I swam in a lake surrounded by forest for about an hour. If I couldn't hydrate my body from the inside I decided I would do it from the outside. The cooling effects of the lake lessened my thirst and helped get me through the afternoon. The water refreshed my body and lifted my spirits. Upon departing the park I asked one of the rangers if she knew of any leaky faucets. She said there were none around, but she did give me the water from the bottom of her cooler that she was not going to drink. This ice-cold 16 ounces of water provided me with great joy. Shortly afterwards I found another 30 ounces in roadside water bottles. At 4:15 p.m. I was feeling good and my mouth was moist. I had collected about three-quarters of a gallon of water, certainly enough to survive.

I believe it is harder to appreciate what you have when you have too much of it or it is too readily available. When we have an excess of something it loses its value in our mind. When water flows from a tap with the turn of a knob we no longer give it the life-giving value it deserves. When light is created by the flick of a switch we do not value it as much as the light of the rising sun after a long dark night. When heat is created by twisting a knob, we do not savor it like we would a fire lit to warm trembling hands. When sweat is evaporated off a hot body by conveniently turning on an air conditioner, we do not appreciate it like a shady spot under an oak tree. When electricity is so easy to use that you forget where it comes from, we no longer feel gratitude the way we do when we harness the energy of the sun from a solar panel.

I called it a day after 50 miles of riding and found a remote beach to pass the rest of the evening. I swam in the ocean and after drying off and eating a half-loaf of bread I sat on a bench overlooking the beach and wrote about my day. This was my first swim in the open Atlantic Ocean since my arrival, and it is truly wonderful to be here. I have no water and haven't had a drop for a few hours now. Oh, how wonderful a few ounces would be. I will savor my next drink in the morning. It is dark now, and I am having trouble seeing the computer screen through the cloud of mosquitoes so I'll end on that note. Hopefully I can find a spot on the beach where these blood-hungry insects won't seek me out.

DAY 94: NEW FRIENDS IN TWO HOURS

After realizing there was no hiding from the mosquitoes last night, I decided to flee the beach to find shelter in the town nearby. I hopped onto the Warm Showers app and there was a host just a few miles away. I sent them an e-mail at 9 p.m. letting them know my situation, and much to my delight I heard back just 15 minutes later as I was riding down the trail to get back to the highway. They said come on over. I used the lights of passing cars to scour the roadside for bottles of water and listened for the sounds of dripping. My ears led me to an AC unit that was dripping like crazy so I collected a Nalgene bottle full to bring with me and purify. As I collected the water I Googled "drinking water from AC units" and found that it is very safe to drink straight up and completely safe if it's purified first. Just one hour after I was being eaten alive I was being welcomed into a wonderful home by wonderful people. Both Meg and Bob were environmentalists. I'm used to becoming friends and staying with people I have just met moments before but this time as I sat in the living room with them I actually thought to myself, "It's crazy that I didn't know these people 20 minutes ago and now here I am spending time with them in their home, eating from their garden and soon to be sleeping in one of their guest beds." There are so many good people out there, and you'll never meet them sitting at home.

Overnight they collected one gallon of water from their dehumidifier and put it into a bottle for me. I woke up at about 7:30 a.m. and spent the early morning writing. I would have slept in but my hosts had places to be so I was out of the house at 9 a.m. I was super tired and in need of rest so I pedaled just a few miles north until I found a spot to relax for the morning. It was a beautiful harbor full of sailboats, and I laid out my sheet in the grass between two benches. I worked on the outline of my documentary but mostly just took the time to relax. I dove into the harbor multiple times and swam amongst all the sailboats floating in the bay. It wasn't the cleanest of water but it was good enough to swim in.

I left in a hurry at 1 p.m. to meet up with a couple of media outlets. ABC Channel 6 wanted to do a story on my adventure but needed me there in the afternoon before the evening news so I jammed up to Providence, about 20 miles away. I met them at the station and had a fun time doing the story. Then I met up with Rich Salis of the *Providence Journal*, who had sent me a text earlier saying to meet him at 75 Fountain Street where he'd be waiting with a pen, a notepad and a leaky faucet. We talked for close to two hours and collected a Nalgene bottle full of water from the leaky bathroom sink. When I got out of there at 6 p.m. I was absolutely exhausted from talking all afternoon.

I went to a park a few blocks away and collapsed onto a bench. I was so tired and just wanted to sleep but first I needed to figure out where. I got in touch with a guy named Fernando on WarmShowers and he invited me to stay in his home just a few miles away. So I pedaled over there ready for bed. It turned out he lived in a co-op, and most of his roommates were Brown University students. There are about 12 people and they all eat together, decide what food to buy together, do house chores, etc. They are very conscious when it comes to food and buy mostly locally sourced items. I had a little bit of dinner with them. It was a very cool house with some great stuff going on.

Hanging out with these bright people reenergized me. Then Fernando invited me to a potluck about a mile down the road, so I decided to make an exception and joined in, eating all sorts of good food. Most of it was local and organic but electricity had been used to cook it. They were technically strangers but they all felt like good friends. It just goes to show you can never know where you're going to be in two hours. Life is so unpredictable and so much easier when you just go with the flow and lose your expectations.

I arrived in New Haven at 5 p.m. and met Rachel Marcotte, who had responded to the Drip by Drip campaign on Facebook. She had a small water bottle (about 20 ounces) worth of water that she had collected from a friend's leaky shower. She had even cooled it off for me in the fridge. I gulped it down with a smile on my face and chatted with this hitchhiking traveler for a while.

I needed to get into a creek or lake and cool off so I pedaled about 2.5 miles north from Yale University. Along the way I met a group of four high-school-age cyclists who took me to this awesome waterfall. I spent a few hours just hanging out in the water and cooling off from the heat of the day. It reached 97 degrees today, and I rode all day long through the worst of it.

I happened to be at the water lab at the Eli Whitney Museum and got close to a gallon of water from a leaking pipe there. What a lifesaver. I would have been okay without it, but this water cured my aching head. A couple of women who worked there explained what they are doing, which is so cool. There have five water tanks for kids to play in and learn about water by experience. The system is emptied daily and waters their garden. The New Haven water treatment plant was right there so I also learned all about how the city gets its water.

I am appreciating every last drop of water that hydrates my body, and I hope that by reading this you can start to appreciate water more also. After all, it does give us life. Your car can't give you life. Your TV can't give you life. You can even live without your house. But you can't live without water, so it makes sense to appreciate it.

DAY 91: LIGHTENING UP

Today was a "rest" day in New Haven and I enjoyed the heat wave from indoors, which was just about as hot as the outdoors, if not hotter. Last night before bed I was pouring sweat

DRIP BY DRIP FINAL SUMMARY

I just went seven days through a heat wave drinking only wasted water. It was everywhere and I found it in many different ways. I drank from spraying fire hydrants, leaky faucets, showers and hoses; chewed on discarded cups of ice; scavenged for bottles of water on the roadside that people had tossed out their windows and drank from dripping AC units and dehumidifiers. I drank just over a gallon of water each day for a total of eight gallons of water and biked 260 miles. The daytime high ranged from 89 to 97 degrees every single day — the heat wave was the most extreme in 60 years on the East Coast.

The only water I used besides those eight gallons was flushing six toilets for a total of ten gallons. The crazy thing is that every time I flushed a toilet I flushed more than an entire day's worth of drinking water down the drain. I bathed in lakes, streams and the ocean when I got a chance and that was the extent of my water usage for the entire week. An average American uses 80 to 100 gallons of water per day. The average European uses 50 gallons per day (about half of what Americans use); the average African uses two to five gallons per day (between one 50th and one 20th of what an Americans uses). I used less than two gallons per day in the middle of a heat wave — about one 50th of the American average. The average American uses 560 to 700 gallons per week; I used less than 20. Look at those numbers and try to say that the average American couldn't cut back on their water consumption.

This week wasn't exactly easy but it was not by any means life-threatening. What I've learned is we've got it so good in America that I can play games with water and come out on top. This is a resource that provides life if you have it and death if you don't. I'm not playing games like this just for the fun of it. I'm doing this to point out our waste of resources and to inspire individuals to start conserving them. Water is a life-giving resource we are blessed to have in abundance. In many other regions around the world water scarcity truly is a life and death matter. Our lack of consciousness and disregard for our resources is magnifying the problems in our own country and sending echoes around the world.

In other countries this campaign of mine is real life. In many countries finding water is a matter of life and death. Imagine that. Here in America we can turn a knob and a seemingly infinite amount of water is at our fingertips. We have so much of it that we take it for granted. Believe me, you wouldn't take it for granted if you only had access to a few gallons per day. We turn on a faucet and we have all the good clean water we need to drink, bathe in, clean our stuff with, brush our teeth with, and even poop and pee in. Imagine not having any of that. Imagine having to search for your water or walk miles to get it and then walk miles home carrying it. That is happening all over the world, and our excess consumption in America has something to do with it. At home in San Diego I rarely thought of the fact that water gives me life, but now that I have gone to this extreme I have realized just how precious and valuable water is.

The solution is simple. Start using only the water you need and inspire others to do the same. If you are not part of the solution you are part of the problem. Realize that, take action, and you will be a part of the solution. Inspire and teach others to take action, and now you're really part of the solution.

DAY 95: DAZED AND CONFUSED

I lay in bed working and then decided to try to get some more news coverage so I called the other newspapers in the area and found a journalist that wanted to cover the story. She said to meet her at noon at Waterplace Park in downtown Providence.

That gave me some time to look for water and food, but I was just so tired and spacey that I didn't use my time well and had to head over to the park in the rain all too soon. This was rain I normally could have drunk, but since I had committed to only drinking wasted water I had to let it drip by. We hung out for a while but I felt like my energy was too low to really enjoy talking. The clouds opened up and dropped a ton of rain on us so we hid under a pavilion as we spoke.

At 1 p.m. I was ready to hit the road, but my cell phone and laptop were both dead and the sun was not shining to charge them up. So I aimlessly headed north not really knowing where I was but just hoping to run into Route 1 that would take me to Boston. I was feeling a little dizzy and disoriented from the hunger and thirst, which did not help me navigate at all. I found a few partially full bottles of water on the side of the road, and the sensation of water in my mouth felt oh-so-good.

Exhausted, I pulled off the road and laid my blanket out by the side of a small lake. The sun had come out some so I put out my solar panels, which charged up my cell phone so I could get my bearings straight. I had only made it five miles out of Providence, had eaten nothing but a few leaves of lettuce and some tomatoes, and found just a few ounces of water to drink. Luckily my phone told me I hadn't gone too far out of the way and had 35 miles to go to Boston. Rather than get right back on the road I decided to clear up my mind and take a nap. The rest was really good for my head, and I woke up at 4 p.m. feeling rejuvenated. I took a swim in the lake and got back on the road.

A short while later, a giant rainstorm was bellowing towards me. The clouds were some of the most impressive I had seen on the trip, a shade of gray so dark they were almost black. I cinched my gear shut and welcomed the rain to come hydrate me through my skin. The storm took its time to arrive, and during that time I found a bakery that had thrown out all the perfectly good end pieces of the loaves. I was pedaling along eating my bread when the storm opened up onto me. I soaked in the water through my skin and sipped the drips of water running off my mustache. My conscience told me I was cheating, but my dehydrated cells couldn't resist. The rain lasted just an hour, but the gloomy cloud coverage held for the rest of the night.

I arrived in the outskirts of Boston at 7:30 p.m. I had an interview planned with a podcast, but my phone microphone wasn't working because water had dripped into it so I had to cancel. I got to my Aunt Myrna and Aunt Michelle's home and found them preparing a magnificent dinner. We had a salad topped with lobster and cheese, and it was all local, organic ingredients. They actually got the lobster from a CSA. It was an on-the-grid meal since water and electricity were used to prepare it, but I am loosening up on the rules a bit to start to acclimate back to "normal" life. This is challenging since I am keeping statistics of everything I do, and I have seen them increasing quite drastically in the last week; for example, I've nearly doubled the packaged food and tripled the non-local food that I've purchased. We hung out and talked for a couple of hours and had a wonderful time. We stayed up close to midnight just hanging out and talking.

My arrival in Boston meant the end of my Drip by Drip campaign so after dinner I rode my bike over to the lake to scoop up a gallon to purify. I was so thankful to have a bounty of water in front of me.

DAY 96: BOSTON

I slept pretty well in the guest bedroom on the comfortable pull-out couch. When I woke up I decided to plug into an outlet and spent most of the morning on the computer catching up with writing and social media.

Myrna and I walked over to the grocery store, and I got milk, bread, honey, and some fruits and veggies. The milk was in a glass bottle that I put a deposit on and will return when I'm done with it. The store was full of good local, organic food and I was happy to be there. I decided to make my day much easier by drinking water from the faucet. So when I needed water I went to the sink and filled up my water bottle, being very careful not to waste a drop. What a luxury it is to have clean drinking water at the turn of a knob, something I've not had for three months. The only other time I used water from on the grid was in Northport, NY, when I had to turn on a faucet to take a photo for the Drip by Drip campaign and ended up filling my water bottles. It is a slippery slope falling back into routines.

Today, after 96 days on the road together, Brent and I decided to part ways. We haven't gotten along a lot of the time on this trip, but together we did create some beautiful images. These pictures will last a lifetime and will continue to tell the story of this journey for many years to come. I'm extremely grateful for his sticking with me through my lack of empathy and all the times I put my interests and my project before him.

When I have a goal in sight I often put so much focus on it I neglect others, and I certainly did that to him. That is something I've been doing forever and probably always will to some extent, but I do intend to work on it. A lot of life comes very easy to me, and I forget that some aspects don't come that easy to everyone else. I get annoyed sometimes when the "easy" things are hard for someone I am working with. That is another thing I intend to work on.

This is Brent's second bike ride across America, and I am so thankful to have had his help, his friendship and his documentation of the journey. I will finish the last 200 miles to Vermont on my own, and Brent is heading back home to Florida after a few days hanging out in Boston. I'm glad we did this together and I know we both gained a lot from it. With that being said, if anyone hears that we are making plans to do something like this again, PLEASE STOP US.

DAY 97: PIONEERS OF SUSTAINABLE BUSINESS

I pedaled over to meet up with James and Aaron from the Boston Collective Delivery at the Patagonia store in downtown Boston. We hung out in the store for a bit talking with all the cool staff and learning about the good things they are doing around town. I visit Patagonia stores because I choose to surround myself with inspiring people, inspiring businesses and positive energy. The way Patagonia uses business to create a healthier planet is a huge inspiration to me and has influenced much of the way I run my own business today.

My business is marketing and Patagonia's is clothing, so you could assume that they can't be much alike. However, I have modeled nearly all of the bases of my company after their ethics. Patagonia founded One Percent for the Planet and were the first members, committing to donate at least one percent of their revenue to environmental organizations. But they don't just cut a big check to a large NGO and call it a day; instead they seek out smaller groups working to save or restore habitat that put the money to extremely solid use. In doing so they have helped small groups win huge battles to save natural habitats and have funded thousands of environmental groups to help them get the good work done.

They are the pioneers of sustainable business and sustainable clothing. They build durable and functional products meant to last a lifetime, have recycling programs for worn wear and teach customers to value their clothing rather than constantly consume the newest fashion. They truly care about their impact on people and the planet and have analyzed their entire footprint and developed some the most sustainable clothing on the market. A good portion of their clothes are made from recycled materials such as plastic bottles or old clothing, and they were the first company to switch over to 100-percent organic cotton. They are one of the biggest influences on the growth of organic versus conventional cotton, which uses a heavy amount of chemicals.

The culture around Patagonia is incredible as well, with flex hours so that employees can really enjoy life while still having a full-time job. They have a policy that allows employees to go surfing when the swell is high. Their accomplishments and their influence on sustainable, responsible business is unparalleled and would take multiple books to explain. There are two books that do exactly that, which I'd highly recommend reading: *Let My People Go Surfing* and *The Responsible Company*.

After leaving Patagonia James, Aaron and I biked over to their office a few miles away. I learned all about their nonprofit and am excited about what they are doing. The Boston Collective Delivery is a messenger service whose goal is to take delivery cars off the road in downtown Boston. Doing so would reduce traffic congestion, fuel consumption and pollution. They love what they are doing and stay active on the job. They also have a delivery bike that has a solar-assist battery hooked up to it, which I played around with in the warehouse. That thing has some serious power. I also met the guys over at Geek House Bikes and watched them work on two custom bikes. They are another great group of guys doing great things with their business. I walked out of that building feeling very inspired by everything inside.

That evening my Aunt Myrna threw a gathering for my arrival in Boston. It was an incredibly enjoyable evening full of good people, good food and tons of fun. Didi Emmons catered the event, and almost everything prepared was local, organic food. She has just created a nonprofit restaurant, and part of the mission is to teach youth about food, so four teenaged kids came over with her to prepare the food and it was fun to watch them in action. Didi has started five restaurants (two are nonprofits) and written three cookbooks, and it was an educational experience to be in her presence. She showed me you can eat in a luxurious manner and still be good to the earth. She was so conscious about making sure I could eat everything, and I was so appreciative of her thoughtfulness.

Myrna and Michelle have really wonderful friends and it was so great to meet them. Friends of mine I hadn't seen for five years since college, friends that I had just made online from this journey, and friends who knew me through other friends came to the party as well. It truly was a night of joy and it reminded me of being back in San Diego with all of my friends.

I love all of my family and the funny thing is how I've come to love and appreciate them more and more over the last years. I guess it's easier to love and get along with someone when you're not cramped up in a small house or car with them year after year, but I am amazed at how much I've grown to appreciate them. The last few days in Boston with Myrna and Michelle was such a fabulous time. Just a few short years ago I felt like I didn't have much in common with my Aunt Myrna, and we didn't have that much to talk about. Now I can hang out and talk with her all evening and still have a long list of things to talk about the next day. Never would I have thought we'd end up having such similar interests and so much in common. People here think it's interesting that her last name is Greenfield because of all the "green" stuff she is doing. I'm so proud and impressed by all of her accomplishments in Boston, from helping to start a farmers' market to working in the nonprofit industry for many years to starting her own marketing company, Good Egg Marketing, that services good businesses and people who are doing good things.

DAY 98: OPEN MIC NIGHT

I slept in until past ten this morning. I am so far behind on sleep and so in need of a long rest. Even when I am not biking I am constantly doing something. I really just need this adventure to come to an end.

It's nice to know that in the future I can ride 40 miles on a Friday night just to go visit a friend. I now have no excuse, and I intend to use this new skill. One cool thing I've learned on this trip is what a great tool the bike can be. I've seen people of every shape and size and every age riding long distances and short distances around the country. I've met people who commute year-round, winter and summer. Biking is something that just about anyone can do. I've met a handful of people who have biked across the country in their 60s and 70s. If they can do that then any 20-something can ride to work or school.

Back in Providence I had met a gal named Emma who told me to visit her parents' café in Nashua and also set me up with a girl name Emily who I could stay with. It was open mic night at the café and Emily told me to meet her there. She introduced me to Emma's parents, the owners of the café. It was a great environment and the 30 or so people watching the musicians were all smiling. I put my name on the list even though I wasn't a musician; I figured they might be interested in knowing I had just rolled up from San Francisco.

It turns out everyone was quite interested and very entertained. I told them what I was doing to create a healthier earth and recounted some of the funny encounters from the last 98 days. I was the last person up, and after my little presentation I talked to about half the people in the café. Then a handful of us walked back to Emily's house where they all played musical instruments together, and I lay on the couch resting my eyes. I was so tired but I didn't want to miss out on the fun. I was grateful to have fallen into such a cool group of people in a town I had never heard of just a few days before.

DAY 99: SLEEPING ON A CHURCH PORCH

A late night and an early morning meant another day of being way too tired for my own good. I had agreed to meet WMUR Channel 9 at 10:30 a.m. in Manchester, which was about 20 miles north, so I got on the road at 8:30 a.m. It was a smooth ride, and I had time to stop at the river in town to freshen up before meeting up with the news people. The river was roaring fast, but I found a spot tucked away behind a few rocks where I could safely submerge myself. As usual, dipping into the river refreshed and rejuvenated me and kicked off the new day. I rode over to the park in time to meet up with the reporter and cameraman, and they did a quick interview that aired on the six o'clock news the next day. I did a story with the *Union Leader* as well.

After a pretty relaxing day I searched out a church to rest my tired head for the night. I rode past a graveyard and contemplated staying there but instead continued on. I was uneasy riding through the somewhat run-down neighborhoods and was not really happy at the thought of sleeping on those streets. I've felt uneasy about this city since the moment I rolled into town. I checked a handful of churches for an open door and eventually just pulled my bike and trailer up the front stairs of a church and set up my sleeping pad on the porch. Fireworks kept me up for a while but I eventually fell asleep around 10:30, which was about three hours earlier than the last four nights. I worried about the slew of people walking the streets up to no good, but I was pretty tucked away and doubted many people would notice me. I had to be up at a decent time since I'd be waking up at a church on a Sunday morning.

DAY 100: TALKING TO PEOPLE

Who would have thought a night on a church porch would be my best night's sleep in a few weeks? I woke up at 7 a.m. after about nine hours of sleep, and although I was still exhausted, I could tell I had had a solid night of rest.

It was a cold night, and I woke up many times with my arms wrapped tight around my chest to conserve heat. Just a week ago I was riding through a heat wave sweating by night and day, and now the temperatures have cooled down drastically and clouds have covered the sun for good portions of each day. I miss the extreme heat a little, and especially miss the warm nights.

I rode away from the church in the early light without much of a plan. I pedaled just a few blocks and found a nice bench in a park to sit, eat bagels and peanut butter, and enjoy the morning. I spent the next few hours talking to people and catching up on my writing. Being behind on sleep and my writing over the last week had my head in a cloud. On top of that, the adventure is in a transitional point of nearing an end but not actually being over. This has changed my habits and thrown me off. But having spent the day writing and getting caught up relieved me greatly, and as I pedaled on I felt my woes lifting.

I got on the road later in the day and had a choice to make when I came to a fork in the road. I had asked for directions earlier and was told of a more-traveled route that avoided the hills and would save me a considerable amount of effort. I had planned to take that route but upon reaching the fork I decided to take the road less traveled. The road that would challenge me and make me feel alive. The road that would have more peaks and valleys full of lush green trees and more water to cleanse my spirit and soul. The road that would give me time alone on my last few days of the adventure. I pedaled on and the cold and cloudiness dampened my spirits a bit, and I felt a bit lonely riding through the countryside. However, the beautiful smells in the air flowing through my nostrils reminded me that life is magical and there is no need to feel alone, as I have the world on my side. I got to the town of Weare at about six o'clock and just about called it a night in the pavilion in the middle of town, but decided to continue on another nine miles to the next town of Henniker.

As I pulled into town I saw a baseball field, which reminded me of a traveler I had met in Nashua who said he often stays in the dugouts of baseball fields. I pulled into the shelter just as the rain was starting to come down. It was dry in there and wet outside so I sat on the bench and watched the rain. I worked on my writing and caught up on some e-mails as I shivered a bit in the damp, cold air. I enjoyed the solitude and hit the sack at a little past nine, ready for another full night of rest. It was just a 25-mile day, but the trailer was feeling heavier than ever before, and I was exhausted.

DAY 101: THE WILDEST RIDE YET

I woke up in the dugout after a pretty good night's rest, a solid ten hours of sleep, which I desperately needed. It rained all night and I was often cold, but the sun was shining through the clouds this morning.

I headed west and stopped at a grocery store in Henniker and checked the dumpster before going inside to shop. Money aside, I have a hard time rationalizing buying something inside that is going to waste outside. Besides that, I just haven't felt like using money lately. So I was peeking into the dumpster when a door opened from above and the boss man came out to throw something in there. If I had ducked he wouldn't even have noticed me, but like a deer in a headlights I just looked up at him in the open door. He said, "What are you doing?"

My response was, "Getting some food."

He rebutted, "Get out of here!"

So I walked around front to buy some groceries and said hello to him with a big smile on my face when I saw him walking down an aisle. I grabbed milk, peanut butter and bread to get me through the day and then sat outside and ate until I had my fill.

I rode through the gorgeous town of Newbury and took a break in Sunapee at a picnic table by a creek. Then I swam in the clear, fast-moving creek while talking with a local man. I filled up my jugs with the water from the picture-perfect, gorgeous river.

I used Google Maps on my phone to continue heading northwest and wound up on some very steep dirt roads. I had to walk up a few because my thin road tires could not get enough traction. It was quite tiring but very pleasant to be riding through such beautiful countryside. The road became less maintained as I continued onwards and

248

in the early evening I stopped at a waterfall to make myself another snack. I leaned against a tree with my legs dangling over a rock ledge and thought to myself, "Aaaah, this is the life." Even though it was a bit chilly I walked down to the beaver pond to take a dip.

Before getting in I discovered that the pond was full of newts. I was as excited to see them as I would have been 16 years ago, at the age of ten. I have always loved newts but never seen them in nature, just in *National Geographic* and on TV programs. Yeah, I've seen plenty of salamanders, lizards, snakes, frogs and toads, but never newts. I was so excited. I sat and observed them for a while and tried to catch them but had no luck. They were quick little creatures. A short while later a school of little black bullheads (similar to catfish), each the size of a dime, swam by in the shallows. It reminded me of the first time I ever saw a school of young bullheads on a vacation in third grade in northern Michigan. We caught a bunch of them, and when I was playing with them back home one of them poked me with its venomous fin spike, and I cried like the little boy I was. I'll never forget that. I don't usually touch them now, but I still love to see these fish that school and swim together in a black ball.

I continued on down the road and it abruptly ended at a country home. I thought to myself, "Dangit, that dead-end sign five miles back was right after all." I stood there for a bit deciding just what to do. I looked around the corner and found the road turned into some sort of a trail about half the width of the road I was on. I stood in front of this steep primitive trail full of huge rocks and dirt and rather than walking up to the house and asking where the trail led I just went for it. Google Maps showed the trail leading through the woods for about four miles and gave me the impression that it would lead me to Highway 120. I pushed my bike up a trail that even a mountain bike would have been challenged by, and there I was in the woods. Then it got rough. Real rough. Like the roughest it's been in the last 4,600 miles.

Instantly I was bombarded by more deerflies than I have ever seen in my life. My brain reacted by pumping adrenaline throughout my body. I couldn't stop for more than a couple seconds at a time, knowing that if I did the swarms of deerflies would be piercing my skin. Considering I was only moving at a few miles per hour I was surprised they weren't biting me more, but the swarm was getting their fair share of bites into my skin. I moved on with adrenaline pumping through my veins, sometimes riding and sometimes running with my bike and trailer by my side. I am very thankful for that adrenaline because without it there is no way I would have been up to the challenge. I pulled my bike up steep hills, pedaled down steep hills and walked when the trail was too rough to handle. At times I was drudging through ankle-deep mud holes and pulling my trailer through puddles almost knee deep. I was never certain this trail wouldn't just end in the middle of nowhere or at a lake, and that is what kept it real interesting. I was yelling out in pain and slapping my body as the deerflies bit into me, often killing two flies at once. I grunted profusely to help me pull my rig through the mud holes and over the rocks. Usually I consider one or two deerflies a nuisance, but I had about 30 swarming around me at a time and was bitten about 20 times in two hours.

I came out at a gorgeous lake so stunning the whole experience was worth it. I was able to enjoy it from atop a beaver dam as I swatted the flies away. Twice I came upon water deeper than I could trudge my trailer through but both times I found that the trail diverted around a corner. Springs spilled clear, cold water out onto the trail, which at times created mud to cover my legs and at other times washed the mud and blood off. It was a wild time, and it reminded me how much I like getting deep into nature — ideally with much less gear, but that just made it all the crazier. Eventually I saw a break in the trees ahead of me and caught site of a dirt road. I came out at a three-way intersection, and since my phone was dead I used my intuition and continued straight, figuring that must be west. The dirt road took me downhill for a few miles and then ended at a local highway that I assumed was Highway 120 north. I rode on it for a while and then it dawned on me to look to see where the sun was. It was indeed setting in the west to my left so I knew I was heading north. A few miles more of riding and I pulled into Lebanon, where an oldtimers' orchestra was playing at the band shell. I collapsed there in disbelief of where I had just come from and where I was now, and enjoyed how spontaneous life can be when you let it be. Biking across America is a great way to live spontaneously — you never know what's going to be around the bend.

I continued on with just eight miles to go to Quechee, voice recording the day into my phone as I rode. I crossed a river into Vermont, my final state, and from there had just five miles to go for the day. I pulled in just after dark to my hosts for the night, David Dougherty and Sheila Powers. David and Sheila welcomed me into their home, and we sat in the kitchen and had a delicious homemade dinner with mostly natural, local foods.

DAY 102: WHY WAIT FOR HEAVEN WHEN YOU CAN GO TO VERMONT RIGHT NOW?

I decided to spend the day in Quechee and stay another night. I only had 70 miles to go but wasn't scheduled to arrive in Waitsfield for two days so I had time to kill. The morning was a relaxing one, and I felt great after a solid night's rest. I spent most of the day at the house, writing, playing with the camera and talking to David and left around 3 p.m.

It was a gorgeous day. I headed to the Ibex Outdoor Clothing headquarters five miles away in White River Junction. On my way over I stopped at a cold, spring-fed creek to wash up. It was a stunningly beautiful day, and I was happy to be out riding the bike without the trailer. My visit with Ibex was really fun, and I learned about some of the sustainability measures they are taking. I met a couple dozen of the employees and was really happy to see that they all seemed to be living the lifestyle they are selling. They make almost everything from 100-percent merino sheep's wool. They are big into sustainability and have some great initiatives going on.

Leaving Ibex I could smell freedom in the air, imagining that, in just over 36 hours, I would be a free man. Free of all my rigorous rules and limitations and free to do whatever I wanted, whenever I felt like it. I have felt great levels of freedom on this journey, and I am in fact a free man, but in just a few days I would be able to turn on a light, take a shower, use a washing machine to wash my clothes, or drink water from the tap. I would be able to hop by in a bus or car, buy whatever I want at the store and plug in my electronics for seemingly infinite electricity. This is the freedom that awaits me. But having immersed myself in these sustainable measures all summer I know I will not lose them or shake them off just like that. Although I will be back to living "normally," these practices will stick with me in moderation. In comparison to the radical life I've been living for the last 102 days, I will be living quite freely.

It turned out a Facebook friend of mine lives just two miles from where I'm staying, which is quite surprising considering I am in the middle of nowhere. Rose and I met online because of a mutual friend, Rebekah, and she invited me over for dinner with her family so I gladly accepted. I pedaled over to Rose's home in Quechee later in the day. It was an absolutely gorgeous two-mile ride. This land is out-of-this-world beautiful and makes me want to cry every time I come around a corner. Rose and her friends and family were so welcoming and enjoyable. She cooked up a small feast of healthy food, and I stuffed myself until my eyes didn't want to stay open anymore. The food was delicious and the conversation was enjoyable. She's really into permaculture and has spent many years out in Hawaii tending to the land. When she was 18 years old, for her senior year in high school, she sailed around the whole world. Her mom was a fun character with a mischievous twinkle in her eye. These women have had no shortage of good living.

DAY 103: ORGANIC MAKING A COMEBACK

The morning ride could not have been more beautiful. Everywhere I looked I saw beauty. The sky was so blue, the clouds were so white, and the trees were so green. The combination would make any grown man cry. The route followed the Ottauquechee River for the first 10 or 15 miles, and I stopped for a swim in its pristine water. I floated down the swift river a bit and found a big rock to clamber up and

PART 6

VERMONT

DAY 104: THE FINISH LINE

Today I just need the finish line so badly. I need to take a break from the long days of cycling, writing and searching for food and water. I set out on the road early, ready for the adventure to end, but the feelings bubbling inside my chest told me that this was only the beginning of my journey.

After the finish line I knew most of my daily actions would remain the same, likely much less extreme though. Rather than dumpster diving I'll probably just get back to the farmers' markets and my local co-op. Rather than searching out leaky faucets and purifying my water from lakes I'll just use water very conservatively from the faucet. Rather than cycling day in and day out across America I'll just cycle wherever I need to go around town. And rather than being so righteously rigorous with my rules I'll live in moderation, still in alignment with my ethics but allowing for exceptions.

The hard work will have paid off. 104 days of paying attention to every action I take will mean that I won't have to think quite so deeply at every moment. Instead, I'll be able to act on the knowledge and experience I've gained and the habits I've formed. This will be my new normal. My way of living and way of being, at ease after putting in the practice. Plus at home, I can establish this low-impact way of life rather than have to find new sources of sustenance every day on the road.

I had 49 miles to go to whatever awaited me on the other side of this adventure; 49 miles to a big rest; 49 miles to many nights of solid sleep; 49 miles to the One Percent for the Planet headquarters. The first 40 miles went very smoothly. I was on track and feeling good. Then the concrete turned to gravel, and I wondered if I'd have a repeat of three days ago. The road got steep, the steepest yet, and my tires were spinning out on the dirt road. Then I nearly flew over the handlebars. The weight of my trailer pulled my rear tire right out of the axle, and I sat there in the road covered in sweat and dirt thinking back to San Francisco. Here I was just a handful of miles from the end and I was having the same problem I had had on Day 1. I could only laugh though, as it just seemed like a perfect ending to the story. With a little handiwork I got the bike back up and running, and a few more steep miles brought me to my last summit. Waitsfield sat in the valley below me.

At the bottom of the hill a few of my friends from One Percent for the Planet were waiting for me, and together we pedaled the last few miles into town, where everyone else awaited. At the finish line I was greeted by my One Percent for the Planet family, who welcomed me to Vermont like mothers and fathers and brothers and sisters. I couldn't have imagined a more beautiful end to the adventure. Today my family grew by a few dozen people, and I smiled profusely in their presence.

With all the excitement and emotions just three words raced through my mind:

I made it!

I made it 4,700 miles across America on my bicycle, over three daunting mountain ranges, through vast expanses of desert, through the wind-beaten Great Plains, and through many of the country's largest cities and smallest towns. I battled freezing cold nights in the West, record heat waves in the East and enough cars to last a lifetime everywhere in between. My days on the road and under the stars ranged from mouth-parching dry to bone-drenching wet. I dodged dozens of thunderstorms and was clobbered by many more and even outran a tornado. I pedaled 375 miles across the state of Iowa with no seat and over 800 miles barefoot mostly just to see if I could do it. I lived off a leaky fire hydrant in Brooklyn for five days and pedaled from New York City to Boston in a heat wave living on wasted water. I tested more preconceived physical and mental notions than I knew I had and came out unscathed.

The trip was downright grueling, but I was almost always happy because I learned that when you have less, you have more. I learned to appreciate a small sip of water, a morsel of food, the last three percent of battery life on my computer, clean clothes, fresh air, smooth roads and clean water to swim in. Now that I can find joy in the simple parts of life I can find sources of happiness for free everywhere around me.

I learned the power of a bicycle. It is a simple machine, but it can take us great distances, both literally and figuratively. Life is good when I'm on a bike. Good for myself, good for the earth and good for the people around me.

I learned that people do genuinely want to help and be a part of something greater than themselves. I learned that many people want to do the right thing for the earth — they just need that extra little push, and need to see someone else do it first. I learned that positivity tends to create more positivity, as does goodness.

I learned that by living simply I can live free. The less complicated I make my life the more time I have to do what I love and what's good for me. Rather than working for money I can spend time with my family and friends, exercising and breathing fresh air in the outdoors, and cooking and eating healthy.

I set out with some seriously challenging goals, and I'm proud to say that I didn't fully accomplish any of them. But I sure did come darn close, and when it comes to earth-friendly living that's what really matters.

To cross America (and then some) I used less than one quarter of a gallon of fossil fuels. I never used a single car, bus, train, or plane; just one ferry into Manhattan. I traveled all but one of 4,700 miles via my own human power. In those 104 days I used 600 times less fossil fuels than the average American uses in that time, just going about life.

More than 90 percent of the food I ate was locally grown, organic and unpack-aged or from the garbage. When I arrived in NYC I had purchased only 22 packaged, 8 non-organicand 12 non-local foods. One trip to the grocery store for the average Ameri-can would involve more packaging, pesticidesand long-distance food than I purchased the entire summer. I ate over 280 pounds of food from dumpsters and was a fruit maniac, eating around 760 servings of the stuff on the ride. I never bought a single sports drink or energy packet, but I ate a whopping 16 pounds of honey. Who needs sports drinks when nature makes honey?

In 104 days I used 160 gallons of water, or about 1.5 gallons per day. The average American uses 80 to 100 gallons of water per day at home, which is about 60 times more water than I used. Of my 160 gallons, only 30 were from on the grid; 60 were purified from natural sources, 50 were wasted water and 20 came from wells. I didn't take a single shower, use a washing machine, or buy a bottle of water, even on the hottest of days.

I set out to not use any outlets but ended up plugging into five for a total of 22 hours. I made it the whole way without turning on a single light switch and no longer have the unconscious habit of turning on a light when I walk into a room. I used 1,000 times less non-renewable energy than the average American.

I created a mere two pounds of trash and nine pounds of recycling in 104 days on the road. The average American produces 4.5 pounds of waste per day (three pounds of which is trash) so I created more than 40 times less waste and 150 times less trash than average person in America.

I kept the most positive attitude I could have hoped for, even through the most challenging of times. I cursed only nine times, when not that long ago I might have sworn that often in one

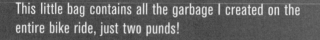

This little bag contains all the garbage I created on the entire bike ride, just two punds!

bask on. Huge logs were wedged into cracks in the rock and made for great planks to jump into the deep hole below. I played as long as I could, but I only had a bit of time to kill this morning as I told the Biedlers I'd be at their farm at noon for lunch.

Off Highway 14 I took a right onto Happy Hollow road, and the paved road ended and turned into dirt. I pedaled hard up a steep hillside with crystal-clear creeks trickling down on both sides, wondering if I'd end up in the woods on primitive trails like I had a few days prior. My stomach was rumbling with so much hunger that I could feel my seat shaking, and I imagined a farm-cooked meal with fresh cold milk awaiting me at the farm. When I wasn't thinking about lunch I thought about the Stollers' farm back in Ohio a 1,000 miles ago. Fond memories of playing with the kids on the farm, hanging out in the kitchen eating homemade pie and looking in the pantry at their bounty of canned goods kept me company as I rode.

Upon arrival I sat down for lunch with Regina, Brent and their daughter Erin and filled my stomach to its threshold. We had a great conversation over lunch, and I learned all about their small family farm. They milk 35 cows and supply the milk to Organic Valley. Their cows eat nothing but grass, spending the entire summer out at pasture except the couple hours it takes to milk them each day.

When they started farming in about 2000 there were 47 organic farms in Vermont. Now there are more than 205, over half of which are part of the Organic Valley co-op. There are a total of 900 dairy farms in Vermont, which means nearly a quarter of them are organic. Regina and Brent expect to see that percentage increase drastically over the next years as farmers start to realize the many benefits of farming organically. They do what is called rotational grazing, which puts the cows on a new patch of grass every day. This is becoming more and more common throughout Vermont and all over the United States as it is a very healthy way of feeding cows and tending to the land.

In just 14 hours, I will be at the One Percent for the Planet headquarters in Waitsfield. My life on the bike will be over soon. For now….

sentence, and I made it across the country without ingesting one drop of alcohol or a single drug.

Ripples have been sent around the world and received by thousands and thousands of people. Most of the ripples are unknown to me but many have come back from lands around the globe such as Russia, Algeria, Kenya, Azerbaijan, Austria, Chile, Australia, and the USA. These ripples are building up inside me to form waves that will be released for years and years to come. I am hearing every day from Americans who are waking up, becoming more conscious and seeing resources in a new light.

Send your ripples far and wide my friends.
We can expect greatness to come in this world.

AFTERWORD

We live in an interesting time, an exciting time. We live in an era where we just may witness the survival or the extinction of the human race. We are destroying the natural world much faster than it can heal itself. We are aware of our destruction, but most humans are just too lazy to do what needs to be done. Most of us are too lazy to think past our own little lives. Billions of humans deny or completely avoid the fact that they are destroying the environment. Maybe that's a way of self-protection, to feel okay about their lives. Maybe it's feeling helpless and hopeless, like their actions don't count.

We cannot deny that we are destroying the earth. Once we are gone I think the earth will repair itself and will be better off without us, the way we are now. But if we could unite to live for more than ourselves, for humankind, for other creatures, for the earth, then maybe the earth would be better off with us. After all, we are a pretty special creature.

Many scientists are pessimistic about the future of the human race. Most people who've deeply analyzed our pattern of treating the earth see an end to life as we know it in the near future. Most corporations have little-to-no plan for the future, just a plan for how to pull in as much money as possible right now at the expense of our earth.

I am, for some reason, optimistic.

Even though I see evil prevailing on most of the streets I walk, I am optimistic. Even though I see evil in most of the homes I visit, I am optimistic. I am optimistic because of the remaining wide-open spaces that exist. Because of the crystal-clear creeks I've drunk from in New Zealand. Because of the kangaroos I've hopped with in Australia. Because of the giraffes I've roamed with and the gazelles I've pranced with in Africa. Because of the vast woods I've been lost in. Because of the otherworldly reefs I've snorkeled through in Indonesia. Because of the poison dart frogs that have mesmerized me in Colombia. Because of the orangutans

I have shared a tree with in Borneo. Because of North America's national parks, vast enough for me to roam freely in for a lifetime.

I'm optimistic because these places will likely live on with or without us. If we change our ways many generations of the human species will get to enjoy life on earth and all the beauty it has to offer. If we continue our destructive path we will die off, as will many of the creatures and plants. We'll have been on the earth for a mere blink of the Mother's eye, but she will recover and life will resume without us. Our destruction could take thousands of years to heal, but the earth will recover from the wounds we've inflicted and she'll be fine. Just as a scab covers a wound on our skin and then slowly fades away, the earth will cover the wounds we've inflicted, and she will return to her magnificent form in one manner or another.

I'm selfishly optimistic because I think the complete destruction will take until I am an old man or more likely dead of old age. We'll run out of fuel for our vehicles, but I'm okay with that because I don't need them anyway. Many of our modern conveniences may be no more. Life may be nothing like we know it today, but that's okay because I'll adapt to the changes. Maybe we'll no longer have a choice and all be forced to start living a more earth-friendly lifestyle because we won't have the resources to over-harvest and over-consume. I've learned to be happy simply by being. I've learned to be happy without access to modern conveniences and luxuries. I've learned to take joy in a grain of sand, a drop of water, a blade of grass, a rundown industrial building, rats scurrying in the subway, or rain falling upon me. I'm happy be alive no matter the circumstances, and I'm going to keep smiling. I'll spread happiness and that will give me joy, no matter my circumstances.

The earth will go on with or without us. But I'd prefer to keep swimming in the cool, clear lakes. I'd prefer to wander through the woods and breathe in the fresh air from nature's trees. I'd prefer to lie in the prairies and watch the fluffy white clouds float by above. I'd prefer to get caught in mid-afternoon storms. I'd prefer to hear the singing of the songbirds, the buzzing of the bees and the laughter of children. I'd prefer to feel my body shivering in the cold and sweating in the heat of the sun. I'd prefer to walk down the street and say hello to my neighbors. I'd prefer for the human race to live on and find harmony and balance with our Mother's other children.

I'm going to be open-minded about the continuation of our race. I'm going to embrace whatever the next decades on earth bring. I'm going to keep on smiling no matter the circumstances. I'm going to continue to do my part no matter how bad or how good things get.

We live in an exciting time. The humans of the 21st century, us, get to choose whether our race will live on or take our last breaths as a species. We get to choose whether our community of seven billion lives or dies. What an exciting time to be alive. We just may get to witness the earth reach its threshold or quite possibly the greatest comeback story of all time.

I'm rooting for the greatest comeback story of all time, but I'll be okay either way because I'll know I did my part. I've dedicated my life to keeping our earth beautiful. I've dedicated my life to waking up our sleepy race and inspiring my fellow humans to take action. I'm going to inspire everyone I can to live a life that revives our Mother. Those people I inspire are each going to inspire a couple of people too, and those people will inspire more. Out of the many that I inspire I hope a few will become great leaders and inspire a great number more. If we started today in this manner the world could be touched, on every corner of every continent, in just a short time. If we can live beyond ourselves we will see a ground swell of inspiration, of love and respect for one another, for our fellow creatures and for our earth. We will see our world come back to life, and we will see true abundance like it has never been seen before.

Be a part of the great earth revival. Be a part of the greatest comeback of all time. This is the start of the greatest greening of the earth since the earth first saw the color green.

It starts with you. It starts with me. It starts with your children, your classmates, your fellow employees, your boss, your parents, the guy biking past you on the street, the person sitting next to you on the train, the clerk behind the counter at the store. It starts with every single one of us taking action and doing what we know is right. To be a part of this revival you must start from within and lead by example. The most powerful way to lead is by showing what must be done. Check to see if your heart is beating faster right now. If it is, you know what to do.

Start today. Start now. Don't waste time. Life is precious. Live it. Be Alive. Embrace life.

Others will see your heart pumping more blood than ever before. Others will see your smile bigger than ever before. Others will see you taking action and leading by example. They will follow you, just as you are following these words right now. You will be a part of this earth comeback and you will live on to tell the next generation of the time when humans nearly destroyed themselves.

The butterflies will still be fluttering their wings. The birds will still be singing their songs. The wind will still blow leaves off the trees in the fall. The bees will still be buzzing. Children will still be laughing. And you'll be proud to know that you were a part of the revolution.

It's not going to be easy, but it is going to be rewarding.

We're going to cry, but we're going to learn to smile like never before.

It's going to be fun and it's going to be the most exciting time of our lives.

But we've got some serious work to do.

We need to use our precious time wisely.

Start the great earth revival today.

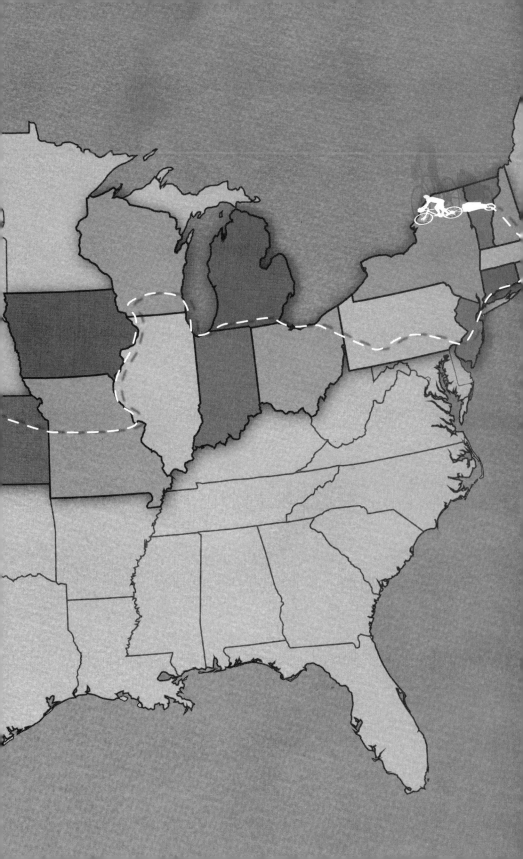

RESOURCES

If you're inspired and want a little help to live a more earth-friendly lifestyle then this resource section is the place for you! Here you will find how-to guides, tips and expanded information for many of the topics covered in the book. It's all hosted on my website, RobGreenfield.tv, where you'll find days' worth of information and stories sure to entertain, educate and inspire you into a happier, healthier existence!

Apply this adventure to your life to reduce your impact on the earth:

TRANSPORTATION: How to reduce your impact from getting around:
RobGreenfield.tv/Transportation

FOOD: Eating earth-friendly:
RobGreenfield.tv/Food

WATER: How to use less water:
RobGreenfield.tv/Water

ENERGY: How to use less electricity:
RobGreenfield.tv/Energy

WASTE: How to create near-zero waste:
RobGreenfield.tv/Waste

CONSUMPTION: How to cause less destruction when buying stuff:
RobGreen-field.tv/Consumption

PERSONAL HYGIENE: Back to the basics:
RobGreenfield.tv/Hygiene

TRAVELING: How to reduce your impact traveling:
RobGreenfield.tv/Traveling

ACTIVISM: How to create your own environmental activism campaign:
RobGreenfield.tv/DIYactivism including:
- How to create an activism campaign
- How to get sponsors and gear
- How to get people to pay attention (social media)
- How to get media attention
- How to do it on a very low budget.

HOW-TO'S:

- **HOW TO DUMPSTER DIVE:**
  RobGreenfield.tv/DumpsterDiving
- **HOW TO FREESTYLE GARDEN:**
  RobGreenfield.tv/HowToFreestyleGarden
- **HOW AND WHERE TO SLEEP FOR FREE:**
  RobGreenfield.tv/SleepforFree
- **HOW TO LIVE OFF WASTE:**
  RobGreenfield.tv/LiveOffWaste
- **HOW TO QUIT A JOB THAT DOESN'T SERVE YOU OR THE EARTH:**
  RobGreenfield.tv/QuitYourJob
- **HOW TO BE A POSITIVE ENVIRONMENTAL INFLUENCE ON OTHERS:**
  RobGreenfield.tv/PositiveInfluence
- **HOW TO GET OUT OF THE ROUTINE AND FOLLOW YOUR DREAM:**
  RobGreenfield.tv/RoutineToDream
- **HOW TO OVERCOME THE FEAR TO LIVE A MORE EARTH-FRIENDLY LIFESTYLE:**
  RobGreenfield.tv/OvercomeFear
- **HOW TO TRAVEL AMERICA FOR FREE (WITHOUT MOOCHING)**
  RobGreenfield.tv/TravelFree

MORE:

- **PREPARATION AND PLANNING FOR THIS ADVENTURE:**
  RobGreenfield.tv/DudesPlanning
- **SAFETY AND TIPS FOR FEMALE TRAVELERS:**
  RobGreenfield.tv/TravelerSafety
- **FOOD WASTE: SOLUTIONS TO THE FOOD WASTE FIASCO:**
  RobGreenfield.tv/FoodWasteSolutions
- **PEOPLE AND NONPROFITS TO FOLLOW:**
  RobGreenfield.tv/GoodGuys
- **DOCUMENTARIES AND BOOKS TO LEARN FROM:**
  RobGreenfield.tv/EducateYourself
- **NEWS STORIES FROM THIS ADVENTURE:**
  RobGreenfield.tv/Dude+news
- **LESSONS LEARNED FROM A YEAR WITHOUT SHOWERING:**
  RobGreenfield.tv/Shower
- **FROM DRUNK TO DUDE MAING A DIFFERENCE:**
  RobGreenfield.tv/Timeline

ABOUT THE AUTHOR

Rob Greenfield is an adventurer, activist and dude making a difference. His purpose is to inspire health, happiness, and freedom on earth, and he's dedicated his life to this mission. He has cycled across the United States twice on a bamboo bicycle, went a year without showering and has dove into more than a 1,000 dumpsters across America, all to inspire positive social and environmental change. When not out adventuring he lives off the grid in a 50-square-foot tiny home in San Diego. His extreme adventures and activism campaigns may appear unattainable to many but within them are an abundance of simple lessons and tips that can be adapted into any life to live with more happiness, health and freedom.

"Live simple and you will live free."

PROCEEDS

I aim for information on sustainable and healthy living to be available to all regardless of whether they use money or have the funds to buy this book.

Following in the footsteps of Mark Boyle, the Moneyless Man (moneylessmanifesto.org), the information in this book has been made available for free. Visit RobGreenfield.tv/DudeforFree for more information on how to get a free version of the book.

One-hundered percent of my proceeds from this book will be donated to One Percent for the Planet nonprofits. These organizations are dedicated to making the world a happier, healthier place for all of us through positive changes in the way we deal with food, water, energy, waste, and transportation. Visit RobGreenfield.tv/DudesImpact to see the positive impacts made through sales of this book.

I am able to donate all my proceeds because I have vastly simplified my existence and have vowed to a life that does not revolve around money. I have vowed to donate 90 percent of my earnings from media to good causes and to keep no more than $15,000 per year for myself. I have also vowed to own few possessions or assets. To learn more about my financial ethics and guidelines visit RobGreenfield.tv/Vows

If you have enjoyed *Dude Making a Difference* you might also enjoy other

BOOKS TO BUILD A NEW SOCIETY

Our books provide positive solutions for people who want to
make a difference. We specialize in:

**Food & Gardening • Resilience • Sustainable Building
Climate Change • Energy • Health & Wellness • Sustainable Living**

**Environment & Economy • Progressive Leadership • Community
Educational & Parenting Resources**

New Society Publishers

ENVIRONMENTAL BENEFITS STATEMENT

New Society Publishers has chosen to produce this book on recycled paper made
with **100% post consumer waste,** processed chlorine free, and old growth free.

For every 5,000 books printed, New Society saves the following resources:[1]

28	Trees
2,551	Pounds of Solid Waste
2,807	Gallons of Water
3,661	Kilowatt Hours of Electricity
4,638	Pounds of Greenhouse Gases
20	Pounds of HAPs, VOCs, and AOX Combined
7	Cubic Yards of Landfill Space

[1]Environmental benefits are calculated based on research done by the Environmental Defense Fund
and other members of the Paper Task Force who study the environmental impacts of the paper
industry.

For a full list of NSP's titles, please call 1-800-567-6772 *or check out our website* at:

www.newsociety.com

new society
PUBLISHERS